INTERPRETING GENRES OF SCRIPTURE
HERMENEUTICS 2

Cover Photo Description

In *Hermeneutics 1* you studied *General Principles for Interpreting Scripture.* Now, in *Hermeneutics 2,* you explore Specific Principles for studying genres (pronounced ZHAN-rez)—various types of writing in the Bible. We will teach you to interpret nine genres :

- Historical narrative (Genesis–Esther)
- Law in the Old Testament (Genesis–Deuteronomy)
- Poetry (Psalms)
- Wisdom (Job, Proverbs–Song)
- Prophetic books
- Gospels
- Acts
- Epistles
- Revelation

On the front and back covers, there are eight pictures that represent genres. Can you match the picture with each genre? (Hint: The harp represents poetry and wisdom.)

Contact Information

Order your copy online from:

Web: www.FaithAndActionSeries.org

Faith & Action
3728 W. Chestnut Expressway
Springfield, Missouri 65802 U.S.A.

E-mail: Info@FaithAndActionSeries.org

Telephone: (417) 881-4698

Interpreting Genres of Scripture
Hermeneutics 2
Student Manual

by
Dr. Quentin McGhee,
Dr. Steve Eutsler
and Dr. Carl Gibbs

Instructional Design by
Dr. Quentin McGhee, Senior Editor

PUT YOUR FAITH TO WORK!

Faith & Action Series

Faith & Action
3728 W. Chestnut Expressway
Springfield, Missouri 65802 U.S.A.

Copyright Information

First Edition 2016

Faith & Action Series—Hermeneutics 2, First Edition
©2016 Faith & Action Team

Course # THE2032
ISBN 978-1-60382-124-7
Item # 4421-23E0

Table of Contents

List of Figures

Faith & Action Series Overview

Bible	Theology	Church Ministries
Survey of the Old Testament	God & the Bible (Theology 1)	Evangelism & Discipleship
Survey of the New Testament	Angels, Man, & Sin (Theology 2)	Marriage & Family
Pentateuch	Christ & Salvation(Theology 3)	Pastoral Ministry
Historical Books	The Holy Spirit & the Church (Theology 4)	Ministerial Ethics
Poetic Books	General Principles for Interpreting Scripture (Hermeneutics 1)	Preach the Word (Homiletics 1)
Major Prophets	Hermeneutics 2	Homiletics 2
Minor Prophets	Unlocking the Treasures of Your Fire Bible	Principles of Teaching
Life & Teachings of Christ (Synoptic Gospels)		Biblical Counseling
John		Children's Ministry
Acts of the Holy Spirit		Youth Ministry
Romans & Galatians		Missions 1
First & Second Corinthians		Cross Cultural Communications (Missions 2)
Prison Epistles		Teaching Literacy
Pastoral Epistles		Leadership
Hebrews		Church Government & Administration
General Epistles		Church History 1
Revelation & Daniel		Church History 2

Faith & Action Series Three-Year Bible School Plan (103 credits)

First Year

First Semester

Course #	Title	Credits
BIB1013	Survey of the New Testament	3
BIB1023	Pentateuch	3
BIB1033	Synoptic Gospels	3
THE1012	God & the Bible (Theology 1)	2
THE1022	Hermeneutics 1	2
MIN3023	Children's Ministry	3
		16

Second Semester

Course #	Title	Credits
BIB1043	Survey of the Old Testament	3
BIB1052	John	2
BIB1063	Acts	3
THE1032	Angels, Man, and Sin (Theology 2)	2
MIN1013	Homiletics 1	3
MIN1033	Evangelism & Discipleship	3
		16

Second Year

First Semester

Course #	Title	Credits
BIB2013	Romans & Galatians	3
BIB2023	Historical Books	3
BIB2072	Hebrews	2
MIN2012	Church History 1	2
MIN2023	Missions 1	3
THE2013	Christ & Salvation (Theology 3)	3
THE2032	Hermeneutics 2	2
		18

Second Semester

Course #	Title	Credits
BIB2043	Corinthians	3
BIB2052	Prison Epistles	2
BIB2063	Poetic Books	3
MIN2032	Church History 2	2
THE2042	The Holy Spirit & the Church (Theology 4)	2
THE2052	Leadership	2
MIN3073	Marriage & Family	3
		17

Third Year

First Semester

Course #	Title	Credits
BIB3012	Pastoral Epistles	2
BIB3022	General Epistles	2
BIB3033	Major Prophets	3
MIN3013	Pastoral Ministry	3
MIN3022	Church Government & Administration	2
MIN3033	Cross Cultural Communications (Missions 2)	3
MIN3043	Homiletics 2	3
		18

Second Semester

Course #	Title	Credits
BIB3043	Revelation & Daniel	3
MIN1032	Teaching Literacy	2
MIN3053	Biblical Counseling	3
BIB3053	Minor Prophets	3
MIN3063	Principles of Teaching	3
MIN3072	Ministerial Ethics	2
MIN3082	Youth Ministry	2
		18

About This Book

1. **The Lesson Headings** divide each chapter into several parts. Each of these lessons focuses on principles related to one theme. We number the lessons consecutively throughout the book.

2. **The Lesson Goals** are listed at the beginning of each chapter. Also, when a lesson begins, the goal for that lesson is printed there. You will find that there is at least one goal for each lesson.

3. **Key Words** are defined in a section called "Definitions" at the end of the book. The symbol * comes before all words that are defined. To help some students, we have also defined a few words that are not key words.

4. **Teaching Method:** These courses are designed for the *guided discovery* method of learning. This method focuses on the student, rather than the teacher. When this course is used in a classroom, lectures are not intended. Rather, most of the class time should be used for students to discuss the questions in the margins and related questions from the teacher and other students. At least 25% of the student's grade should be on how faithfully the student has tried to answer questions *before* class.

   It is VERY important for each student to own his or her book. We encourage Bible schools to require students to buy their texts at the time they pay tuition. It is a shame for students to leave school without their books, because they need them for a lifetime of ministry. Owning the book enables a student to write notes in it and underline important ideas. Also, when students own their books, they do not waste class time by copying things that are already written in the text. Rather, they spend their time discussing questions related to the Bible and ministry.

   In a classroom the teacher and students should discuss key questions together. The best teachers never answer their own questions. Some students will complain at first when the teacher requires them to think, read, and search for answers. But a good teacher knows that children who are always carried never learn to walk. And students who are always told the answer learn to memorize, but not to think and solve problems. In many ways, a good teacher is like a coach—guiding others to succeed.

   The questions in this course are like a path that leads straight to the goal. If the questions are too hard for a student, the teacher can ask easier questions that are like stairs toward harder questions. Also, the teacher should ask questions that guide students to apply the text to local issues. Often, a good teacher will add a story or illustration that emphasizes a truth for students.

5. **Schedule:** This *Faith & Action Series* course is for two credits. For a Bible school course, it is good to plan 26 contact hours between the teacher and students. This allows one lesson for a class hour.

6. **The Questions:** Most questions in the margins are identified by the hammer ➤ and nail ➤ symbols. Questions are steps toward a goal. As a student answers the questions, he or she is sure to reach the goals. The hammer introduces *content questions* and the nail precedes *application questions*. Our logo for this book includes the hammer hitting the nail. A student must grasp content before being able to apply it. The answers to all content questions are in the text, near the question. We encourage students to answer nail or application questions from their local settings.

   In some books there is the symbol of a shovel ➤ before certain questions. Questions beside the shovel symbol are inductive questions. The word *induce* means "to lead." These questions lead students to discover truth for themselves.

7. *Sabio* is a Spanish word that means "wise man." This symbol in the margin signifies a proverb or wise saying.

8. **The Illustrations,** such as stories and examples, are preceded by the candle symbol.

9. **Figures** include pictures, photos, charts, and maps. We number the figures in order throughout the chapter. For example, the first three figures in chapter one are numbered 1.1, 1.2, and 1.3. There is a list of maps and charts near the front of the book.

10. **The Test Yourself** questions come at the end of each chapter and are indicated by the balance symbol . There are always ten of these questions. As a rule, there are two test questions for each goal in the chapter. If students miss any of these questions, they need to understand why they missed them. Knowing why an answer is right is as important as knowing the right answer.

11. **Essay Test Topics** are at the end of each chapter, indicated by the pencil symbol . Note that these essay topics are the lesson goals of the chapter. A student should be able to summarize these goals, writing 50-100 words on each one. These essay topics test students at a much higher level than the multiple choice, Test Yourself questions.

12. **Sample Answers** to the hammer questions, some comments on the nail questions, and answers for the Test Yourself questions and Essay Topics are in the Teacher's Guide. Students should answer questions so they will grow and become strong in their mental skills.

13. **Bible quotations** are usually from the New International Version (NIV). We also use the New American Standard Bible (NASB) and the King James Version (KJV). We encourage students to compare biblical passages in several versions of the Bible.

14. **The Scripture List** includes key Scripture references in this course. It is located near the back of the book.

15. **The Bibliography** is near the endnotes page. It is a complete list of books the author refers to in this course. Some students will want to do further research in these books.

16. **Endnotes** identify the sources of thoughts and quotes. They are listed by chapter at the end of the book.

17. **The Unit Exams and Final Exam** are in the Teacher's Guide. In the Teacher's Guide there are also other useful items for the teacher and potential projects for the students.

18. **Course Description** (THE2032): In *Hermeneutics 1,* students discovered general principles for interpreting Scripture, and practiced using them. In *Hermeneutics 2,* we build on the previous course, and emphasize specific principles for nine genres of the Bible, including Old Testament historical narrative, Law, poetic books, wisdom books, and the Prophets; and New Testament Gospels, Acts, Epistles, and apocalyptic writings. About half of the course provides exercises for the student to practice applying the principles of Hermeneutics 1 and 2.

19. **Course Goals**

Genre	Global Goals
1. Historical Narrative	Explain the five parts of a story, and summarize how analyzing characters helps us interpret a story. Summarize Kaiser's six themes of salvation, noting *already* and *not yet* aspects of each. Answer three questions for interpreting a historical narrative: • What is God telling us about Himself? • How does this story relate to the larger story of salvation in Christ? • What does God want us to be and do?
2. Law	Explain that salvation in the Old Testament and in the New Testament is by faith in God—and explain how this faith expresses itself. Explain and illustrate: Law is not over, under, or behind us, but in us. State the three types of Old Testament laws, and give examples of each.
3. Poetic Literature	Explain the value and way to find the historical context of a psalm. Identify and illustrate five types of parallelism in Hebrew poetry. Analyze the parts, parallelism, figurative language, and message of Psalm 1. Explain ways we can use the psalms today.

Global Goals continued on next page

Genre	Global Goals
4. Wisdom Literature	Use the six forms of proverbs to interpret them. Defend the idea that proverbs are principles, not promises. Illustrate how to interpret a proverb in the context of the whole book of Proverbs.
5. Prophets	Analyze the common standards of the 16 prophets, the 300-year period in which they lived, and the three kingdoms that ruled during their times. Summarize the character, anointing, and authority of the prophets. Apply this. Contrast and illustrate forthtelling and foretelling in the ministry of the prophets. Analyze the two roads of blessings and curses that run through the Old and New Testaments.
6. Gospels	Define kingdom of God, and compare the revelation of God's kingdom to three phases of light. Compare the *already* and *not yet* aspects of the Kingdom on five topics. Explain the Gospels as combination of stories *about* Jesus and teaching *of* Jesus. Draw a diagram of Matthew 1–28 to illustrate this. Analyze the role of ethics in the Kingdom, and the reasons for various views on ethics. Identify the parts of a story, and answer three key questions on any historical narrative.
7. Acts	Summarize the relationship of history and theology in Luke's writings. Compare and contrast what Luke, John, and Paul emphasize about the Spirit. Contrast descriptive and prescriptive aspects of a passage in Acts, related to church expansion. Support your positions with parallel passages.
8. Epistles	Use the historical and cultural background, literary context, word usage and relationships, and literal and figurative language to interpret a passage in the Epistles.
9. Apocalyptic Passages	Illustrate how the historical context and the biblical authors help us interpret apocalyptic literature. Identify at least ten characters in Revelation. Summarize their roles. Compare parallel passages to discern the big story of apocalyptic writings. Identify five contrasts in Revelation that help you interpret apocalyptic passages.

20. Authors

Dr. Quentin McGhee is the founder and senior editor of the *Faith & Action Series*. He earned a B.A. from Southwestern College in Oklahoma City, and a B.S. from Oral Roberts University (ORU). Later he completed an M.Div. at the Assemblies of God Theological Seminary, where he taught beginning Greek. He earned a D.Min. from ORU in 1987 and in 2015 was inducted into the ORU Hall of Fame in the College of Science and Engineering. Dr. McGhee and his wife, Elizabeth, pioneered a church in Oklahoma. They went on to serve as missionaries in Kenya for 15 years. There they helped start many churches, developed an extension Bible school for full-time ministers, and assisted in curriculum development. Currently, Dr. McGhee serves as Director for the *Faith & Action Series*, while Elizabeth assists with graphics, desk-topping, translations, and sales.

Dr. Steve D. Eutsler has a rich ministerial background as a teacher, pastor, preacher, and writer. He serves as a mentor for students of Global University in the areas of Bible and Practical Theology. Also, he has served as adjunct professor at Central Bible College and Evangel University for 12 years, teaching courses on Bible, practical ministry, and preaching. Steve has pastored 18 years. He is the author of four books, *Light for the Darkened Heart, Clothing the Mind, Planning Pentecostal Preaching,* and *The Prison Epistles.* Steve is known for being an outstanding expository preacher. He has contributed sermons to *Preaching On-Line* and illustrations to *PreachingToday.com.* His sermon outlines often appear in *Enrichment Journal* and *Pulpit Helps.* Also, he serves as a Dale Carnegie trainer. He contributed significant research and notes for this *Faith & Action* course on *General Epistles.* He earned his Doctor of Ministry degree at the Assemblies of God Theological Seminary in Springfield, Missouri, where he and his wife, Jackie reside. They have two grown children, Tabitha and Jeremy.

Dr. Carl Gibbs earned a B.A. degree from Northwest College and an M.Div. and D.Min. from Western Seminary in Portland, Oregon. He has served under Assemblies of God World Missions for over 30 years. From 1977-1989 he directed curriculum development for the Brazilian Extension School of Theology (BEST), which now has more than 16,000 degree-level students in six countries. From 1991-1998 Dr. Gibbs served ICI University as Dean of the School of Bible and Theology. He is also known as founder of the Barnabas Series, supplemental notebooks for instructors. Dr. Gibbs has served as a member of DETC and as President of ACCESS. He has taught and lectured throughout Africa, Europe, and Asia. College courses he has written include: Historical Books, Major Prophets, Prison Epistles, Exegesis of Colossians, Hebrews, Soteriology, and Hermeneutics. From 2001-2006 Dr. Gibbs was Dean of Graduate Studies for Global University in Springfield, Missouri. He presently serves as the Director of Educational Resources at Africa's Hope.

21. Contributors and Consultants

Dr. James Hernando has earned the following degrees: B.S. in Education (State University of New York), B.A. in Bible (Northeast Bible College), M.S. in Education (State University of New York), M.Div. (Assemblies of God Theological Seminary), M. Phil. and Ph. D. (Drew University, 1990). Jim and his wife, Moira, have three sons: Matthew, Eric, and Daniel.

Jim taught at Trinity Bible College and served as Chair of Biblical Studies (1980–1986). He has been Associate Professor of New Testament at AGTS from 1990–2014, and Chairs the Biblical Theology Department. Jim has preached and taught Hermeneutics and New Testament Theology in Ukraine, and Costa Rica.

His recent publications are: 2 Corinthians in *Full Life Bible Commentary to the New Testament* (Zondervan), *Dictionary of Hermeneutics: A Concise Guide to Terms, Names, Methods and Expressions* (GPH), *Studies in the Letters of Paul* (Global University), and *First and Second Corinthians* (Faith & Action Series).

Jim has been awarded many honors, such as: Who's Who in American High Schools, Who's Who in American Colleges and University, FTE Hispanic Doctoral Scholarship, Outstanding Alumnus of Valley Forge Christian College, Member of the Advisory Board for the Foundation of Pentecostal Scholarship, and Assemblies of God Distinguished Educator's Award for 25 years of service.

Faith Lund is the daughter of Dr. Quentin and Elizabeth McGhee. She has a B.S. in Biblical Studies from Southwestern Assemblies of God University and an M.Div. (concentration in Biblical Languages) from the Assemblies of God Theological Seminary (AGTS). She is also a candidate for a Ph.D. in Biblical Interpretation and Theology from AGTS. Faith taught in Honduras for a year before joining the Faith & Action team, first as an editor and later as an M.A. She currently serves in Northern Asia with her husband Danny and their two children, Caleb and Viola.

Kelly Iseman is a Ph.D. Candidate at the Assemblies of God Theological Seminary. Her concentration of studies is Luke–Acts. She graduated from Hope College with a B.A. in Social Work, and from Regent University with an M.Div. Kelly is a licensed minister with the Church of the Brethren. In her 10 years of ministry experience, she has served in the roles of adjunct professor with the Caribbean School of Theology, associate pastor, worship leader, Bible teacher in various middle school and high schools, and guidance counselor. She is a passionate preacher and teacher who loves pouring into the next generation of Christian leaders. Kelly is married to Mike Iseman and currently teaches at Lake Mead Christian Academy.

16

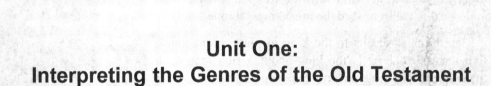

Unit One:
Interpreting the Genres of the Old Testament

Chapter 1 coaches you to interpret Old Testament historical narratives.
- *Explain the five parts of a story, and summarize how analyzing characters helps us interpret a story.*
- *Summarize Kaiser's six themes of salvation, noting "already" and "not yet" aspects of each.*
- *Answer three questions for interpreting a historical narrative: What is God telling us about Himself? How does this story relate to the larger story of salvation in Christ? What does God want us to be and do?*

Chapter 2 gives you practice interpreting Law.
- *Explain that salvation in the Old Testament and New Testament is by faith in God—and explain how this faith expresses itself.*
- *Explain and illustrate: Law is not over, under, or behind us, but is in us.*
- *State the three types of Old Testament laws and give examples of each.*

Chapter 3 guides you to interpret poetry (Psalms).
- *Explain the value and way to find the historical context of a psalm.*
- *Identify and illustrate five types of parallelism in Hebrew poetry.*
- *Analyze the parts, parallelism, figurative language, and message of Psalm 1.*
- *Explain ways we can use the psalms today.*

Chapter 4 helps you interpret Wisdom Literature (Proverbs).
- *Use the six forms of proverbs to interpret them.*
- *Defend the idea that proverbs are principles, not promises.*
- *Illustrate how to interpret a proverb in the context of the whole book of Proverbs.*

Chapter 5 mentors you to interpret prophecy (Major and Minor Prophets).
- *Analyze the common standards of the 16 prophets, the 300-year period they lived in, and the three kingdoms that ruled during their times.*
- *Summarize the character, anointing, and authority of the prophets. Apply this.*
- *Contrast and illustrate forthtelling and foretelling in the ministry of the prophets.*
- *Analyze the two roads of blessings and curses that run through the Old and New Testaments.*

Chapter 1:
Interpreting Historical Narrative—
True Stories of What Happened in History

Imagine you are a servant of the king. All day long you deliver messages for him. Then one day the old prophet demands to see the king, and you let him in. The old prophet—dressed in heavy brown robes that smell of dust and sweat— walks toward the great king's throne.

Figure 1.1   The account of the prophet Nathan confronting King David is an example of historical narrative—a biblical story of history.

The prophet speaks to the king in plain, blunt tones, like a farmer. He tells the king about a rich man with many sheep who stole the only lamb a poor man had. Your king's jaw clenches and his eyes flash with fire. He himself was once a shepherd, and the prophet's story strikes him deeply. He stands and speaks in a voice shaking with anger. The king declares that this rich man deserves death, and demands that the rich man pay back four lambs. Other servants and friends admire the king for his justice and kindness. But the old prophet does not speak at first. When he does, the king staggers backward in shock. "You are the man!" declares the prophet Nathan.

King David grows pale and silent. He slumps back to his throne and puts his hands over his face. At once, he realizes that his sins are known.

The power of this story in 2 Samuel 12 illustrates why God chose to use historical narrative. Most of the Old Testament, as well as the Gospels and Acts, are historical narratives—history that is narrated or told as a story. These stories put human faces on truth. Through characters, settings, and events, a story invites readers to share in the experience—as if they were a part of the story. Stories of the Bible do not just tell us truth, they show truth to us, and help us experience it.

Lessons:

Discern the Lessons of a Story
Goal A: *Review how to find the historical/cultural background and literary context.*
Goal B: *Use 3 questions to separate good actions from bad ones.*

Discern the Message God Intends
Goal A: *Explain why many cultures prefer stories, instead of direct truth.*
Goal B: *Explain why interpreters must find the author's meaning, rather than allegorize.*

Discern the Author's Meaning by Examining the Story
Goal A: *Explain how historical narratives differ from fables, myths, and parables.*
Goal B: *Identify and explain the 5 parts of a story.*
Goal C: *Summarize how analyzing characters helps us interpret a story.*

Discern the Author's Message Through the Big Picture
Goal A: *Explain how small stories in the life of Abraham are part of his bigger story. Apply this to us.*
Goal B: *Summarize Kaiser's 6 themes of salvation, noting "already" and "not yet" aspects of each.*

Discern the Author's Message Through Answering Three Final Questions
Goal: *Demonstrate the skill of answering the three final questions for interpreting a historical narrative.*

historical narrative—true stories of history; scholars tend to refer to biblical stories as historical narrative

genre—type of writing; a distinctive literary type

plot—the storyline; the plan, scheme, or main story; includes the introduction, conflict, crisis, resolution, and conclusion of a story

historical context—the setting of a story. The three aspects are *physical* [the place, objects, and people], *cultural* [customs, values, beliefs, attitudes, and actions], and *temporal* [politics, government, and events].

foil—a person or thing that makes another seem better by contrast

parallel passages—passages on the same subject or topic

 Lesson 1

Discern the Lessons of a Story

Goal A: *Review how to find the historical/cultural background and literary context.*
Goal B: *Use 3 questions to separate good actions from bad ones.*

Review: Please take a few minutes to review *Hermeneutics 1: General Guidelines for Interpreting Scripture.* You will need to use these same guidelines to interpret any passage. In this course, we will consider *specific guidelines* for each *genre* or literary form—such as historical narratives, law, poetry, and gospels.

General Guidelines for Interpreting Scripture (Hermeneutics 1)

A. *Historical/cultural background—Answer these questions:

5 questions about the author of the book or letter:

Who was he? When did he write the book? What setting was he in?
What relationship did he have with those to whom he wrote? What was his purpose?

3 questions about the receivers of the book:

Who were they? What was their city or town like? What was their social status?

3 questions about the passage in the book:

How does the specific passage relate to the author's purpose? Are there any specific historical details to explain?
Are there any specific cultural details to explain?

B. Circles of *literary context (Note that circles 4, 5, and 6 are *parallel passages.)

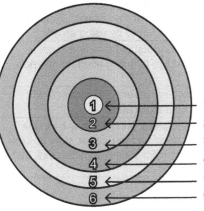

1. **Paragraph context:** *Give the chapter and verse references for your passage.*
2. **Subdivision context:** *Identify the subdivision and its theme that helps explain your passage.*
3. **Book context:** *Relate your passage to the book's theme, outline, and parallel passages.*
4. **Bible context:** *Compare parallel passages: same author/different book.*
5. **Bible context:** *Compare parallel passages: different author/same testament.*
6. **Bible context:** *Compare parallel passages: other testament.*

C. Word usage and relationships: Explain key words, phrases, conditions, and promises.

D. Language—literal and figurative: Does the literal meaning of your passage make sense? Does the context explain the meaning of your text? Are there figures of speech to explain?

Figure 1.2 Review of *Hermeneutics 1:* Some general guidelines for interpreting Scripture

A word to the wise (teachers and students): For an overview of where we went in *Hermeneutics 1* and where we are going in this chapter, look at Figure 1.2.

Introduction. The hundreds of stories in the Bible make it interesting to read. At the same time, it is a challenge to interpret this *genre (pronounced ZHAN-reh), or type of writing. The interpreter needs to separate the lessons or morals from the details of history.

About 40 percent of the Old Testament and much of the New Testament is *historical narrative—true stories of history. Since many stories outside the Bible are not true, scholars tend to refer to biblical stories as historical narrative or biblical narrative. **Story** is the most common type of writing in the Bible. God has chosen to reveal Himself and His will to us through extraordinary stories involving ordinary people in ordinary circumstances. Stories are the heart and soul of the biblical witness about God. So some refer to the Bible as *the story of the relationship between God and people.* God put stories in the Bible because they are powerful and delightful. Stories are interesting and inviting. They draw us in. As we listen to a story, we experience its emotions and identify with some of the characters. We see ourselves in parts of the story. Through stories, we do more than hear about truth—we experience it and participate in its application. So let us *appreciate* stories for the reasons why God chose to use so many of them.

When we interpret the Bible, we must pay careful attention to understand and apply stories. Figure 1.3 lists some guidelines to help us interpret stories of the Old Testament. Please read through these guidelines. Then we will explore them as you study through the chapter.

Seven Guidelines to Help Us Interpret Stories of the Old Testament[1]
1. The *setting* of a story is its *historical context*. This setting has **three** dimensions. The *physical* dimension includes a place, objects, and people. The *cultural* dimension has customs, values, beliefs, attitudes, and actions. The *temporal* dimension includes politics, government, and events. To interpret a story, we must consider this three-fold setting in relation to the characters and the plot.
2. Reading the story itself is the starting point for understanding it. So *first* climb into the story, and understand it from the inside out—rather than bringing explanations with us to the story. Then, *after* reading a story, the larger story of the Bible may enlighten our understanding. For example, we read in Genesis that God created man in His own image, and gave him dominion over creation. Yet the larger story of Scripture helps us understand more fully the meaning and benefits of being created in the image of God. He made us, not only to rule over creation, but to fellowship with Him and to be like Him. Our destiny is to grow and be transformed into His glorious likeness.
3. The *plot* of a story includes the introduction, problem/conflict, climax, resolution, and conclusion (Figure 1.5). The plot and flow of a story help us understand the main point (message). Stories of the Bible do not tell us everything that happened. God led the writer to tell *certain* things, for the purpose of communicating a *message* to us. So let us enjoy each story, but keep in mind that what God wants to share is the <u>message</u> of the story. We should not try to make all the details into little messages. Rather, let us understand that the little details were necessary to bring us the big message. For example, in the story of Noah and the ark, let us not search for the significance of the type of wood Noah used, or the number of stories on the ark. These details are interesting, but the main message is that God saved Noah and his family by using an ark.
4. The story itself is the messenger. There may be clues in the tone of the story that help us understand it—clues such as sorrow, joy, sarcasm, or irony. If these clues are lacking, we should not distort God's message by using allegory or types that move away from the story God gave.
5. Biblical stories, by themselves, are not teachings. Teachings and doctrines must be based on several passages. God's people must study the Scriptures and apply them in various circumstances, under the Spirit's guidance.
6. To apply the message of a story, it is helpful to state the message as a cross-cultural principle. A principle may be in the form of a command, a promise, a warning, or a timeless truth. For example, a principle based on the Exodus story is: *God delivers His people.* There are many applications of this one principle, such as deliverance from slavery to bitterness, lust, greed, food, work, power—or any form of slavery.
7. Always answer three questions about historical narrative (biblical stories): • What is God revealing to us about Himself? • How does the story relate to God's plan of salvation that reaches completion in Christ? • What does God want us to be and do?

Figure 1.3   Guidelines for interpreting biblical stories

A. In a biblical story discern good examples from bad ones.

A lady once complained to a pastor that some of King David's actions in the Bible offended her. And even though his actions were wrong, the Bible did not condemn him.

Like the lady, many of us have wondered about some of the stories in the Bible. With the great stories of faith and righteousness, we find accounts of incest, lying, adultery, cruelty, deceit, suicide, and murder. Often, the Bible records sinful acts without condemning those who sinned. Still, as readers, we must discern that all sin is wrong. In the Bible, God expects readers to recognize that evil is evil. Each night when the sun goes down, God does not have an angel announce, "It is dark." Likewise in Scripture, whenever someone sins, God does not say, "This is sinful." There are some things, such as darkness and sin, that God expects us to recognize!

In Scripture, we must discern what is a good example to follow, and what is only the historical record of a person's actions. Not everything a biblical hero does is an example for us to follow today. Most of the time, the Bible records righteous acts without praising them. Likewise, it describes sins without condemning them.

David committed adultery with Bathsheba (2 Sam. 11). The Bible describes what David did, but his actions are not a good example for us to follow. Likewise, the Gibeonites deceived Joshua (Josh. 9). The Bible describes their deceit, but their actions are not a good example for us.

Q 1 ✎ *Do the Gibeonites teach us to lie (Josh. 9)? Explain.*

Biblical writers seldom tell us which actions or commands are good to follow. So we may struggle to discern good from bad. Centuries ago, some from Europe killed the local people in the Americas and South Africa. They said they were obeying God's order to Joshua to slay the Canaanites. These Europeans claimed that God's command to kill the local people was a command for them to follow.

Q 2 ✎ *Should we, like Joshua, kill unbelievers and take their land? Explain.*

And just a few decades ago, in Nazi Germany, ministers said that murdering the Jews was God's will—because the Jews had asked for Christ's blood to be on the heads of their children (Matt. 27:25).

Even today some claim that having many wives is biblical, because the patriarchs had several wives. Look at the following examples and determine if each example is good or bad for us to follow.

Q 3 ✎ *Complete Figure 1.4 by explaining why we should not follow these examples.*

Bible	Action	Your Explanations Why We Should Not Follow These Examples
Gen. 6:14	Noah built an ark.	Bad. Obedience is good, but we do not need to build a physical ark.
Gen. 12:1	God told Abraham to leave home and move to a new land.	
Gen. 19:30-38	Lot had incest with his daughters.	
Gen. 29:31–30:24	Jacob had four wives.	
Exod. 1:19	The midwives lied to save the babies.	
Deut. 20:16-18	Israel killed their enemies because they were instructed by God to do so.	
Josh. 2:4–6	Rahab lied to save the spies.	
Ruth 3:9	Ruth proposed marriage to Boaz.	
Esther 2:15-18	Esther married an unbeliever.	
Ezek. 4:4-8	Ezekiel preached, lying on his side.	

Figure 1.4   Practice explaining actions we should not follow.

We gave you some easy practice discerning good and bad examples. But some examples in the Bible are harder to evaluate. Should a modern believer test God as Gideon did with a *fleece*? Is a believer allowed to marry an unbeliever as Esther did? Should a new convert divorce an unbelieving mate as Ezra commanded the Jews to do (Ezra 9:1-2, 10:2-5)? Will a Christian leader be punished as David was (1 Chron. 21) if he counts those who attend church?

Q 4 *List 3 questions for determining if a biblical action or command is for us to follow today.*

Q 5 *How should believers in your culture greet each other?*

Q 6 *Should believers today divorce unbelievers, as Ezra commanded (Ezra 10:1-5)? Explain.*

Q 7 *Should a believer marry an unbeliever, based on Esther's actions? Explain.*

Q 8 *Why did the author of Numbers not explain Balaam's sin?*

Q 9 *Does Rahab's lie to save the Israeli spies teach believers to lie in extreme circumstances (Josh. 2; Rev. 21:8)?*

Q 10 *Is the Bible's description of Hosea's marriage a pattern for believers today? Explain.*

Q 11 *Is it sinful to count God's people? Explain.*

Q 12 *Give an example of an Old Testament practice that is an example for believers today.*

How can we discern when Scripture gives us an action or command to follow? Here are three questions to clarify what a *story* is *teaching*—and what it is *not teaching*.

- Does the Bible condemn this action in other passages?
- Does the Bible confirm and repeat this action, promise, or command in other passages?
- Is the action or command just part of a local culture, but not a practice for all believers?

Test a passage with all three questions as you seek to interpret it. For example, does Scripture teach all believers to greet each other with a holy kiss?

- Greeting each other with a holy kiss passes the test of question 1, for the Bible does not condemn it.
- Greeting each other with a holy kiss passes the test of question 2, for several passages in the New Testament refer to it (1 Pet. 5:14).
- But on question 3, we find that greeting with a kiss was *only* a cultural practice. Even today, some parts of the world greet with a kiss on the cheek, but other parts of the world greet with a handshake, a bow, or in another manner. Kissing as a greeting is not an example for all believers. The type of greeting depends on the culture. So be sure to apply **all three questions** when interpreting a passage. Now, let us take a closer look at each of the three questions.

1. Do other passages of the Bible condemn the action? The action of a biblical hero cannot guide us if it contradicts other Scripture. Biblical stories may describe lying, adultery, deceit, and other sins. In these cases, the biblical writer assumes that his readers know the Scriptures and commands of God. He does not feel the need to repeat what is clear from other Scriptures.

For example, Numbers 22 does not tell us the sin in Balaam's heart. But Peter says Balaam loved the wages of wickedness (2 Pet. 2:15). Likewise, Jude condemns Balaam's error (Jude 11).

2. Do other passages of the Bible repeat and confirm the action, promise, or command? You have learned that a doctrine must not be based on a single passage. For all believers to follow a practice, several places in the Bible must teach us to do it.

Some events are <u>not</u> an example for us to follow—they are unique in history.

- God told Hosea to marry an adulterous wife (Hos. 1:2). The Bible never repeats this command to believers. Rather, Hosea's marriage was an example of God's relationship to unfaithful Israel.
- David numbered his people and suffered God's wrath (1 Chron. 21:1-30). There is no biblical command against numbering the people of God. In fact, Numbers and Ezra contain several examples where leaders numbered God's people and were blessed. The Gospels mention the number of people Jesus fed. Acts mentions the number of new believers on the Day of Pentecost. David's sin was not that he numbered the people, but that he was proud and trusted in the large army of Israel.

Other practices <u>are</u> good examples in Scripture.

- Elijah prayed for a sick boy (1 Kings 17:17-23), and God healed him. Many passages—in both the Old and New Testaments—teach us to pray for the sick to be healed (James 5:14-15).
- The Israelites lifted up their hands to God in praise and prayer (Ps. 28:2; 134:2). Likewise, Paul tells us to lift up holy hands in prayer, without anger or disputing (1 Tim. 2:8).
- The Lord's Supper was not just a one-time event in Christ's life. Rather, it was still a practice in the early church 30 years later (1 Cor. 11:23-26).

3. Is the action or command only part of a local culture? Sometimes the actions of people in the Bible reflect a cultural practice of their time. Even though a cultural custom was common in Israel, it may lack meaning today in the same or other cultures.

- Rachel's generation believed that a *mandrake plant assured that a woman would conceive a baby (Gen. 30:14-16). This reflected her culture—not a medical pattern for modern believers.
- Ruth asked Boaz to show he would marry her by throwing a corner of his robe over her (Ruth 3:9). The way she proposed marriage and the way he responded were part of an old Jewish custom. These practices are not patterns for single women today.

B. An example of using the three questions

Let us apply the three questions to Gideon's fleece—seeking a sign to know God's will (Judg. 6:36-40). Is Gideon's method a pattern for believers today? Or did he already know God's will, but lacked the courage to act on it?

Question 1: Other verses in the Bible discourage us from asking God for signs. God prefers that we trust Him without signs. Jesus encourages us to walk by faith, not by sight and signs.

Perhaps Zechariah wanted a sign when he refused to believe the message from Gabriel about his wife giving birth to John the Baptist in her old age. As a result of not believing, Zechariah could not speak for 9 months (Luke 1:19-22, 63-64). It is better to believe God's Word than to ask Him for a sign.

Question 2: In the Old Testament, signs are mentioned a few times. God gave signs to Moses and to Pharaoh (Exod. 4:1-9, 7–10). Isaiah invited Ahaz to ask for a sign (Isa. 7:10-11). Likewise, Hezekiah asked Isaiah for a sign that God would heal him (2 Kings 20:8). But in Gideon's case, God had already sent an angel to talk with him. Still, Gideon asked for signs. Gideon's request seems to reveal doubt, rather than faith.

Question 3: Gideon's fleece may have been a cultural practice. In the New Testament, we see others asking for signs (Matt. 12:38; 16:1; Luke 23:8; John 6:30). Seeking and following signs seems to be common in many cultures. False christs and false prophets deceive many with signs (Matt. 24:24). The Antichrist will lead the whole world astray with the signs he does (2 Thess. 2:9; Rev. 13:13-14). *"A wicked and adulterous generation asks for a sign!"* (Matt. 12:39). It is wise to believe the Bible and to walk with God by faith, rather than seeking signs to guide us.

Conclusion. God gave some signs to guide and assure His people under the old covenant. In contrast, under the new covenant, it is easier for us to know God's will. He puts His Spirit within us to guide and assure us. He has given us an entire Bible to help us know His will. Likewise, He guides us through wise counsel, circumstances, and spiritual events such as dreams and visions. So under the new covenant, God has many ways to guide believers without using signs.

Q 13 ✎ *Is the old Jewish custom of greeting with a kiss part of your culture (1 Pet. 5:14)? Explain.*

Q 14 ✎ *Does the old Jewish custom of washing feet have meaning in your culture (John 13)? Explain.*

Q 15 ✎ *How does the old Jewish custom of wearing a veil relate to your culture (1 Cor. 11:5-6)? Explain.*

Q 16 ✎ *In Matthew 16:1-4 what did Jesus teach about asking for signs?*

Q 17 ✎ *Did Jesus encourage us to ask for signs (John 4:48)?*

Q 18 ✎ *In John 20:29, whom does Jesus say is blessed?*

Q 19 ✎ *What 2 advantages for guidance do believers have under the New Testament?*

Lesson 2

Discern the Message God Intends

Goal A: *Explain why many cultures prefer stories, instead of direct truth.*
Goal B: *Explain why interpreters must find the author's meaning, rather than allegorize.*

A. Stories are an indirect way of communicating a message.

In many cultures people avoid speaking truth directly. And they avoid saying something negative to an equal or superior. They will tell a story or a proverb that hints at their feelings—without directly stating how they feel. The prophet Nathan used this indirect method with King David. Nathan told a story that expressed how God felt about David.

Q 20 ✎ *Why do some tell stories instead of speaking truth directly?*

A missionary asked the principal of a Bible school to give his opinion about the school's new books. For years the school had used notes that the teachers copied for the students. But now, the students had textbooks written at a much higher reading level.

"What do you think of the new books?" asked the missionary. The principal answered with a story. He said that when he was a young man, he was invited to a fellowship meeting in a town nearby. He wanted to impress his friends by wearing shoes. He had never owned a pair of shoes, so he went to the market looking for his first pair. He found a pair he liked, at a good price, but they were one size too small. The seller warned him they would hurt his feet, but he insisted on buying the shoes.

He walked 15 miles to the meeting, and had pain with every step. On the way home, he took out his knife and cut the end off each shoe. This allowed his toes to have more room. Later he threw the shoes beside the road, and walked home barefoot. With that the principal stopped talking. Smiling, the missionary understood. The new books did not fit the students!

Q 21 *Would you know the purpose of the story about the new shoes if you did not know the missionary's question? Explain.*

Like the story about the shoes, stories of the Bible are often told without an explanation. The interpreter must examine the story to discern what the author meant. Then—after the author's meaning is clear—it is possible to apply the truth to others. If we had the story about the shoes, but did not know the missionary's question, we would not understand the purpose of the story. Likewise, to understand the purpose of biblical stories, we must examine the context of a story, the story itself, and the way a story is told. Then, and only then, can we discern the author's purpose in telling a story.

Q 22 *What are the 2 most important tasks of interpreting a biblical story?*

B. Discern the author's point.

The two goals of hermeneutics are: Get the author's point, and apply it. The point of a biblical story is the point the author intended. When we preach the author's point, we are preaching the Word of God. Otherwise, if we misinterpret a story and do not preach what the author meant, we are twisting the Scriptures. Man or woman of God, preach the Word of God, not your own imaginations. As Paul charged Timothy, "Preach the word" (2 Tim. 4:2). God has called you to preach His holy Word. You are studying Hermeneutics because you want to be faithful to your calling. God has promised to anoint His Word. He has promised that it will accomplish its purpose, and not return to Him void [empty] (Isa. 55:11). As there is life in a seed, there is life in the Word of God Almighty. When you preach the messages that God sent to earth, it will take root, grow, and bear fruit. But take heed that you preach His Word—the message that He sent. For there is no life or power in the words of humans. The best speeches will not change lives. The most creative talks will not bring conviction for sin. Minister of God, beware, lest you substitute your thoughts for God's thoughts. *"Do your best to present yourself to God as one approved, a worker who ...correctly handles the* **word of truth**" (2 Tim. 2:15).

Q 23 *Whose word are you preaching if it is not the author's point?*

Preach the true message of God! This is the most important lesson in this course. Preach God's Word, not your own imaginations. Preach the message God sent from heaven to earth. Be content to be God's messenger. Your task is to deliver the message God sent. But be sure you have understood His message. Otherwise, who will give that message to your people? And if you do not preach the message He sent, what excuse will you give when you stand before Him at the end of your days. Approach the Bible with reverence, fear, and trembling. Search and study the Bible with total sincerity. For your calling is to stand before people and deliver the message God has sent to them from heaven. Jesus turned water into wine. But take heed, lest you turn the wine of His Word into water!

Q 24 *How do some preachers turn wine into water?*

Q 25 *Do you think there is a hidden truth in the boards of the ark, or the stripes of a zebra? Explain.*

As we saw in *Hermeneutics 1,* the Church has at times suffered from the *spiritual disease of allegorizing.* Recall that those who use allegory try to find hidden meanings in the details of history and stories. These unfaithful messengers abuse their calling. They lack humility and reverence for God. If they preach on Noah's ark, they must say that the three levels of the ark represent something. Their imagination knows no limits. Perhaps they must even find a spiritual meaning for the stripes of the zebra that was on the ark. Nonsense! If you want to entertain people with your own thoughts, go do it outside the church, without a Bible in your hand. The message of Noah's ark is that God judged the world for sin, but saved Noah because he was righteous and found grace in God's eyes. There is no hidden truth in the boards of the ark, or the three levels of the ark. The levels were so the people and animals would have enough room. Preach the message God sent. Avoid letting your mind wander away from your calling to preaching your imaginations. Preach the Word!

Even today, some preachers lead believers astray with allegory. These unbiblical interpreters believe that every Old Testament story has two meanings: the author's meaning, and a spiritual meaning based on the New Testament. But it is wrong and dangerous to change the meaning of the author.

God inspired the biblical authors to write the stories He gave them. It is **wrong** to take away the meaning God intended, and add a meaning God did not want. Those who replace God's meaning with their own meanings are very proud. Imagine a messenger so proud and unfaithful that he adds to or takes away from the meaning God Almighty wanted us to have, preaching his own thoughts!

Q 26 ↖ *What can we say about a messenger who substitutes his ideas for God's ideas?*

Some say this error of using allegory is preaching the right message from the wrong passage, but it is worse than that. Using allegory cheats believers—it steals from them the great truths God intended in His stories. Allegory also sets a bad example. It teaches believers to misinterpret the Bible. Allegorizing shifts the focus from God to humans. It turns attention away from God's message to human imagination. Using allegory, there are no guidelines or control of the interpretation. False teaching can result, and teachers claim these teachings are based on the Bible. So we must be Bible-centered—finding the one purpose of a biblical story, the meaning God Himself wants us to have.

Q 27 ↖ *What is the difference between being "Bible-centered" and "reader-centered"?*

The stories of the Bible—its historical narratives—are NOT allegories. When the Bible presents a story as history, we should not search for hidden meanings—meanings that the author never imagined. All true interpreters of the Bible begin with the same goal—to find the author's meaning. The faithful interpreter does not dare suggest what a story means to us today **until** he or she understands what the story meant to the writer and those who first heard it.

Q 28 ↗ *What is the first goal of all true interpreters of the Bible?*

This does not mean that every biblical story has only one interpretation. Nor does it mean that a pastor can preach only one sermon from a biblical story. But we are saying that the author's purpose is the basis of all interpretation. Pastors may preach a thousand messages from one passage. But all of these messages should be based on the one true message God sent through a human writer.

At times, a biblical writer may not have understood the full application of his message. For example, Moses wrote the story of Abraham receiving promises of a covenant. Perhaps Moses did not fully understand this truth. His understanding of the scope of the promises was limited. Moses may not have realized *how* the Messiah would bless all of the nations. But Moses did understand that God would give Abraham many children. These descendents would have a land. And one of the children of Abraham would bless the nations. The Holy Spirit led writers of the New Testament to fully explain to us the promises God gave to Abraham. God did not leave us to interpret His stories, using our own imaginations. Rather, He inspired New Testament writers to clarify the full meaning of Old Testament stories. So we should be humble enough to preach the plain truth, and not preach things the apostles did not write about. Yet some proud preachers today think they have more insight than the apostles of Christ!

Q 29 ↖ *If a story in the Old Testament was not clear, what did God do for us under the new covenant?*

Q 30 *Why is it dangerous to use allegory as a method to find hidden meaning in the Old Testament?*

Q 31 *Explain the proverb: A lion should not hunt for a mouse!*

Q 32 *What do the oxen represent in 1 Samuel 6?*

Q 33 *What does the oil represent in 2 Kings 4?*

Q 34 *Did Paul use allegory to interpret the story of Hagar and Sarah? Explain.*

Finding the author's meaning in biblical stories is not easy. Seldom does the biblical writer explain his story. This has caused some readers to add their own meanings to the story, based on the New Testament. For example, a pastor was preaching about the time that Abraham sent Eliezer to search for a wife for Isaac. The preacher said that Abraham was a symbol of the Heavenly Father, and that Eliezer was a symbol of the Holy Spirit—sent to search for the bride of Christ (Gen. 24). When Eliezer found her, he placed her on a camel and brought her to the son. Likewise, the preacher claimed that pastors—like camels—bear the church to Christ. Like the camels, these pastors may drink in the Holy Spirit. Then, they must travel for days without study or prayer, because the work of the Lord is heavy. This is bad preaching and bad interpreting. The preacher was not preaching the Word of God; he was preaching his own imaginations! Those who use allegory as a method to interpret should not claim to speak for God! **The main truth is the plain truth, and the plain truth is the main truth**! Pastor, preach the plain truth. A lion should not hunt for a mouse!

Using allegory to interpret the Old Testament lacks the authority of God. One pastor preached about the ark of God coming back to Israel from the Philistines. He said returning the ark was a symbol of pastors, who like the oxen, lead the church back to God. He stopped his message when God's people killed the oxen as a sacrifice (1 Sam. 6:14)! This pastor was not preaching the plain truth. He was wasting people's time and abusing his calling. To find the main truths of this passage, you must read 1 Samuel 5–6. Review the story. It tells about God's judgment on the Philistines. When their gods were near the ark, they fell and broke into pieces. And God struck the Philistines nearby with deadly tumors. Then the Philistines—not the spiritual leaders of Israel—sent the ark home. The oxen do not represent anything! Some principles we might draw from the story are:

- God will judge those who use holy things in an unholy manner.
- God finds ways to speak to those who do not know Him.
- God finds ways to bring His people back into fellowship with Him.

Another pastor preached on the story of the woman who filled many vessels with oil. He said that the oil was a symbol of the Holy Spirit coming in Pentecostal power. But the pastor did not continue to compare the oil to the Holy Spirit when Elisha told the woman to sell the oil (2 Kings 4:7)! Nonsense! Pastor, do not hunt for a mouse in 2 Kings 4. Instead, preach on great principles that are there, such as:

- The best thing to do with a great need is to bring it to God.
- God delights to help those who come to Him.
- To receive a miracle, we must obey God in faith.
- Those who receive a miracle should continue to honor God.

Some say that Paul gave Christians an example of allegorizing the Old Testament stories. These note that Paul compared the children of Hagar and Sarah to children of the Law and Promise (Gal. 4:21-31). But Paul did not ignore the purpose of Moses. Rather, Paul used the story of Abraham to teach a lesson. Ishmael, the child of Hagar, was born in the normal manner. Ishmael was born because Abraham tried to fulfill God's promise in a fleshly manner. But the child of Sarah was born by the Spirit. It took a miracle of the Spirit for Sarah to give birth. Like Sarah's child, we are children of the Spirit. We are *not* born in the normal way as a result of human efforts, like Hagar's son. Rather, we believers are those who have *a supernatural birth* by the Spirit. Paul uses the story of Hagar and Sarah to emphasize a great principle:

> *FLESH GIVES BIRTH TO FLESH, BUT THE SPIRIT GIVES BIRTH TO SPIRIT* (JOHN 3:6).

Paul discerned the principles in the Old Testament story of Hagar and Sarah. Then, he applied those principles to believers of his day. He did not create a second meaning for the story. In the same way, modern pastors should find the principles within a biblical story. Then, we should apply these principles to believers today, in our own culture and time. Many of the events of the Old Testament are examples for us today (1 Cor. 10:6). Still, we must not ignore the author's meaning. Rather, we begin by discerning the meaning of a biblical writer, and then apply the same principles of the story to believers today. In the next lesson, we will give you some guidelines for identifying the true message in historical events and stories of the Bible.

Q 35 *What principle did Paul teach based on the story of Hagar and Sarah?*

Lesson 3 — Discern the Author's Meaning by Examining the Story

Goal A: *Explain how historical narratives differ from fables, myths, and parables.*
Goal B: *Identify and explain the 5 parts of a story.*
Goal C: *Summarize how analyzing characters helps us interpret a story.*

A. View characters and miracles as real in historical narrative.

It is important for interpreters to discern four types of stories.

1. *Fables are stories that a person creates or invents to teach a principle or moral truth.

Q 36 *Give an example of a fable?*

Aesop was an ancient Greek teacher who knew the power of a story. He created fables. The fable he made up about the sun and the wind has lasted over 2000 years. In the story, the sun and the wind debate about who is stronger. When they saw a traveler walking on the road, the wind suggested a test. The one who could remove the traveler's coat would be strongest. The wind tried first—blowing with all his force. But this caused the man to hold his coat tighter. Then the sun tried. He gently shined on the man and soon the coat was off. After telling this fable, the teacher asked: What is the principle or moral of the story? After discussion, people discerned that the moral was: "Kindness has more power to change a person than force."

2. Myths or **legends** are traditional or cultural stories that never happened. These are often about heroes or nature. People imagined them to entertain, or to explain something, often in nature. For example, an elder in Africa created a *myth* to explain why people are different colors. This myth or legend says that God created all people black. Then, He created a small pond of water for people to wash in, so they would become white. God used different animals to carry the message about the water. To the Europeans, he sent a gazelle as a messenger. This animal ran quickly, so the Europeans arrived first and washed completely. But to the Africans, God sent the chameleon—which travels even slower than a turtle. So the African arrived last. There was only enough water left to wash the palms of their hands and the soles of their feet!

3. Parables (and allegories) are earthly stories that a leader—like Jesus—created to teach a spiritual lesson. Listeners recognize that parables may not have happened—but could have happened—and are a method of teaching. For example, Jesus used the parable of the sower to teach a spiritual lesson. The main principle is that as the fate of the seed depends on the soil, the fate of the gospel depends on the type of person who hears it.

Q 37 *Did the story of the 10 virgins occur, or was it a story Jesus created to teach a truth? Give your opinion.*

4. Historical narratives are true stories that tell what happened in history. These days, there are many who call themselves Christian theologians. But there are also many views about inspiration. Liberal teachers confuse or destroy believers. These liberal teachers call the Bible inspired, but claim that it does not have authority over our lives. Likewise, they say the Bible does not contain principles that are true for every generation. Those who believe in inspiration without authority tend to see the Bible

Q 38 *How do those who do not believe in miracles interpret the feeding of the 4,000?*

stories as myths or legends that illustrate truth. In the past, they say, people used fables, myths, and legends about miracles to teach deeper truths.

Review *Hermeneutics 1*, chapter 1, Lesson 2. There we studied the qualifications of a biblical interpreter. Those who do not believe that the Bible is inspired are not able to interpret it correctly. We believe that all Scriptures are:

- inspired by God in a *verbal*, *plenary* way;
- the *revelation* of God to us;
- *infallible* and *inerrant* (true and without error on matters of history, science, and doctrine);
- the *authority* over our faith and living.

Liberal teachers deny miracles of the Bible. But they encourage readers to look beyond the account of a miracle to the principle or moral it illustrates. For example, false teachers say the feeding of the 4,000 was not a miracle. They claim that Jesus never multiplied the loaves and fishes. Rather, they say that first, the small boy was generous—he shared his fish and bread. Then, these false teachers say that all of the people followed his example and shared their fish and bread. In contrast, the Scriptures say that the people had been with Jesus 3 days, and had nothing to eat (Matt. 15:32). Those who do not believe that Jesus multiplied the loaves and fishes interpret the event in a strange way. They say the lesson of this story is sharing—not the power of Jesus to provide for his people.

Q 39 ↗ *How would you respond to a person who said the story of Abraham is true, but Abraham never lived?*

These liberal teachers see the characters in the Bible as legends. For example, they claim that people such as Adam, Eve, and Abraham never lived in history. Likewise, these false teachers do not believe in prophecy. They claim that biblical writers deceived people—writing prophecies about things that had already happened—to give the Bible a sense of authority.

Q 40 ↖ *What are some truths that liberal Bible teachers deny?*

These same teachers do not believe that Jesus was God in the flesh. They do not believe He did signs and wonders. **And they do not believe Jesus rose from the dead!** These are wolves in sheep's clothing. They carry Bibles, but do not believe that biblical stories in them are true history. They define inspiration in a way that is different than we do. They claim, for example, that the story of Adam and Eve is true, although they deny that Adam and Eve ever lived on the earth. Do they believe that north is south, and water is fire? They remind us of Pilate who asked, *"What is truth?"* (John 18:38). Imagine a person in court, claiming to tell the truth, but just making up stories? Would these false teachers say his stories were true? Would they say the person was telling the truth? **Paul put it plainly. He said if Jesus is not raised from the dead, our preaching is useless, and we are false witnesses about God** (1 Cor. 15:14-15).

Q 41 ↗ *Did Jesus believe that Jonah was a real person who was swallowed by a fish? Explain.*

Q 42 ↖ *How does the principle of John 14:2 encourage believers?*

Q 43 ↖ *How is believing related to interpreting?*

Inspiration without divine authority lowers the Bible to the level of Greek myths and Aesop's fables. The Pentecostal interpreter should accept biblical stories in the same way that Christ and the apostles accepted them. When Christ spoke of Old Testament characters, He accepted them as real and their actions as historical. Jesus accepted the story of Jonah and the great fish as a true story of history (Matt. 12:40). Peter accepted Noah and the saving of his family as a real event (1 Pet. 3:20). Likewise, Peter refers to the biblical account of the time when Balaam's donkey spoke, and the apostle considers it to be a historical fact (2 Pet. 2:16). Paul says that the events and people of the Exodus were real examples for us (1 Cor. 10:5-6). Likewise, Jesus said that heaven is a real place. Our Lord said: *"If it were not so, I would have told you"* (John 14:2). It is important to believe that the historical stories of the Bible really happened. As we believe this, we will be able to interpret the stories correctly.

B. Examine the plot of a story to discern the author's point.

To find the author's purpose, we must analyze the plot. *Plot* refers to the plan of a story—including all the parts in the beginning, middle, and end of a story. The longer stories in the Bible have a line of action —like a climb up a mountain. Many stories have five parts in the plot (Figure 1.5).

Q 44 *What are the 5 parts of a story? Name and explain them.*

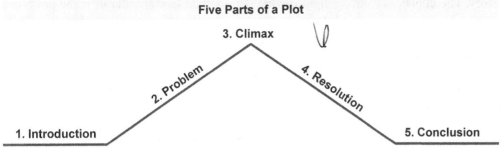

Figure 1.5   Many stories have five parts in the plot.

1. The introduction includes the setting and some characters of the story. The author may introduce more later, as the story develops. For example, see Ruth 1:1-2 for the *setting* and introduction of the characters Elimelech, Naomi, and their two sons. And then, as the introduction transitions to the problem, the author introduces Naomi's daughters-in-law, Orpah and Ruth (Ruth 1:3-4).

Q 45 *In the Introduction of Ruth, when and where was the setting of the story (Ruth 1:1-2)?*

Q 46 *How many characters does the author introduce in Ruth 1:1-4??*

2. The problem or need. This is where the climb up the mountain begins. We see a conflict. (See Ruth 1:3-22, where Naomi's husband and sons all die. Ruth clings to her, but they have no one to help them as they return to Bethlehem.) Sometimes the problem gets worse. The author gives us more information as the story unfolds. See Ruth 2:1-19, as Ruth gleans in the field of Boaz.

3. The climax (Ruth 2:20). We have reached the top of the mountain.

4. The solution. This is the climb down the mountain (Ruth 2:21–4:12). The main character is either informed, confirmed, transformed, or judged. Ruth stays close to Boaz and asks him to marry her, as her kinsman-redeemer. Boaz agrees.

5. The conclusion (Ruth 4:13-22). Naomi is honored as Ruth bears a son named Obed, the father of Jesse, the father of David.

We have examined the five parts of a story, using the example of Ruth. Now, it is time for you to practice identifying the parts of a story, using the stories of Abraham and Elijah.

Q 47 *Complete Figure 1.6 on the story of Abraham offering Isaac.*

Part of the Story	Description	Genesis
1. Introduction		21:32-34
2. Problem		22:1-10
3. Climax		22:11-12
4. Solution		22:13-18
5. Conclusion		22:19

Figure 1.6   The parts of the story: Abraham being tested to offer Isaac as a sacrifice (Gen. 21:32–22:19)

Q 48 *Complete Figure 1.7 on the story of Elijah on Mount Carmel.*

Part of the Story	Description	1 Kings
Introduction		18:16-20
Problem		18:20-21
Rising action		18:22-29
Turning point		18:30-31
Problem increases		18:32-37
Climax		18:38-40
Result		18:41-45
Post-script		18:46

Figure 1.7   The parts of the story: Elijah challenges the prophets of Baal on Mount Carmel (1 Kings 18:16-46)

Q 49 ⬚ *Complete Figure 1.8 by filling in the empty boxes.*

To interpret a story correctly, we must identify its climax—the top of the mountain. Although the climax is usually near the end of the story, it is the emotional center of the story. The climax is a strong sign of what is important to the writer. It is the point in a story where the hero responds to a test, overcomes a struggle, or makes a decision. Three examples of the climax of a story follow (Figure 1.8).

Scripture	Climax	Lesson
1 Sam. 17:46-49	David defeats Goliath.	There is a God in Israel who saves by His power.
Esther 7:1-3	Esther saves the Jews; she reveals her identity.	Esther was willing to identify with her people and faith.
Neh. 6:15-16	Jews finish rebuilding the walls.	Even the enemies of the Jews recognized that God helped the Jews rebuild the walls.
Gen. 22:11-12		
1 Kings 18:38-40		
Judges 7:17-21	Gideon and his 300 men, with trumpets and lamps, attack thousands of Midianites.	

Figure 1.8   The climax of a story helps us recognize the author's purpose—the main lesson he wants us to know.

C. Discern the author's message and meaning by analyzing the characters of a story.

Studying the characters is another key to understanding the meaning of a biblical writer. Learn to answer three questions about a main character.

Q 50 ⬚ *Name 5 round characters in Genesis.*

1. Is a character flat or round? A flat character is one whom a story describes little. In contrast, a round character is described much, with many details. Bible stories tend to use few words, so when a character is described much, the reader should pay attention. Three examples of **round** characters are:

- **Esau.** From the beginning, Moses describes Esau as one who cared little about his birthright. When Esau sold it for a bowl of soup, the author gives us seven verbs that describe his attitude: swore, selling, ate, drank, got up, left, and despised (Gen. 25:33-34). There is no doubt what the author thinks of Esau's actions.

  [33] *"But Jacob said, 'Swear to me first.' So he <u>swore</u> an oath to him, <u>selling</u> his birthright to Jacob.* [34]*Then Jacob gave Esau some bread and some lentil stew. He <u>ate</u> and <u>drank</u>, and then <u>got up</u> and <u>left</u>. So Esau <u>despised</u> his birthright"* (Gen. 25:33-34).

- **Jacob** is shown to be a deceiver. He dresses to look like his brother, lies to his father, and plots with his mother (Gen. 25:27-34; 27:1-36).

- **Joseph** is described over and over in positive ways. The Bible tells us that God was with Joseph (Gen. 39:3, 21; 41:52). Those in authority gave Joseph honor and responsibility. The author describes him as a blessed father. And we see him as a person filled with faith and love—able to forgive his brothers.

Q 51 ⬚ *Name a Bible character who did not change, and one who did change.*

Q 52 ⬚ *Fill in the blanks in Figure 1.9.*

2. Is a character changing (dynamic), or remaining the same (static)? The Bible has many stories of people who change greatly during a story. Seeing how they change helps us discern the writer's purpose. A person may change for the better or for worse. **If** a character's choice results in a **negative result**, the biblical writer **means** for us to recognize the folly of this example. **If the character's choice results in a positive, good result,** the writer means for us to recognize the wisdom of the character's decision. In Figure 1.9, practice discerning the meaning of the author.

Bible	Action of a Character	Writer's Meaning
Gen. 45	Joseph is filled with sorrow, but forgives his brothers. The result is that God blesses him and his family.	Wise, godly example

Figure 1.9   Continued on next page

Continued from previous page

1 Sam. 13:8-14	Saul's choice to sacrifice without Samuel resulted in defeat. Saul changed from being small in his own eyes to being big.	Example of foolishness
	Job changed and became even better.	
	David changed, and repented for his sin.	
2 Chron. 20:35-37	King Jehoshaphat made an alliance with Ahaziah, an evil king of Israel. They agreed to build a fleet of ships. But they never sailed because of the evil alliance.	
2 Chron. 26:16-21	King Uzziah changed for the worse; he became proud, so God struck him with leprosy.	
	Esther changed and testified about her faith	
	Nebuchadnezzar changed and became a better king.	
	Jonah changed and obeyed God.	

Figure 1.9   Practice discerning the writer's meaning through a character's actions and attitudes

Watch for three types of positive changes in a biblical hero.

Q 53 ⋏ *What are 3 good ways a Bible hero may change?*

- The hero may be **transformed** by the changing of his heart (Gideon went from fear to courage),
- The hero may be **informed** by receiving new revelation or promises from God (Abraham received the promise after agreeing to offer Isaac as a sacrifice), or

Q 54 ⋏ *Why should we pay attention to the way a biblical hero changes?*

- The hero may be **confirmed**, crowned, or established as God's person for a position or responsibility (David killed Goliath and was *confirmed* as the future leader of Israel).

Noting how the hero is changed from the beginning to the end of the story is a powerful tool to discern the author's purpose in a story.

Q 55 ⋏ *In Figure 1.10 decide whether the change was transformation, information, or confirmation.*

Scripture	Change	Type of Change
Gen 12:1-5	Abraham receives the promise.	
Gen 32:27-28	Jacob has his name changed to Israel.	
Exod. 3–4	Moses responds to the call to challenge Pharaoh.	

Figure 1.10   Practice analyzing the type of change in a character of a story.

3. Is a character contrasted with someone (a *foil), as we contrast light with darkness? Biblical authors use contrast to emphasize good and bad. A foil is a person used as a contrast, as Mordecai is contrasted with Haman. The contrast in a story may be between persons, actions, or attitudes. In the story of the birth of Christ, the foil of the wise men is King Herod (Matt. 2:1-18). Long ago, jewelers put a very thin piece of metal foil under a stone in a piece of jewelry. The foil caused the stone to shine more brightly.[2] Likewise, in a story a foil emphasizes the good characteristics of the hero.

Q 56 ⋏ *Complete the last line of Figure 1.11.*

Hero (Good Example)	Foil (Bad Example)	Scripture
Abraham chose the hill country.	Lot chose the valley near the cities.	Gen. 13
Joseph was faithful, sexually.	Judah committed adultery with Tamar.	Gen. 38–39
Ruth clung to Naomi's God and people.	Orpah left Naomi.	Ruth 1
David had a sling and stones.	Goliath had great armor and weapons.	1 Sam. 17
David sought God's counsel.	Saul sought a witch.	1 Sam. 28; 30:7-8
Elijah		1 Kings 18:16-46

Figure 1.11   Bible stories often contrast a good and bad example—a hero and a foil.

Lesson 4: Discern the Author's Message Through the Big Picture

Goal A: *Explain how small stories in the life of Abraham are part of his bigger story. Apply this to us.*
Goal B: *Summarize Kaiser's 6 themes of salvation, noting "already" and "not yet" aspects of each.*

A. Relate small stories to bigger stories—the parts to the whole.

Sometimes a small story is part of a bigger story. (Some call this a multi-plot story—one big story with many smaller plots.) In this case, we must interpret each small story as a chapter in an entire book. The life of Abraham is an example of many small stories that are part of a big story or theme—walking by faith. At first, some of the small stories seem to lack meaning:

- Abram lied about Sarai.
- He allowed Lot to choose the best land.
- He took Hagar as a wife.

But later, we see that these small stories are good steps, and bad steps, in Abraham's journey of faith.

Q 57 ✎ *Identify at least 4 small stories in the life of Abraham that show steps of faith.*

Q 58 ✎ *Have you ever tried to fulfill God's promise in a fleshly manner? Explain.*

> [1]*The LORD had said to Abram, "Leave your country, your people and your father's household and go to the **land** I will show you. [2]I will make you into **a great nation** and I will **bless** you; I will make your name great, and you will be a **blessing**. [3]I will **bless** those who bless you, and whoever curses you I will curse; and all peoples on earth will be **blessed** through you." [4]So Abram left, as the LORD had told him; and Lot went with him. Abram was seventy-five years old when he set out from Haran. [5]He took his wife Sarai, his nephew Lot, all the possessions they had accumulated and the people they had acquired in Haran, and they set out for the **land** of Canaan, and they arrived there* (Gen. 12:1-5).

God promised Abraham a land, a seed, and a blessing for the nations. In these small stories we see Abraham either accepting the promise by faith <u>or</u> trying to fulfill God's promise by his own efforts.

Q 59 ✎ *Complete the final column in Figure 1.12.*

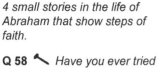

Genesis	Story or Event in the Life of Abraham	Promise	Genesis	Did Abraham Walk by Faith?
12:1-9	He travels to Canaan.	Land, seed, blessing	12:2-3, 7	Yes
12:10-20	He lies about Sarai.	Land		
13	He separates from Lot.	Land	13:14-17	
14	He rescues Lot.			
15	He believes God's Word.	Seed	14:17	
16	He marries Hagar.	Seed		
17	God changes his name.	Seed	17:1-8	
18–19	He intercedes for Sodom.	Seed, blessing	18:17-19	
20	He lies about Sarah.	Seed		
22	He offers his son.	Land, seed, blessing	22:15-18	

Figure 1.12   Small stories in the life of Abraham are part of his bigger story—walking by faith.

Q 60 ✎ *Complete Figure 1.13 on small stories in the life of Joseph.*

Like Abraham's story, the life of Joseph contains many small stories (sub-plots). These are part of Joseph's bigger story in Genesis 37 to 50.

Small Story or Event in the Life of Joseph	Chapters in Genesis
Joseph goes from his father's house to the pit.	
Joseph goes from Potiphar's house to the prison.	
Joseph goes from Pharaoh's house to his father's tent.	

Figure 1.13   Small stories about Joseph are parts of the big story of his life: saving many people.

A. Relate small stories to the big story of redemption.

Many believers read the stories of the Old Testament, but they do not see how these stories relate to the big picture. Instead, they just read a story and apply it to themselves. For example, they read about David and Goliath, and then say, "God can help me slay the giant of unbelief." The Old Testament stories have a lot to teach us about faith, family, and God. But the Old Testament is more than a collection of devotional stories. Together, the stories of the Old and New Testaments form God's big story of salvation.[3] Every story in the Bible is like a piece of the puzzle. Each story is part of the story of salvation. Likewise, the story of each believer—of every generation—is a part of God's story of redemption. Abraham is a part of the salvation story, and so are you and I!

Q 61 *The story of Abraham is part of which 2 larger stories?*

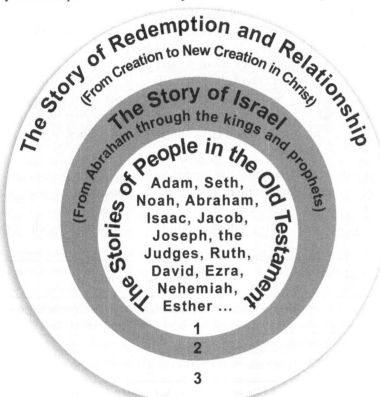

Figure 1.14   All small stories in the Old Testament are part of the big story of salvation—that includes both testaments.

Walter Kaiser has summarized the story of salvation with **six themes**.[4] Kaiser teaches that each story of the Old Testament supports one or more of the six themes. We may divide the six themes into two groups. The first group of three tells what God promises to do for His people. The second triad tells what God promises to be for His people.

Q 62 *Of Kaiser's 6 themes, which one emphasizes our participation and cooperation?*

Theme 1, 2, 3, 4 & 6
I (God)

Six Themes About God's Relationship With His People	
Theme 1: I will give you a **land**—a kingdom.	*Theme 4:* I will be **your God**.
Theme 2: I will give you a **Seed**—a Messiah.	*Theme 5:* You will be **my people**.
Theme 3: I will **bless** the nations—through the Messiah.	*Theme 6:* I will dwell **with you**.

Figure 1.15   The Old Testament stories support six themes of salvation.

Themes 1–3 are in God's promise to Abraham in Genesis 12:1-5. God promised Abraham a **place**, a **Seed**, and a **blessing** for all nations. God repeats this three-fold promise throughout Abraham's life. Sometimes Abraham accepts the promise by faith, but other times he tries to fulfill this promise by his own efforts. Note how these three themes—the land, the Seed, and the blessing—are woven into each major event of Abraham's life. In each step or event of Abraham's life, he is tested to respond by faith.

The three great themes of what God will do —the land, the Seed, and the blessing— relate to promises.

Q 63 *In themes 1–3, what did God promise to do for Abraham and his children?*

A land.   At the Exodus, the people leave Egypt and travel toward the Promised Land. In Deuteronomy 30, Moses reminded Israel that God would give them the Land of Canaan. God promised the land *if* they obeyed Him. In contrast, God warned that He would remove them from the land *if* they disobeyed. Captivity stories reflect this warning. Israel did conquer the land. But in time they turned from God to idols. This led to the destruction of the Northern Kingdom. Later, Judah was conquered and suffered 70 years in the captivity of Babylon. Still, God brought a remnant of Jews back to their land. The prophets spoke of a coming kingdom—a renewed land in the future. This prophecy will be further fulfilled when Christ rules on the earth. And in eternity we experience the ultimate *Promised Land*—the substance of what is now just a shadow.

A Seed.   The promise of a Seed was about one special Son—Christ (Gal. 3:16). God repeated this promise to David (2 Sam. 7). There, God declared that the special Seed would be a son of David—and that His kingdom would never end. This prophecy of David's special Son is behind many stories about protection of the Seed. For example, God protected Josiah, the only son of David alive in his days. In the New Testament, the promise of God giving Abraham a Seed is partly fulfilled in Christ's first coming. But a greater fulfillment will be when Christ returns to rule the earth. And eternity will bring the highest level of God giving Abraham and His children a Seed—when, in Christ, we live and fellowship with God forever.

Q 64 ➚ *How did God use Abraham to bless the nations?*

A blessing.   God promised Abraham that the special Seed would be a blessing to the nations. This promise is repeated in Jeremiah 31. The Old Testament often emphasizes the theme that God delights to bless other nations. For examples, see the stories of Ruth, Naaman, Rahab, Jonah, and such. This promise is fulfilled today in the Church—made of believers from every tribe and tongue.

Promise God Gave to Abraham—Genesis 12:1-5	Promise Repeated	Promise Fulfilled
A land	Deuteronomy 30 Israel will possess Canaan.	Partly fulfilled in Canaan, but it looks to Christ's kingdom on earth, and our eternal dwelling with Him.
A Seed	2 Samuel 7 David will have a Son who will reign forever.	This was partly fulfilled by Christ's first coming (Gal. 3:16), but it also looks to His second coming, and eternity.
A Blessing	Jeremiah 31:31-34 A new covenant with the Law written on human hearts	This blessing to all nations is being fulfilled today in the Church (Heb. 8:10), and will continue for eternity (Rev. 21:3, 7).

Figure 1.16   **God promised Abraham and his children a place, a Seed, and a blessing (Gen. 12:1-5).**

Themes 4–6 are in many passages of the Bible (Exod. 6:7; Lev. 26; Jer. 31:31-33; Ezek. 36:26-28; Zech. 2:10-13; 2 Cor. 6:16; Heb. 8:10; 1 Pet. 1:15; Rev. 21:3, 7). Let us look at the first reference to this three-part promise.

Q 65 ➚ *What are some actions that fulfill "I will be your God"?*

I will be your God.   12 *"I will walk among you and be your God, and you will be my people.* 13*I am the* LORD *your God, who brought you out of Egypt so that you would no longer be slaves to the Egyptians; I broke the bars of your yoke and enabled you to walk with heads held high"* (Lev. 26:12-13).

Through stories of the Old Testament, we see God fulfilling His promise "I will be your God." As Israel's God, we see Him redeeming, saving, delivering, healing, protecting, and providing for His people—in many passages of Genesis, Exodus, Numbers, Joshua, Judges, Samuel, Kings, Chronicles, Ezra, Nehemiah, and Esther.

Q 66 ➚ *What contrast is there between theme 5 and the other 5 themes?*

You will be my people.   Notice that five of the six themes begin with "I" and focus on God. And of course, this theme emphasizes that we are *God's* people—we belong to *Him*. But unlike the other five themes of the Old Testament, this theme begins with "You." Throughout the Old Testament, the historical narratives emphasize that as God's people, we must relate to Him in ways He requires. One of the great themes of the Old Testament and the New Testament is that to be God's people, we must be like Him. To be the possession of a holy God, we must be holy. To fellowship with a righteous God, we must live righteously. Hundreds of verses in the Bible emphasize what it means *to be God's people*. Above, we looked at Leviticus 26:12-13, which emphasizes *"I will be your God."* But attached to these two verses of the covenant is the part, *"you will be my people."* Thus for 32 verses in Leviticus 26:14-46, God emphasizes that to be His people we must obey His voice, and live according to His laws. Children of God cannot live like children of Satan, God's enemy. God is light, and to fellowship with Him, we must walk in the light (1 John 1:7-9). We must be holy in the way we live, because God is holy (Lev. 11:44; 1 Pet. 1:15). *"You are to be holy to me because I, the Lord, am holy, and I have set you apart from the nations to be my own"* (Lev. 20:26).

Yet even as we practice being holy and righteous, we depend on God to enable us. He is our God from A to Z. God made it clear to Israel that He will be our God *as* we will be His children. In our relationship, He gives us all we need for life and godliness as we walk in faith, love, obedience, and dependence on Him (2 Pet. 1:3).

Q 67 What makes it possible for us to live holy and righteous as God's people?

Some of our brothers and sisters in Christ object to us seeing any illustrations of good behavior in the stories of the Old Testament. For example, one helpful book on hermeneutics (in some ways) says that if you look for something Joseph *was* or *did* that Christians today should imitate, "you will not find any such thing in the narrative."[5] Gordon Fee and Douglas Stuart are respected scholars. They want our interpretation of Old Testament stories to focus completely on God, not humans. We agree that God is the focus of our faith. But we agree with Dr. Steve Mathewson who believes that excluding moral lessons from historical narrative is "unnecessarily reductionistic."[6] Writers of the New Testament saw moral lessons and examples for us in Old Testament stories. Jesus told believers *"Remember Lot's wife!"* (Luke 17:32). Paul and James use Abraham as an example of living by faith (Rom. 4; James 2:20-24). Paul refers to stories of Israel's failure, and says *"these things were written as an example"* (1 Cor. 10:11). Likewise, the writer of Hebrews recalls stories of the Old Testament and urges us to learn moral lessons from these stories, so that we do not fall as the Israelites fell (Heb. 3–4). And Hebrews 11 names 15 Old Testament examples of faith to encourage and instruct us. Likewise, James guides us to suffer *like* the prophets (James 5:10), be patient *like* Job (James 5:11), and pray *like* Elijah (James 5:17-18). And these are but a few of a long list of examples from the Old Testament that the apostles use to instruct and encourage our moral behavior. We agree to keep the focus of our faith on God. But there are many examples in the Bible that God has given to instruct us—some whose behavior we must avoid, and others whose behavior we will do well to imitate, as the Corinthians were to follow Paul's example (1 Cor. 11:1). Is it possible that some theologians do not see virtues to imitate in the life of Joseph because their theology does not include the importance of human choices?

Q 68 Do you believe God gave us biblical stories to show us examples to imitate and avoid? Illustrate.

For those of us who are open to seeing it, we recognize a helpful contrast between Judah's immoral behavior and Joseph's purity. The biblical author puts these accounts side by side in the historical narrative of Genesis 38–39.

I will dwell with you. This promise of God to be with His people appears often in the Bible. Some examples are God's promise to be with Moses and to help him deliver Israel from Egypt (Exod. 4:12-13). Likewise, God was with all of His servants, including prophets, kings, and priests. And we see His presence with His people as a group—through the pillar of fire and the cloud that went with Israel to Canaan. His presence filled the temple of Solomon in a visible, dramatic way. And even in exile, God's presence was with the remnant of Jews in Babylon. God has promised to be with us always, and to never leave or forsake us (Matt. 28:20; Deut. 31:6; Heb. 13:5).

Q 69 ✎ *In what sense is the final theme fulfilled already, but not yet?*

This promise has been fulfilled in part. But it will be fulfilled completely at the climax of the salvation story when God lives with His people in the New Jerusalem.

> ³*And I heard a loud voice from the throne saying, "Now the dwelling of God is with men, and he will live with them. They will be his people, and God himself will be with them and be their God. ⁴He will wipe every tear from their eyes. There will be no more death or mourning or crying or pain, for the old order of things has passed away"* (Rev. 21:3-4).

Q 70 ✎ *In Figure 1.17, draw an arrow to show where Ezra was in God's big story of salvation.*

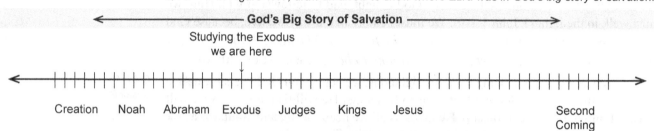

Figure 1.17   The Exodus is a small story in God's big story of salvation.
When we read any story of the Bible, such as the Exodus, we should think about how it relates to
God's big story of salvation, and remind ourselves, "Reading this story, we are *here* ↓ on God's timeline of salvation."

Lesson 5

Discern the Author's Message Through Answering Three Final Questions

Goal: *Demonstrate the skill of answering the 3 final questions for interpreting a historical narrative.*

A. Three final questions to answer about any story of the Old Testament

Q 71 ↗ *What are the 3 final questions to ask about any story of the Old Testament?*

What we have said up to this point is to help you succeed at this final step.

> **5.** Answer the three questions.
>   • *What is God revealing about Himself in this story?*
>   • *How does this story relate to God's big story of salvation in Christ?*
>   • *What does the story teach that God wants us to be and do?*
> **4.** Relate small stories to bigger stories and themes.
> **3.** Analyze the story: key words, literal or figurative language, tone, plot, and characters.
> **2.** Analyze the literary context (including parallel passages, circles 4-6).
> **1.** Analyze the historical and cultural background.

Figure 1.18   Five steps to interpreting a story of the Old Testament

Dr. Steve Mathewson, and the Gospel Coalition, encourage us to answer **three questions** as we interpret and apply each story of the Old Testament.[7] These three questions offer a balanced perspective for the relationship between God and His children. Here are the three questions to answer about each Old Testament story:

- **What is God revealing to us about Himself in this story?** Does the story emphasize God's love, holiness, mercy, righteousness, faithfulness, judgment, patience, provision, sovereignty? Does it reveal Him as Creator, King, Judge, Father, or Missionary?

- **How does the story relate to God's big story of salvation that reaches completion in Christ?** Note that God's plan of salvation spans from *creation* to *new creation*, from Genesis to Revelation. Together, the small stories of the Bible make up one big story about the relationship of God to humans. So as we interpret a small story, it is helpful to see how it relates to the big story. For example, we understand the story of the Passover in Exodus as we relate it to Jesus, *"the Lamb of God who* *takes away the sin of the world"* (John 1:29). So one of the main questions we must ask about any story of the Old Testament is: How does this story relate to the larger story of salvation that God completes in Jesus Christ? (Figure 1.18)

- **What does the story teach that Gods want us to be and do?** When interpreting a story, start with its theology and ethical thrust, *not* with the characters' behavior. Then point out what characters did right or wrong. Stories of the Bible seldom state the main point or points. Rather, God expect us to study the stories and discern His message. Biblical stories contain good characters to imitate, and bad characters whose behavior we should avoid. Likewise, there are characters who are good at times, and bad at other times, or who are partly good and partly bad. Biblical characters, like all of us, had their strengths and weaknesses—their best times, normal times, and worst times. Yet, in a biblical story, there are characters who may illustrate what God wants us to *be* or *do*.

Hermeneutics and homiletics that center on God **do not preclude** *imperatives* (commands, exhortations, and warnings). Rather, Scripture always bases the *imperative* (what we must do) on the **indicative** (facts: what God has *surely* done *for us* in Christ and will *surely* do *in us* by the power of His Spirit). A message that calls listeners **to be** or **to do** *without* **God's enablement** is sub-gospel and sub-Christian.[8] Likewise, a message is sub-Christian if it focuses *only* on what God has done for us in Christ, and *does not call us* to a Spirit-led life—worthy of a relationship with Christ (See Phil. 1:27). When our hermeneutics and homiletics answer the three questions about a story, we present a balanced message.

Q 72 ⬉ *Does a gospel that includes obedience to God's commands subtract from the message of grace? Explain.*

As an example, let us answer the three questions on **the story of Cain and Abel** (Gen. 4:1-16).

Question 1: *What is God revealing about Himself in this story?* This historical narrative reveals several truths about God.

Q 73 ⬈ *In the story of Cain and Abel, what are 2 things that God reveals about Himself?*

- *God requires that we approach Him in a certain way.* We cannot come to God on our own terms. We must approach God in a way that pleases Him. Abel and his offering pleased God. But God did not look with favor on Cain and his offering. Note that the biblical text links the person *and* his offering (Gen. 4:4-5). Something in Cain's attitude or his offering did not please God. The text indicates that Cain and Abel knew what would please God.
- *God is merciful.* Cain rejected God's counsel and encouragement. Then he murdered Abel, his brother. It was necessary for God to judge Cain. But even in judgment, God showed mercy. He put a mark of protection on Cain. He extended Cain's life, giving him time to repent.

Question 2: *How does the story relate to God's plan of salvation that reaches completion in Christ?* When Adam and Eve sinned in Eden, recall God's promise as He spoke to the serpent: *"I will put enmity between you and the woman, and between your offspring and hers; **he will crush your head**, and you will strike his heel"* (Gen. 3:15). The hostility between people and snakes represents the great battle between God and Satan throughout history. The seed or offspring of the woman would one day crush the head of the evil one. And all believers will one day share in this victory—when God crushes Satan's head beneath our feet (Rom. 16:20). Through Cain, Satan killed the godly son of Adam and Eve. But God is faithful to His promise of salvation. And by the end of Genesis 4, we see that a new son is born to continue the godly lineage. And men once again begin to call upon the Lord (Gen. 4:25).

Question 3: *What does the story teach that God wants us to be and do?*

Q 74 ⬈ *From the story of Cain and Abel, what can we see that God wants us to be and do?*

- *God wants us to be righteous and do what is right—even if we get it wrong the first time.* God is for us, not against us. He wants us to succeed. God cheers for us. He wants us to repent and accept forgiveness when our attitude is wrong. He desires a relationship with us. When Cain was discouraged, God encouraged him to do what was right, and be accepted (Gen. 4:6-7).

• *God wants us to master sin* (Gen. 4:7). With sin, there are only two possibilities: It will master us, or we will master it. Sin crouches at the door like a wild animal, eager to destroy us (Gen. 4:7). God desires for us to accept a relationship with Him on His terms. Then He will empower us to be the masters of sin, not the slaves of sin (Rom. 6:1-14). The power to overcome is God's, but the choice to overcome is ours.

Answering the three questions about a story helps guide us on the path of good hermeneutics. And it keeps the passage in perspective—focusing on God, His plan of salvation, and our cooperation with Him. When you preach a story, be sure to answer the three questions. But let the story guide your outline. It does not matter in which order you answer the three questions. Preach the story in all of its beauty and power. Let the scenes and parts of the story shape your message. Answer the three questions and preach the principles as you move through the story—as God gave it to us. Then the power of the story will capture the hearts of your people. They will learn the story itself—in relation to God, His plan of salvation, and our cooperation with Him. If we preach about Cain and Abel, our final point would be that even in judgment, God is merciful.

B. Practice answering the three final questions about an Old Testament story.

Figure 1.18 summarizes all we have covered in this chapter. On any story of the Old Testament, we want students to practice answering three final questions. We have done this for you in the example of Cain and Abel. Now it is your turn to practice.

First Practice: The Tower of Babel (Gen. 11:1-9). (Read the helpful notes in the NIV Study Bible.)

Question 1: *What is God revealing about Himself in Genesis 11:1-9?*

Question 2: *How does Genesis 11:1-9 relate to God's plan of salvation that reaches completion in Christ?*

Question 3: *What does Genesis 11:1-9 teach that God wants us to be and do?*

Second Practice: Abraham and Abimilech (Gen. 20:1-18).

Question 1: *What is God revealing about Himself in Genesis 20:1-18?*

Question 2: *How does Genesis 20:1-18 relate to God's plan of salvation that reaches completion in Christ?*

Question 3: *What does Genesis 20:1-18 teach that God wants us to be and do?*

How does this small story relate to the bigger story of Abraham's call and destiny?

Was Abraham a good example for us in this small story? Explain.

Test Yourself: Circle the letter by the ***best*** completion to each question or statement.

1. To identify the historical/cultural background
a) analyze the 6 circles of context.
b) compare Old Testament and New Testament cultures.
c) contrast ancient and modern history.
d) answer questions about the author and readers.

2. An example of a merely cultural practice is:
a) tithing.
b) honoring parents.
c) foot washing.
d) communion.

3. Why do many cultures prefer stories?
a) They are creative.
b) They are easy to understand.
c) They are indirect.
d) They are hard to change.

4. A key to interpreting Scripture is:
a) allegorizing the original meaning.
b) understanding the author's meaning.
c) comparing our times with the past.
d) contrasting various passages.

5. What is a historical narrative?
a) A biblical story
b) A version of history
c) A recording of history
d) An interpretation of history

6. The third part of a story is:
a) the problem.
b) the climax.
c) the solution.
d) the postscript.

7. Which is TRUE of King David?
a) He changed.
b) He remained the same.
c) He was a flat character.
d) He was not contrasted.

8. How many small stories of Abraham are in the Bible?
a) Only 1
b) 3 or less
c) 3 to 5
d) More than 5

9. Five of Kaiser's six themes focus on:
a) a land and a seed.
b) humans.
c) God.
d) the Messiah.

10. The middle of the final three questions for interpreting a historical narrative is about:
a) God.
b) repentance.
c) character.
d) salvation.

Essay Test Topics: Write 50-100 words on each of these goals that you studied in this chapter.

- Review how to find the historical/cultural background and literary context.
- Use 3 questions to separate good actions from bad ones.
- Explain why many cultures prefer stories, instead of direct truth.
- Explain why interpreters must find the author's meaning, rather than allegorize.
- Explain how historical narratives differ from fables, myths, and parables.
- Identify and explain the 5 parts of a story.
- Summarize how analyzing characters helps us interpret a story.
- Explain how small stories in the life of Abraham are part of his bigger story. Apply this to us.
- Summarize Kaiser's 6 themes of salvation, noting *already* and *not yet* aspects of each.
- Demonstrate the skill of answering the three final questions for interpreting a historical narrative.

Chapter 2:
Interpreting Old Testament Law

Introduction

On her radio program, a woman spoke against homosexuality. She used an Old Testament law to support her belief. A listener was offended, and published a letter criticizing her. He said she quoted one law from the Old Testament to condemn homosexuals, but ignored many other Old Testament laws. He said that if she obeyed one Old Testament law, she should obey other laws such as:

Figure 2.1   God gave to Moses the Law on Mount Sinai.

- Stone a person who works on the Sabbath (Exod. 35:2).
- Kill and burn a bull on an altar as a sacrifice (Lev. 1:9).
- Do not eat shrimp or lobster (Lev. 11:10).
- Do not sew two types of cloth together (Lev. 19:19).
- Do not trim off the sides of your hair (Lev. 19:27).

This brings us to *two* of the most difficult questions about interpreting the Old Testament:

- **First question:** How do the laws of the Old Testament relate to believers today? For example, which laws does God require us to keep?
- **Second question:** What is the purpose of laws under the old covenant?

The Law spans from Exodus 20 to Numbers 10:10, and through much of Deuteronomy. From these small parts of the Old Testament, believers have made many strange interpretations. So in this chapter we will take a closer look at the Law and what God wants us to learn from it.

Lessons:

Salvation Under the Old and New Covenants—Part 1

Goal A: *Explain what a covenant is, and why God's people can be under only one covenant.*
Goal B: *Explain that salvation in the Old and New Testaments is by faith in God—and explain how this faith expresses itself.*

Salvation Under the Old and New Covenants—Part 2

Goal: *Explain and illustrate: Law is not over, under, or behind us, but it is in us.*

Old Testament Laws: Ceremonial, Moral, and Civil—Part 1

Goal A: *State the 3 types of Old Testament laws, and give examples of each.*
Goal B: *Explain why believers live by the ethical principles of the Law.*

Old Testament Laws: Ceremonial, Moral, and Civil—Part 2

Goal: *Explain that some civil laws illustrated eternal principles. Give examples.*

Key Words

ceremonial laws—laws that pertain to religious rituals such as circumcision, laws for priests, concerning the tabernacle, sacrifices, and cleansing

civil laws—laws that guide relationships; laws forbidding the religious practices of the Canaanites and guiding the Jews in relating to each other

moral laws—laws that teach what is always right or wrong, such as the Ten Commandments

progressive revelation—the advancement of light or revelation from God in stages; God's provision to mankind of more understanding concerning Himself through time. The old covenant often revealed an infant form of truth, but the new covenant reveals mature, full-grown truth.

Lesson 6 Salvation Under the Old and New Covenants—Part 1

Goal A: *Explain what a covenant is, and why God's people can be under only one covenant.*

Goal B: *Explain that salvation in the Old and New Testaments is by faith in God—and explain how this faith expresses itself.*

In this lesson and the next, we explore five truths about salvation under the old and new covenants. Let us consider these five truths (A–E), one by one.

A. The Old Testament Law is part of a covenant.

Our Bible is divided into two major parts: the Old Testament (covenant) and the New Testament. The Old Testament contains 39 books that are often grouped into four parts: the 5 books of the Law, the 12 Historical Books, the 5 books of Poetry and Wisdom, and the 17 books of the Major and Minor Prophets.

All of the 39 books of the Old Testament are built upon the foundation of the Law. But only four books contain laws—Exodus, Leviticus, Numbers, and Deuteronomy. The Law was the basis of God's relationship to Israel. The prophets spoke to the people about keeping God's Law. Most of the Old Testament is the story of a covenant based on the Law.

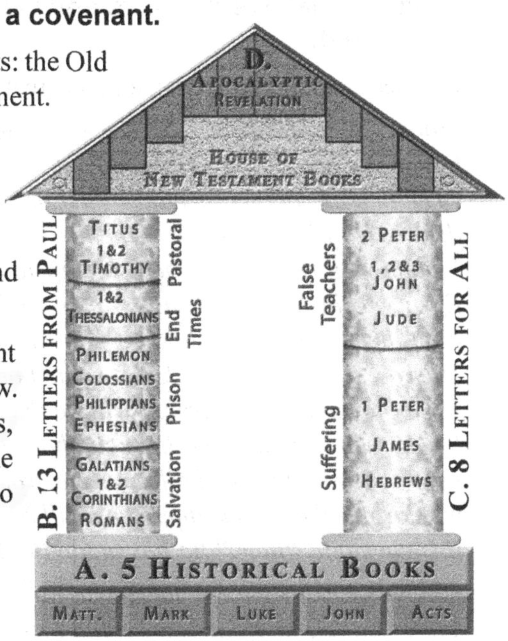

A *covenant* is an agreement between two *parties*—with duties and promises that each side agrees to perform.[1] Today, two parties sign a contract when a piece of ground is sold. The contract states conditions—what the *seller* and *buyer* agree to. *Both* must keep their parts of the conditions, or the agreement is not valid (binding). In the Bible, the only covenant without conditions is the one God made with Noah.

> [11] *"I establish my covenant with you: Never again will all life be cut off by the waters of a flood; never again will there be a flood to destroy the earth."* [12]*And God said, "This is the sign of the covenant I am making between me and you and every living creature with you, a covenant for all generations to come:* [13]*I have set my rainbow in the clouds…"* (Gen. 9:11-13).

There were no conditions on the covenant God made with Noah. However, all other covenants in the Bible have conditions.

In an agreement between humans, there may be bargaining. But when God creates a covenant, there is no bargaining—God alone decides the conditions and blessings. Humans cannot change God's covenant, but they may choose to accept or reject it. (For a thorough treatment of covenants, see *The Full Life Study Bible* articles on Genesis 26:3-5 and Deuteronomy 29:1).

God made a covenant with Abraham (Gen. 12). The Lord renewed this covenant with Isaac and Jacob. About 400 years later, God expanded the covenant through Moses. Moses wrote down the Law—which had over 600 commandments. These laws were the basis of the Old Testament (or covenant). *If* the Israelites obeyed the 600 laws, God agreed to bless and protect them. If they broke laws accidentally, there were sacrifices

Figure 2.2
House of Old Testament books

Figure labels:
D. APOCALYPTIC REVELATION
HOUSE OF NEW TESTAMENT BOOKS
B. 13 LETTERS FROM PAUL — TITUS 1&2, TIMOTHY 1&2, THESSALONIANS, PHILEMON, COLOSSIANS, PHILIPPIANS, EPHESIANS, GALATIANS, 1&2 CORINTHIANS, ROMANS
Pastoral, End Times, Prison, Salvation
False Teachers — 2 PETER, 1,2&3 JOHN, JUDE
Suffering — 1 PETER, JAMES, HEBREWS
C. 8 LETTERS FOR ALL
A. 5 HISTORICAL BOOKS — MATT., MARK, LUKE, JOHN, ACTS

Q 1 *How were the books of the Major and Minor Prophets built upon the Law?*

Q 2 *What is a covenant?*

Q 3 *In a covenant with God, can humans bargain? Explain.*

Q 4 *God's covenant with the Jewish nation was based on _____.*

for forgiveness. If the Israelites broke the laws through rebellion, God promised to curse them. These laws are contained in Exodus 20 through Deuteronomy 33.

When we study the Old Testament, we should remember that it is about a covenant between God and the Jews, based on the Law of Moses. The Law was like a road. If they walked on it—not turning aside to the right or the left—God would bless them (Deut. 28:14). If they disobeyed and took another road, God would be angry and curse them (Deut. 28:15-68). (See a diagram of the two roads in Figure 5.7.)

B. Today, all believers—Jews and Gentiles—are under the new covenant, not the old.

God set aside the old covenant and created a new covenant.

*[7]For if there had been nothing wrong with that first covenant, no place would have been sought for another. [8]But God found fault with the people and said: "The time is coming, declares the Lord, when **I will make a new covenant** with the house of Israel and with the house of Judah. [9]It will not be like the covenant I made with their forefathers when I took them by the hand to lead them out of Egypt, because they did not remain faithful to my covenant, and I turned away from them, declares the Lord. [10]This is the covenant I will make with the house of Israel after that time, declares the Lord. I will put my laws in their minds and write them on their hearts. I will be their God, and they will be my people. [11]No longer will a man teach his neighbor, or a man his brother, saying, 'Know the Lord,' because they will all know me, from the least of them to the greatest. [12]For I will forgive their wickedness and will remember their sins no more." [13]**By calling this covenant "new," he has made the first one obsolete; and what is obsolete and aging will soon disappear*** (Heb. 8:7-13; Jer. 31:31-34).

Christ is the end of the law so that there may be righteousness for everyone who believes (Rom. 10:4).

Christians are **not** under the old covenant based on Law. We see this clearly in several New Testament verses:

- *"For sin shall not be your master, because you are **not under law,** but under **grace**"* (Rom. 6:14).
- *[16]"From the fullness of his grace we have all received one blessing after another. [17]For the **law** was given through Moses; [but] **grace** and truth came through Jesus Christ"* (John 1:16-17).
- *"Clearly no one is justified before God by the **law,** because, 'The righteous will live by **faith**'"* (Gal. 3:11).
- *[3]"Again I declare to every man who lets himself be circumcised [to keep the Law] that he is obligated to obey the whole law. [4]You who are trying to be justified by the **law** have been alienated from Christ; you have fallen away from **grace**"* (Gal. 5:3-4).

The Old Testament is not our covenant with God. *"Christ is the end of the law so that there may be righteousness for everyone **who believes** [in Him]"* (Rom. 10:4). The New Testament is *our* testament or covenant.

C. Salvation in the Old and New Testaments is by faith in God.

God is, and has always been, the only One who saves people. God is love, and His love reaches out with salvation. No person has ever earned his or her salvation. Salvation is, and has always been, something that God offers humans by His grace. He allows us to accept or reject the salvation He offers. Some choose to accept salvation, and so they live to please and obey Him. Others reject God's offer of salvation and live a life of rebellion and disobedience. But even those who seek to obey and please

Q 5 ↖ *How was the Old Testament Law like a road?*

Q 6 ↗ *When God made a new covenant, what did He do with the old one?*

Q 7 ↗ *Give the reference for the Scripture: "Christ is the end of the law …"*

Q 8 ↖ *Contrast what Moses brought with the things that Jesus brought (John 1:16-17).*

Q 9 ↖ *Explain: The Old Testament is not our covenant with God.*

Q 10 ↖ *Can a believer be under both the Old Testament and the New Testament? Explain.*

Q 11 ↗ *Explain: Throughout the Old Testament, salvation was by faith in God.*

God do not earn their salvation.[2] *"Noah was a righteous man, blameless among the people of his time, and he walked with God"* (Gen. 6:9). Still, it was not Noah's works that saved him. Noah found grace and favor in the eyes of the Lord (Gen. 6:8). And he sought to please God by building an ark. God's love and grace have always been the basis of man's salvation. He loves people and wants to save them—long before they know Him. Still, let us remember that grace is easier to find in some places than others. For example, grace is easier to find kneeling in God's house, than kneeling to an idol. Finding grace is always related to the places we are looking for it. Noah found grace while living a righteous life and walking with God. We always have an abundant supply of grace walking *with* God or *toward* Him. In contrast, since God is the source of grace, it is hard to find grace walking *away* from God. But as we move near to God, He moves near to us (James 4:8).

In the Old Testament and in the New, God forgives through a sacrifice of blood.[3] He has always required a blood sacrifice to pay the penalty for a person's sins. This is clear throughout the Bible—from the early chapters of Genesis through Revelation. God's justice demands human death as a payment for human sin. But His grace accepted the temporary death of animals, until Jesus died for all as our substitute (John 1:29).

- In the case of Adam and Eve, God brought them skins to cover their nakedness (Gen. 3:21). So it appears that their sin caused the death of animals—sacrificed for them.

- Many think Cain and Abel knew that God required them to sacrifice an animal as an offering to Him (Gen. 4:1-7). We are certain that Abel knew God approved of an animal sacrifice.

Q 12 Give some examples of people who came to God with faith that He would accept their sacrifice.

- Noah, after the flood, sacrificed animals to God (Gen. 8:20-21).

- Abraham sacrificed animals to God (Gen. 15:9). He sacrificed a ram—instead of his son, Isaac—on or near the same mountain where Jesus died (Gen. 22).

- Job, who may have lived during the time of Abraham, sacrificed animals to atone for sin (Job 1:5).

- The children of Israel, before the Law was given, sacrificed the Passover lamb as a substitute for the firstborn.

- The Law of Moses required a blood sacrifice for a person to be saved from God's judgment. *"For the life of a creature is in the blood, and I have given it to you to make atonement for yourselves on the altar; it is the blood that makes atonement for one's life"* (Lev. 17:11).

  In fact, the law requires that nearly everything be cleansed with blood, and without the shedding of blood there is no forgiveness (Heb. 9:22).

- Jesus was the Lamb of God, slain for the sins of the world (John 1:29).

  [8]*...The four living creatures and the twenty-four elders fell down before the Lamb. Each one had a harp and they were holding golden bowls full of incense, which are the prayers of the saints.* [9]*And they sang a new song: "You are worthy to take the scroll and to open its seals, because you were slain, and with your blood you purchased men for God from every tribe and language and people and nation"* (Rev. 5:8-9).

Q 13 Under the Law, why did God accept the blood of animals?

Q 14 On what basis were the believers of Hebrews 11 saved?

Remember: We know that believers today are saved through faith in Jesus, the Sacrifice God provided for our sins. But it is good to remember that even under the Old Testament, people were **saved by faith in God**. Hebrews 11 lists many who pleased God as they lived by faith—including Abel, Enoch, Noah, Abraham, Isaac, Jacob, Joseph, Moses, the Israelites crossing the Red Sea, Rahab, Gideon, Barak, Samson, Jephthah, David, Samuel, and the prophets (Heb. 11:1-32). And Hebrews 11:39-40 tells us that all of these believers under the old covenant will be made perfect with believers under the new covenant. Faith in God is, and has always been, the only way of salvation. And as Moses and the prophets emphasize, true faith expresses itself in obedience to the God who saves us. We will emphasize this theme in chapter 5.

Q 15 ✎ *Complete Figure 2.3 by summarizing the passages mentioned (which are printed below).*

Reference	Your Summaries
Rom. 4:1-5	
Gal. 3:6-9	
Gal. 3:10-14	
James 2:20-22	

Figure 2.3   Practice summarizing verses that show we are saved by faith that expresses itself through obedience.

[1]What then shall we say that Abraham, our forefather, discovered in this matter? [2]If, in fact, Abraham was justified by works, he had something to boast about—but not before God. [3]What does the Scripture say? "Abraham believed God, and it was credited to him as righteousness." [4]Now when a man works, his wages are not credited to him as a gift, but as an obligation. [5]However, to the man who does not work but trusts God who justifies the wicked, his faith is credited as righteousness (Rom. 4:1-5).

[6]Consider Abraham: "He believed God, and it was credited to him as righteousness." [7]Understand, then, that those who believe are children of Abraham. [8]The Scripture foresaw that God would justify the Gentiles by faith, and announced the gospel in advance to Abraham: "All nations will be blessed through you." [9]So those who have faith are blessed along with Abraham, the man of faith (Gal. 3:6-9).

[10]All who rely on observing the law are under a curse, for it is written: "Cursed is everyone who does not continue to do everything written in the Book of the Law." [11]Clearly no one is justified before God by the law, because, "The righteous will live by faith." ... [13]Christ redeemed us from the curse of the law by becoming a curse for us, for it is written: "Cursed is everyone who is hung on a tree." [14]He redeemed us in order that the blessing given to Abraham might come to the Gentiles through Christ Jesus, so that by faith we might receive the promise of the Spirit (Gal. 3:10-14).

[20]You foolish man, do you want evidence that faith without deeds is useless? [21]Was not our ancestor Abraham considered righteous for what he did when he offered his son Isaac on the altar? [22]You see that his faith and his actions were working together, and his faith was made complete by what he did (James 2:20-22).

All of the sacrifices by believers of the Old Testament were types or symbols of Christ—whose blood makes forgiveness possible for all.

Someday, all who have been saved by faith will be together. *"I say to you that many will come from the east and the west, and will take their places at the feast with Abraham, Isaac and Jacob **in the kingdom of heaven**"* (Matt. 8:11). This will include all of those who lived by faith (Heb. 11). When that great day comes, we will all worship the Lamb who was slain for our sins!

Lesson 7

Salvation Under the Old and New Covenants—Part 2

Goal: *Explain and illustrate: Law is not over, under, or behind us, but it is in us.*

We are studying five principles about salvation under the old and new covenants. In Lesson 6 we studied principles A–C. In this lesson we study the final two principles.

D. Salvation expresses itself through good works—keeping the spirit (principles) of the Law.

Faith and works. Our salvation and relationship with God is not based on the laws we keep. Still, the grace that brings the New Testament and the Spirit's power within us enables us to live the righteous principles of the Old Testament (Rom. 8:4).

[3]*For what the law was powerless to do in that it was weakened by the sinful nature* [flesh]*, God did by sending his own Son in the likeness of sinful man to be a sin offering...* [4]***in order that the righteous requirements of the law might be fully met in us, who do not live according to the sinful nature*** [flesh] ***but according to the Spirit*** (Rom. 8:3-4).

Believers today are saved by grace through faith in Christ (Eph. 2:8). And the Spirit guides those with saving faith to live by God's ethical principles and produce good works. Faith without works is as dead as the body without the spirit (James 2:14-26).

Q 16 ↗ *If Professor Grace is our teacher, what do we learn?*

[11]*For the **grace** of God that brings salvation has appeared to all men.* [12]***It teaches us*** *to say "No" to ungodliness and worldly passions, and to live self-controlled, upright and godly lives in this present age* (Tit. 2:11-12).

*"This is the covenant I will make with the house of Israel after that time, declares the Lord. I will **put my laws in their minds** and **write them on their hearts**. I will be their God, and they will be my people"* (Heb. 8:10).

Q 17 ↖ *Does the new covenant replace law with grace?*

Some think God liked laws in the Old Testament, but converted to love and grace in the New Testament. But God does not change (Num. 23:19; Mal. 3:6; James 1:17). Jesus did not come to replace law with grace. He did not come to abolish the Law but to fulfill it (Matt. 5:17-18). A Jewish teacher told Jesus that the Law instructs us to love God and neighbors. Jesus told him, *"You are not far from the kingdom of God"* (Mark 12:34). There is law in God's kingdom—from north to south and east to west. There is as much law in God's kingdom as there is grace, love, and light in it. The New Testament teaches us four truths about law.

Q 18 ↖ *Complete Figure 2.4.*

Law is not over us as:	Your Explanations
A master	
A judge	
A savior	

Figure 2.4   Practice explaining that law is not over us as a master, a judge, or a savior.

Law is not *over* us as a master, a judge, or a savior. Law is not a *master* who imposes his will on us. We have only one Master, Jesus Christ, who is altogether kind and good.

Neither is law a *judge* who accuses and hands down a sentence of condemnation on us. *"Who will bring any charge against those whom God has chosen? It is God who justifies"* us in Christ (Rom. 8:33-34). Neither law nor anything else can condemn those in Christ. Paul teaches that Christ has cancelled the role of the Law as judge (Col. 2:14). Therefore, we should not let anyone judge us by laws about eating, drinking, feasts, or even the Sabbath day (Col. 2:16). Law is not a judge over believers.

Nor is law a *savior*, reaching down to lift us up. The early church did not require Gentiles to seek salvation through circumcision and the law of Moses (Acts 15:5). Rather, the apostles rebuked the Judaizers and affirmed that Jews and Gentiles are saved by grace (Acts 15:11). We are saved by Christ alone, not Christ and Moses. *Law is not a ladder we can climb to heaven.* For no one will be declared righteous by keeping the Law (Rom. 3:20). Law saves no one, under the Old Testament or the New Testament. Paul emphasized being clothed with a righteousness that is not our own—the righteousness that comes through faith in Christ (Phil. 3:9). Thank God, law is not over us—as a master, a judge, or a savior.

Law is not *under* us. Believers are not above the Law. We do not trample God's laws under our feet and live as rebels—as though law does not apply to Christians. Jesus rebuked teachers who *ignored* big laws—such as *"justice, mercy and faithfulness"* (Matt. 23:23, see Amos 5:15; Mic. 6:8; Zech. 7:9).

Q 19 What does this mean: "Law is not under us, and we are not above the law"?

There is law in God's kingdom. For lawlessness—disobeying the Law—is the essence of sin (Matt. 7:23; 1 John 3:4). Paul rebukes those who use grace as a cloak to cover their sins. These deceived people sin while claiming that sinning gives God the opportunity to give more grace (Rom. 6:15-18). But Paul says of such people, *"Their condemnation is deserved"* (Rom. 3:8). In some countries, government officials say they are above the law, and that certain laws do not apply to them. Likewise, some Christians falsely claim that they are above the Law—that in grace, law does not apply to us. Theology calls this *antinomianism [against the Law]. At the final judgment, Jesus will say to all workers of *lawlessness* (Greek: *a-nomian*): *"Depart from me, I never knew you"* (Matt. 7:23). Law is not something that believers treat with contempt and walk upon. Law is not beneath us.

Q 20 Is law behind us, outdated, obsolete—a thing of the past?

Law is not *behind* us. It is not something we can ignore. Even though we are under the New Testament, this does not mean we have outgrown the Law. Jesus did not fulfill the Law so that we could turn our backs on it. We have not graduated from law, as a student moves from one grade to the next. Law is not outdated. It is not a thing of the past. As Hebrews says, the old covenant is obsolete and fading away (Heb. 8:13). We no longer sacrifice animals, and we do not depend on earthly priests. But law is not obsolete. Paul practiced forgetting those things that were behind him (Phil. 3:13). But he did not forget the Law, because it was not something the New Testament left behind (Acts 24:14, 16; 25:8). So if God's law is neither over, under, or behind us—where is it?

Q 21 What promise did Jeremiah prophesy about law in the new covenant?

Law is *in* us. Hallelujah! This is the promise Jeremiah foretold:

> *"This is the covenant I will make with the house of Israel after that time,"* declares the LORD. *"**I will put my law in their minds and write it on their hearts**. I will be their God, and they will be my people"* (Jer. 31:33).

Law is **in** us! Under the new covenant, law has the most central place in our being. God puts His law in our minds, and writes it on our hearts! The law of God rules our thoughts. Day and night our heart beats with the joy of God's rule over us. He is our God and King who reigns over us. He is our Savior who freed us from lawless living. He is our Lord whom we obey. This is the promise the writer of Hebrews underlines (Jer. 31:31-34; Heb. 8:10; 10:16). Instead of law on cold, hard tablets of stone, under the new covenant God writes His laws in living letters in our minds and hearts. Law was "added" to show how sinful we were without Christ (Rom. 5:20; see also Rom. 3:19-21). It served *to lead us to Christ that we might be justified by faith.* But law does **more** than show us we were sinful. It teaches us what pleases and displeases our Father. As His children, we delight to please Him. In our inner being we *love* what His law declares is right. We *hate* and abhor what His law says is wrong. God's law is in us, because the Lawmaker is in us. And the righteous requirements of the Law are *"fully met in us, who do not live according to the sinful nature but according to the Spirit"* (Rom. 8:4). God created us in His image. God is our Father and our pattern. Under the new covenant we grow in His likeness—in love and compassion for others (Matt. 7:12) and in holy and righteousness living (Matt. 22:37-40). And we keep growing until the day He transforms us to shine like the sun (Rom. 8:18; 2 Cor. 3:18; 1 John 3:2-3).

Q 22 Is the Law of the Old Testament the same as the Law of the New Testament? Explain.

Law in the Old Testament and New Testament represents the rule of God to which we submit and obey. But God's law or rule over us in the New Testament does not require obeying *the letter* of the Old Testament law—such as animal sacrifices, physical circumcision, earthly priests, death by stoning, or rigid rules about feasts and the Sabbath. Rather, under the New Testament we fulfill the *spirit* of the Law by practicing love.

> [8]*Let no debt remain outstanding, except the continuing debt to love one another, for he who loves his fellowman has fulfilled the law.* [9]*The commandments, "Do not commit adultery," "Do not murder," "Do not steal," "Do not covet," and whatever other commandment there may be, are summed up in this one rule: "Love your neighbor as yourself."* [10]*Love does no harm to its neighbor. Therefore love is the fulfillment of the law* (Rom. 13:8-10).

Q 23 ⬉ Complete Figure 2.5.

Bible	Questions to Answer
Matt. 7:12	How did Jesus summarize the Law and Prophets in one short sentence?
Matt. 22:37-40	Which 2 commandments summarize the essence of the Law?
Rom. 13:8-10	How did Paul say we fulfill the Law?

Figure 2.5   Practice explaining how we fulfill the Law of the Old Testament.

Law is not over us, under us, or behind us—but it is in us! Under the old covenant, God wrote His laws on stone. Under the new covenant, God writes His laws in our hearts. Desires come from the heart. Since God's laws are written on our hearts, we desire to do what pleases Him.

So we see that the ethical principles of the Old Testament are for us today. We fulfill God's laws and ethical principles as we walk in love. God Himself is the source of our love through His Spirit—*"but the fruit of the Spirit is love"* (Gal. 5:22).

E. God's revelation of salvation is progressive.

*Progressive revelation.   We say that light or revelation from God **progresses**—like a child progresses each year in school. The old covenant often revealed an *infant* form of truth. But the new covenant reveals *mature, full-grown* truth.

> [17]*"Do not think that I have come to abolish the Law or the Prophets; I have not come to abolish them but to fulfill them.* [18]*I tell you the truth, until heaven and earth disappear, not the smallest letter, not the least stroke of a pen, will by any means disappear from the Law until everything is accomplished.* [19]*Anyone who breaks one of the least of these commandments and teaches others to do the same will be called least in the kingdom of heaven, but whoever practices and teaches these commands will be called great in the kingdom of heaven.* [20]*For I tell you that unless your righteousness surpasses that of the Pharisees and the teachers of the law, you will certainly not enter the kingdom of heaven* (Matt. 5:17-20).

Matthew	Fruit of Sin (Letter of the Law)	Root of Sin (Spirit and Principle of the Law)
5:21-22	Murder	Anger
5:27-28	Adultery	Lust
5:31-32	Divorce	Selfishness
5:33-34, 37	Breaking oaths	Being dishonest
5:38-39	Revenge	Unforgiveness
5:43-48	Hating enemies	Lack of love

Figure 2.6   Jesus taught that both the fruit and the root of sin are wrong. He emphasized the letter and the spirit of the Law.

At the core of many Old Testament laws were principles.[4] Jesus taught that those in His kingdom should be guided by these Old Testament principles of truth (Matt. 5:19). He emphasized the *principles*, the *spirit* of the Law, rather than the *letter* of the Law (Figure 2.6). So we see that grace does not do away with the moral and ethical teachings

Q 24 ⬉ *How do Christians fulfill the Old Testament Law?*

Q 25 ⬉ *If a hoe you borrow breaks while you have it, what would Jesus want you to do? (See Exod. 22:14)*

Q 26 ⬉ *Explain: progressive revelation.*

Q 27 ⬉ *Does grace replace the ethical principles of the Law? Explain.*

Q 28 ⬉ *What is the difference between the letter and the spirit of the Law?*

of the Law. Rather, it brings into the light the principles *beneath* the Law. To enter the kingdom of God, our righteousness must be greater than that of the Pharisees who kept only the *outer* letter of the Law. From the Old Testament to the New Testament, God's revelation of salvation progresses as light increases from dawn to noon.

In the next lesson, we will look more closely at laws in the Old Testament and the principles upon which they were based.

Lesson 8 — Old Testament Laws: Ceremonial, Moral, and Civil—Part 1

Goal A: *State the 3 types of Old Testament laws, and give examples of each.*

Goal B: *Explain why believers live by the ethical principles of the Law.*

Setting

Q 29 *Give 2 examples of what Jesus called "the heavier [weightier, more important] matters of the law" (Matt. 23:23).*

In this lesson and the next one, we will examine laws of the Old Testament. For purposes of study, we may put these laws into three groups: ceremonial, moral, and civil. There is some overlap in this grouping. For example, a moral law forbidding adultery is also a civil law that guides relationships. Still, it is helpful to consider three types of laws.

- **Ceremonial laws**—on religious rituals such as circumcision, laws for priests, the tabernacle, sacrifices, and cleansing.
- **Moral laws**—such as the Ten Commandments that teach what is always right or wrong.
- **Civil laws**—forbidding the religious practices of the Canaanites, and guiding the Jews in relating to each other. For example, what should a person do if his ox killed the ox of another person?

Figure 2.7   It is helpful to consider three groups of laws in the Old Testament: ceremonial, civil, and moral.

Q 30 *Complete Figure 2.8.*

Type of Old Testament Law	Your Explanations
Ceremonial	
Moral (ethical)	
Civil	

Figure 2.8   Practice explaining three types of Old Testament laws.

The Jews divided the laws of Moses into two groups: *light* commands and *heavy* commands. The light commands were the ceremonial and civil laws. The lightest of these was the command not to remove a mother bird sitting on her eggs (Deut. 22:6). The moral commands—such as those forbidding idolatry and murder—Jews considered to be heavy.[5] Christ agreed that some commands were "heavier" than others. He accused some leaders of emphasizing the light commands and ignoring the heavy ones:

> [23] *"Woe to you, teachers of the law and Pharisees, you hypocrites! You give a tenth of your spices—mint, dill and cummin. But you have neglected the more important matters of the law—justice, mercy and faithfulness. You should have practiced the latter, without neglecting the former.* [24] *You blind guides! You strain out a gnat but swallow a camel"* (Matt. 23:23-24).

The chart in Figure 2.9 divides the Old Testament laws into three groups—and gives examples of each law. It comments on the *duration of laws—the length of time laws endured. We call laws that were just for the old covenant *temporary*. Laws for all time are called *eternal*. Refer to this chart often as you study the three types of laws in this lesson.

Type of Law	Examples	Length of Time	Purpose
1. **Ceremonial** Laws about religious rites	Laws about sacrifices, priests, the tabernacle, holy days, feasts, fasts, cleansing, and circumcision	Temporary	To prepare people for Christ's coming; To give us illustrations of spiritual truths
2. **Moral** (ethical) Laws about right and wrong	Ten Commandments Love your neighbor. Do not seek revenge.	Eternal	To give us eternal, moral laws that do not change; the New Testament repeats moral laws of the Old Testament.
3. **Civil** Laws against practices of unholy, pagan neighbors— the Canaanites	Laws about food and farming	Temporary	To keep God's people separate from pagan worship and customs
Laws about relating to holy, Jewish neighbors	Laws about penalties, slavery, marriage, war, judges, and courts	Temporary	To explain what God said was just and fair; these illustrate moral truths.

Figure 2.9   Three types of laws in the Old Testament had different purposes.

A. Ceremonial laws are about Israel's worship.

*Ceremonial laws** are the largest group of Old Testament laws. They are found throughout Leviticus, and in many parts of Exodus, Numbers, and Deuteronomy. These ceremonial laws are **vertical* in nature. They told the Israelites what God expected them to do with regard to worship. What size must the tabernacle be? What type of furniture should be in it? Which colors should be used? How should the priests dress? When should they wash? Which sacrifices were for each sin or occasion? The ceremonial laws answer all these questions. These laws applied *only* to citizens of Israel *before* Christ died for all.

Q 31 ↖ *Explain: The ceremonial laws are "vertical" in nature.*

None of the ceremonial laws are renewed in the New Testament. Today, the Old Testament temple, sacrifices, and priesthood are replaced. Jesus came to be the Lamb of God (John 1:29). He sacrificed Himself for our sins—*"once for all"*—so that there is no need to sacrifice animals (Heb. 10:10). Jesus is our High Priest in heaven, so we do not need a priest on earth. Believers are now the temple in which God lives.

The Old Testament ceremonial laws are <u>not</u> renewed in the New Testament. And Christians are not under any laws that are not repeated in the New Testament. Jesus fulfilled all of the ceremonial laws and set them aside.

Q 32 ↗ *Why do we not offer animal sacrifices today?*

¹*The law is only a shadow of the good things that are coming—not the realities themselves. For this reason it can never, by the same sacrifices repeated endlessly year after year, make perfect those who draw near to worship. ²If it could, would they not have stopped being offered? For the worshipers would have been cleansed once for all, and would no longer have felt guilty for their sins. ³But those sacrifices are an annual reminder of sins, ⁴because it is impossible for the blood of bulls and goats to take away sins. ⁵Therefore, when Christ came into the world, he said: "Sacrifice and offering you did not desire, but a body you prepared for me; ⁶with burnt offerings and sin offerings you were not pleased. ⁷Then I said, 'Here I am—it is written about me in the scroll—I have come to do your will, O God.'" ⁸First he said, "Sacrifices and offerings, burnt offerings, and sin offerings you did not desire, nor were you pleased with them" (although the law required them to be made). ⁹Then he said, "Here I am, I have come to do your will." **He sets aside the first to establish the second**. ¹⁰And by that will [testament], we have been made holy through the sacrifice of the body of Jesus Christ once for all* (Heb. 10:1-10).

Q 33 ✎ *Does sex between a husband and wife cause them to be spiritually unclean for a time?*

Q 34 ✎ *Does giving birth, or a woman's monthly flow of blood make her spiritually unclean today? Explain.*

The laws about being "clean or unclean" were old, ceremonial laws. These confuse some today. It is helpful to discern that these were temporary. For example, circumcision for males was a temporary ceremonial law. It was a sign of God's covenant with Abraham, and all of the Jews. After Christ died, this sign was no longer necessary, because Jesus made a new covenant.

- *"For in Christ Jesus neither circumcision nor uncircumcision has any value. The only thing that counts is faith expressing itself through love"* (Gal. 5:6).
- [12]*"Those who want to make a good impression outwardly are trying to compel you to be circumcised. The only reason they do this is to avoid being persecuted for the cross of Christ.* [13]*Not even those who are circumcised obey the law, yet they want you to be circumcised that they may boast about your flesh.* [14]*May I never boast except in the cross of our Lord Jesus Christ, through which the world has been crucified to me, and I to the world.* [15]*Neither circumcision nor uncircumcision means anything; what counts is a new creation"* (Gal. 6:12-15).
- *"A man is a Jew if he is one inwardly; and circumcision is circumcision of the heart, by the Spirit, not by the written code. Such a man's praise is not from men, but from God"* (Rom. 2:29).

So we see that physical circumcision has no religious value. Doctors tell us that circumcision—for males only— has value for cleanliness and good health in marriage. So if a male is circumcised, it should be for physical, not spiritual, reasons. (Note that under the Old Testament, circumcision was only for males, and never for females. Those who practice female circumcision destroy the beauty of sex for women, and damage the relationship of a husband and wife in marriage.)

The Old Testament laws about being clean and unclean covered every part of life from birth to death. So the laws helped people think about their relation to God throughout life. Cleanness meant the worshiper met the standards for coming into the presence of *Yahweh;* unclean meant a person did not meet the standards to come before the Lord.[6]

Q 35 ✎ *The Old Testament required that Israel have priests. Do you feel the New Testament church should have priests? Explain.*

Q 36 ✎ *Should ethical principles of the Old Testament guide believers today? Explain.*

Q 37 ✎ *Explain: Jesus fulfilled the Law by completing what it started.*

Q 38 ⚒ *Was cooking or going out of the house allowed on the Sabbath? Explain.*

B. Moral (ethical) laws are about what is right or wrong.   02.08

The study of morals and ethics is about what is right and wrong. The Law contained many ethical principles such as, *"You shall not steal"* (Exod. 20:15). Moral laws and principles of the Old Testament have not changed—they are renewed in the New Testament. For example, the Ten Commandments are moral laws. All of these commands are repeated in the New Testament—except for keeping the letter of the Law on the Sabbath. God still expects us to honor the spirit of the Sabbath law; that is, to set aside one day a week for rest. The Sabbath or seventh day was Saturday. In the New Testament, we see the Sabbath day being replaced by the Lord's day—Sunday, the day Jesus rose from the dead. It was common for believers to gather for worship on Sunday, the first day of every week (1 Cor. 16:2). Paul reminds us that we should not allow anyone to judge or condemn us for not keeping the Sabbath (Col. 2:16).

Some claim to keep the Old Testament Sabbath, but they are breaking it. Recall that to keep the letter of the Sabbath law meant not starting a fire (Exod. 35:3). On the Sabbath, one man picked up sticks, so Israel stoned him for breaking the Sabbath (Num. 15:32-36). And on the Sabbath, no one was allowed to go out of the house (Exod. 16:29). Today, we are not under the letter of the Sabbath law. Jesus Himself did some work to help people on the Sabbath (Mark 2:23–3:6; see also Matt. 12:1-14). The Pharisees wanted to kill Jesus for healing on the Sabbath! As His followers, we keep the spirit of the Sabbath— taking time to worship and rest one day each week. The early church was concerned about which days were the most special. Paul's response was that the day on the calendar was not as important as the principle itself—living by faith, and loving each other (Rom. 14:1–15:13).

137.02.09

Jesus did not come to *abolish the ethical principles of the Law, but to fulfill them. That is, He came to complete what the Law only started. The Law gave a little light, showing us that things such as murder, adultery, and divorce are wrong. Jesus gave us more light, teaching us that the roots of these sins are wrong (Figure 2.6). So Jesus fulfilled or completed what the Law taught about adultery—He emphasized the full, deeper meaning of God's Law. The Savior taught us that God looks beyond our actions and searches our hearts.

Q 39 ╲ *Explain: Jesus came to fulfill the Law.*

God's moral laws are eternal and universal—timeless and true for all people. Moral laws are the basis of all the other laws. They are just as valid for us today as they were for the ancient Jews.

Moral laws are often stated as a direct command—such as "you shall" or "you shall not." The interpreter must remember that these laws are double-sided—like a sword that cuts with either side. Some moral laws guide us away from one thing and toward another. If a moral law forbids something bad, the other side of the truth is that it requires something good. The command *"You shall not steal"* guides us away from stealing and toward working for what we need. The command *"Do not commit adultery"* guides us away from adultery and toward being faithful in marriage.

As we noted earlier, moral laws of the Old Testament are repeated—in some form—in the New Testament.

For example, Figure 2.10 compares Leviticus 19:11-18 with commands in James. Many think James was thinking of this passage in Leviticus when he wrote.

[11] *" 'Do not steal. Do not lie. Do not deceive one another.* [12]*Do not swear falsely by my name and so profane the name of your God. I am the LORD.* [13]*Do not defraud your neighbor or rob him. Do not hold back the wages of a hired man overnight.* [14]*Do not curse the deaf or put a stumbling block in front of the blind, but fear your God. I am the LORD.* [15]*Do not pervert justice; do not show partiality to the poor or favoritism to the great, but judge your neighbor fairly.* [16]*Do not go about spreading slander among your people. Do not do anything that endangers your neighbor's life. I am the LORD.* [17]*Do not hate your brother in your heart. Rebuke your neighbor frankly so you will not share in his guilt.* [18]*Do not seek revenge or bear a grudge against one of your people, but love your neighbor as yourself. I am the LORD"* (Lev. 19:11-18).

Moral Command	Leviticus	James
Do not steal.	19:11	5:4
Do not lie to or deceive one another.	19:11	5:4
Do not swear falsely.	19:12	5:12
Do not defraud/rob your neighbor.	19:13	5:4
Do not pervert justice.	19:15	5:6
Do not show partiality.	19:15	2:1
Judge your neighbor fairly.	19:15	5:6
Do not go about spreading slander.	19:16	3:9
Do not seek revenge or bear a grudge.	19:18	4:7-18
Love your neighbor as yourself.	19:18	2:8

Figure 2.10   Most of the moral laws of Leviticus 19 are repeated in James.

As we close this lesson, let us return to the question of the young man in the introduction. None of the commands to which he referred are repeated in the New Testament. They were all either ceremonial laws—fulfilled in Christ—or civil laws for the time of the Old Testament. By contrast, the law against being a homosexual is a moral law that the Old and New Testaments repeat many times. The Bible says that homosexuality is:

Q 40 ╲ *Give 2 reasons why homosexuality is wrong today.*

- detestable [an abomination in KJV] (Lev. 18:22, 26-27, 29-30).
- not allowed—with stoning as a penalty (Lev. 20:13).
- part of the reason why Sodom and Gomorrah were judged (Gen. 19:4-5, 12-13).
- a cause of the wrath of God (Rom. 1:26-27).
- the reason why some will not inherit the kingdom of God (1 Cor. 6:9).
- against the Law of God (1 Tim. 1:9-10).

Lesson 9 — Old Testament Laws: Ceremonial, Moral, and Civil—Part 2

Goal: *Explain that some civil laws illustrated eternal principles. Give examples.*

We are studying three types of Old Testament laws. We have covered the ceremonial and moral laws (points A and B in Lesson 8). We discuss civil laws *after* moral laws because they often illustrate moral or ethical principles.

C. Civil laws are about how to relate to others.

Q 41 ↖ *What is the difference between ceremonial and civil laws?*

Q 42 ↖ *Give 2 examples of civil laws.*

The civil laws told the Israelites how to live with their Jewish neighbors. These laws related to daily life. They governed topics such as food, farming, slavery, marriage, society, courts, and war. What did God allow people to eat? What if an ox killed a man? What if a child cursed his father? What if a thief was caught? The civil laws answered these questions and many others.

Q 43 ↖ *Are believers today under the ceremonial or civil laws of the Old Testament? Explain.*

The civil laws were temporary, for those under the Law of Moses. Under the New Testament, does God require that we go by the Old Testament civil laws? No. For example, all food is holy (1 Tim. 4:1-5).

> ¹*The Spirit clearly says that in later times some will abandon the faith and follow deceiving spirits and things taught by demons.* ²*Such teachings come through <u>hypocritical liars</u>, whose consciences have been seared as with a hot iron.* ³*They forbid people to marry and <u>order them to abstain from certain foods</u>, which God created to be received with thanksgiving by those who believe and who know the truth.* ⁴*For <u>everything God created is good, and nothing is to be rejected if it is received with thanksgiving</u>,* ⁵<u>*because it is consecrated by the word of God and prayer*</u> (1 Tim. 4:1-5).

In a vision from God, Peter learned that all animals are clean to eat. Soon afterward, he learned that God wants all people to be saved (Acts 10:9-23).

Q 44 ↖ *Does God care if a believer eats pork today? Explain.*

One believer said he did not eat pork because in Matthew 8 the demons went into the pigs. His friend replied, "Since the pigs went into the water, do you also avoid drinking water?"

We have said that food laws of the Old Testament do not apply under the New Testament. Likewise, believers today are not *under* any of the Old Testament civil laws. For example, we still believe it is wrong to curse, but we do not stone someone today for cursing a parent. As we saw earlier, law is not over, under, or behind us—God's Law is in us, written on our hearts. We avoid cursing because it does not please our Father.

The civil laws helped separate Israelites from Canaanites. These laws include restrictions on farming, sewing, and eating. Often these are the laws that seem the strangest to modern Christians. For example, why did God tell the Israelites **You must not:**

- plant two different types of seeds together—such as corn and wheat?
- mate two different types of animals—such as a cow and a goat?
- sew two different types of thread together—such as cotton and wool?
- eat the meat of a goat boiled in its mother's milk?
- eat pork?

We may never understand the reason for every command in the Old Testament. Why? Because there are many things about the religions of Canaan that are lost in history. But we do know that some of the civil laws forbade practices of the Canaanites. For example, as the people of Canaan worshiped, they mixed types of seeds together, and types of threads together as an offering to their gods. So *Yahweh*, the God of Israel, did not want His people following in the footsteps of the pagans.

Likewise, one civil law put limits on how a priest could cut his hair or trim his beard. Another law forbade him to have tattoos or cut his flesh. The problem in both cases related to religious rituals in Canaan. **A priest of Canaan** would either shave the hair on his face, or make designs in the hair *as an act of worship to his god* or *goddess*. As God's people avoided the appearance of evil, they would be safer—and not give sin a chance to take root in their lives. Today, it is not correct to use Leviticus 21:5 as a basis for forbidding haircuts and tattoos. However, any practice is wrong that makes believers look like they share the sinful values of society. And any practice is wrong—even a hair style—if it leads people into temptation.

Q 45 *How does the historical context help you understand why no priest of Israel could trim the hair on his face (Lev. 21:5)?*

We must recognize that the laws about food were **not** *rules for healthy eating*. As we noted above, today God says all food is holy (1 Tim. 4:4-5). God commanded Peter to kill and eat all kinds of animals (Acts 10:13-15). And the early church freed Gentile believers from all laws about food, except food offered to idols, blood, and the meat of strangled animals (Acts 15:28-29; Col. 2:20-22).

Q 46 *Do believers in big cities have the same values about hair and clothing as believers in the rural areas? Explain.*

The laws about food—like the laws against mixing seeds or threads—helped keep Israel separate. Some foods were part of the cults and worship of Canaan. For example, boiling a goat in its mother's milk was part of a worship service to a god in Canaan (Exod. 23:19). Likewise, the Canaanites sacrificed pigs, and then ate them as an act of worship. It also appears that the Canaanites ate shellfish—such as shrimp and lobster—as a part of their culture and religion. Thus, the civil laws from God helped keep Israel separate and safe from the culture and religions of Canaan.

Today, *spiritually*, believers live separated—apart from the world and its values. But *physically*, God sends us toward the world—into it to evangelize unbelievers. We do not conform to the ways of the world. But to evangelize, we seek ways to influence unbelievers. So under the New Testament, the Spirit and the apostles guided the church to drop the civil laws.

Q 47 *How does Peter's vision and conclusion relate to modern missions (Acts 15:8-11)?*

SOME CIVIL LAWS WERE A TEMPORARY EXAMPLE OF AN ETERNAL PRINCIPLE.

The first group of civil laws kept Israel separate from pagan neighbors and cults. A second group of civil laws give temporary examples based on eternal principles. Christians do not need to observe the temporary laws. But we should seek to find the principle behind a law. The Israelites were rural, so many of the laws were about life in the country. Likewise, Israel was a *theocracy—a nation ruled by God. This government required unique penalties that related to Israel's laws. Even though believers today are not under these civil laws, they can teach us (2 Tim. 3:16). What then can we learn from laws such as these?

- The command to put a rebellious son to death (Deut. 21:18-21)
- The command to leave some grain in the fields (Lev. 19:9)
- The command to care for a neighbor's donkey or ox (Deut. 22:4)

Figure 2.11 An outer peel often hides inner fruit. Likewise, beneath a civil law there is often an inner, lasting principle.

Many civil laws of Israel were like the peel of a fruit. The best part of a fruit is under the peel. Likewise, beneath some civil laws there was a principle. We often need to remove the cultural "peel" (specific law) to find the "fruit" (principle) hidden under it.

Q 48 How can Christians benefit from laws of Israel that we are not under today?

Q 49 What is the principle behind the law forbidding farmers to reap the corners of their fields (Lev. 19:9)?

One civil law forbade farmers of Israel to harvest the corners of their fields (Lev. 19:9). God commanded the Israelites to leave behind a few handfuls of grain on purpose. This law may seem odd today, but in the old days of Israel, it kept the poor from starving. The poor who lacked food, like Ruth, were allowed to glean grain from the corners of a field. So what is the principle under the peel of this law? *A believer should be kind to the poor.* This is the spirit of the law that commanded the Israelites to leave some grain in their fields. It is the principle or fruit beneath the peel.

Q 50 Complete Figure 2.12 by identifying the fruit (principle) under the peel (civil law). (Scriptures are written below.)

Reference	Topics of Old Testament Civil Law	Spirit of the Law: Lasting Principles
Exod. 22:14	Restitution	
Lev. 19:14	Abusing the handicapped	
Num. 35:30; Deut. 19:15	Death penalty	
Deut. 19:21	Vengeance	
Deut. 22:1-2	Straying ox	
Deut. 22:8	Safety	
Deut. 25:4	Working ox	

Figure 2.12   Practice identifying the lasting principle beneath the civil law (the fruit beneath the peel).

- *"If a man borrows an animal from his neighbor and it is injured or dies while the owner is not present, he must make restitution"* (Exod. 22:14).

- *"Do not curse the deaf or put a stumbling block in front of the blind, but fear your God. I am the LORD"* (Lev. 19:14).

- *"Anyone who kills a person is to be put to death as a murderer only on the testimony of witnesses"* (Num. 35:30).

- ¹*"If you see your brother's ox or sheep straying, do not ignore it but be sure to take it back to him. ²If the brother does not live near you or if you do not know who he is, take it home with you and keep it until he comes looking for it. Then give it back to him"* (Deut. 22:1-2).

- *"Do not muzzle an ox while it is treading out the grain"* (Deut. 25:4). Paul asks, ⁹...*"Is it about oxen that God is concerned? ¹⁰Surely he says this for us, doesn't he?"* (1 Cor. 9:9-10). Paul explains that God cares about animals, but He cares even more about humans (compare Matt. 12:11-14). Just as the ox worked and deserved a share of its labor, so a minister of the gospel deserves financial blessings (1 Cor. 9:9-12). Beneath many civil laws of the Old Testament are abiding principles to help us relate to others.

- *"When you build a new house, make a parapet [guard rail] around your roof so that you may not bring the guilt of bloodshed on your house if someone falls from the roof"* (Deut. 22:8). This law may not have an application in many cultures, but it applies a principle to obey: We should help provide safety for our family and friends.

Figure 2.13
In Israel's culture most roofs were flat. Family and friends slept on the roof in the hot season of the year.

Eye for eye. To limit vengeance for injury, a judge might order a tooth for a tooth—a similar injury on the guilty person. Only a judge had this right. His judgment of an eye for an eye or tooth for a tooth was to prevent personal vengeance and prevent future fighting (Deut. 19:21). Such laws as a tooth for a tooth prevented personal vengeance and excess—such as taking a life for a tooth, as Lamech did (Gen. 4:23). This civil law taught that justice came through a judge, and the penalty should match the crime, not exceed it. We will explore this principle again in the genre of the Gospels. Jesus teaches us that, instead of demanding an eye for an eye, we should turn the other cheek (Matt. 5:38-39). The deep truth of this law is that vengeance belongs to a judge, not those who are hurt (Rom. 12:19). Sabio says: "If we all demanded an eye for an eye and a tooth for a tooth, most of us today would be blind by 15 and toothless at 30!"

Death penalty. Crimes that resulted in the death penalty under the old covenant seem harsh. Sixteen different sins led to the penalty of death by stoning. But these strong laws were for the good and protection of a society—to purge evil (compare Deut. 19:19). Not many were willing to commit crimes they knew led to death. The Law was plain about the death penalty, so those who committed serious crimes condemned themselves. The death penalty was without favoritism—no one could pay a ransom to escape it (Num. 35:31). And the sentence of death was only possible with two or more witnesses to a big crime (Num. 35:30; Deut. 19:15).[7] Also, keep in mind that the death penalty was not the final judgment. Knowing they were about to die, people still had the opportunity to repent and pray for the mercy of God.

Slavery. Civil laws that allowed slavery are hard for a modern believer to understand. But the slavery in the Bible was different from other kinds of slavery. Slavery in the Old Testament meant being a temporary servant. Since there were no prisons, a debt was often paid by serving, rather than going to prison. Figure 2.14 compares servants and slaves.

Q 51 ↖ *How would you answer a person who condemned the Old Testament for allowing slavery?*

Servants Under the Old Testament	Slavery Outside of Israel
Temporary (no more than 6 years)	Until death
The servant had rights.	The slave was a human tool.
The servant could not be hurt.	The slave could be killed.
The servant could not be forced to do immoral acts.	The slave was at the mercy of the master.

Figure 2.14   A contrast of being a servant in Israel and a slave in other cultures

Conclusion

We have studied the three types of laws in the Old Testament: ceremonial, moral, and civil.

Jesus summarized all of the laws with two chief laws: [37]*"Love the Lord your God with all your heart...* [39]*Love your neighbor as yourself"* (Matt. 22:37, 39). Jesus looked under the peels of the laws to the deeper *principles*.

Test Yourself: Circle the letter by the ***best*** completion to each question or statement.

1. What is a biblical covenant?
a) An agreement two parties create and agree to its terms
b) An agreement God creates and offers to us
c) A declaration that is binding, whether chosen or not
d) An agreement that people must ratify

2. Which statement on a biblical covenant is TRUE?
a) It is possible to be under the Old Testament and the New Testament.
b) One may choose to be under the Old Testament today.
c) God enforces the New Testament, even if most do not agree.
d) Salvation is possible without the new covenant.

3. Under the old covenant,
a) people were saved by keeping the Law.
b) people were not able to be saved.
c) people were saved by sacrifices.
d) people were saved by faith.

4. How does biblical faith express itself?
a) By trusting in God and avoiding responsibilities
b) By seeking to love, obey, and please God
c) By a verbal declaration of what God has done
d) By focusing on the sacrifice that God provided

5. Which is TRUE about God's Law?
a) Law is over us.
b) Law is under us.
c) Law is behind us.
d) Law is in us.

6. Which prophet foretold Law in a new covenant?
a) Hosea
b) Isaiah
c) Jeremiah
d) Daniel

7. Which laws governed human relationships?
a) Civil
b) Ceremonial
c) Moral
d) National

8. Which 2 roads run through both covenants?
a) Faith and works
b) Blessings and curses
c) Right and wrong
d) Law and grace

9. Why do believers keep God's moral laws?
a) As a condition of salvation
b) As an expression of faith and gratitude to God
c) As a presentation of the gospel
d) As a transformation of society

10. What principle did leaving grain in the field illustrate?
a) We should be kind to the poor.
b) We reap what we sow.
c) He who sows sparingly will reap sparingly.
d) We should give some grain as an offering to God.

Essay Test Topics: Write 50-100 words on each of these goals that you studied in this chapter.

- Explain what a covenant is, and why God's people can be under only one covenant.
- Explain that salvation in the Old Testament and New Testament is by faith in God—and explain how this faith expresses itself.
- Explain and illustrate: Law is not over, under, or behind us, but it is in us.
- State the 3 types of Old Testament laws, and give examples of each.
- Explain why believers live by the ethical principles of the Law.
- Explain that some civil laws illustrated eternal principles. Give examples.

Chapter 3:
Interpreting Poetry

Introduction

Psalms relates God to our deepest feelings and needs. The songs of praise in Psalms rise like tall mountains. And the cries of help in Psalms come from the deepest valleys. Psalms, more than any other book of the Bible, connects us with God. He wants to share our brightest times of rejoicing and our darkest days of sorrow. About half of the Psalms include prayers of faith in hard times.

Figure 3.1   Various musical instruments spoken of in the Psalms

The New Testament quotes Psalms 186 times. This is far more than it quotes any other Old Testament book. Jesus and the writers of the New Testament were filled with the Psalms. The Holy Spirit often guided them to teach from these hymns of Israel.

I once asked a friend, "Besides preaching and Bible study, how can we teach doctrine?" After thinking for a few moment he answered, "Another great way to teach doctrine is through songs and hymns."

- We can repeat songs and hymns hundreds of times—year after year—and not tire of singing them. In fact, the more years believers sing a hymn, the more they enjoy it.

- We sing songs and hymns that create joy and strong feelings of praise that few sermons create.

- We find it easy to remember songs. For example, I often recall the song *Amazing Grace.* A verse in the song says "I once was lost, but now I am found; was blind but now I see." These words often come to my mind, like a visitor knocking at the door. We remember the melodies of songs and the words that belong to each melody. I have sung the words in church hundreds of times.

Figure 3.2   Lines of poetry are often parallel, like the tracks of a train.
Together, they will take you to the author's thought.

- We see what we sing because songs tend to use figurative language—leaving a picture in the mind of the singer. The pictures—images in the mind—stir feelings of gratitude to Christ our Savior.

In this lesson, we will study the book of Psalms, the hymnbook of ancient Israel. Psalms are the most well known examples of Hebrew poetry. More than a third of the Old Testament is written as poetry. Poetry is also scattered throughout most books of the Bible. Although we know Psalms and wisdom literature as poetry, almost all the prophets wrote poetry.

Lessons:

Keys to Interpreting Psalms: Historical Context

Goal: *Interpret a psalm by examining its historical context—including its superscript, author, date, and setting.*

Keys to Interpreting Psalms: Parallelism, Figurative Language

Goal A: *Identify and give examples of 5 types of parallelism in Hebrew poetry.*
Goal B: *Explain how to interpret figurative language in poetry.*

Keys to Interpreting Psalms—Part 1

Goal A: *Identify the 3 parts and purposes of a praise psalm—to help you interpret it.*
Goal B: *Use the 6 parts of a lament to help you interpret it.*
Goal C: *Analyze the parts of a thanksgiving psalm to help you interpret it.*

Keys to Interpreting Psalms—Part 2

Goal A: *Illustrate and explain ways the apostles used the messianic psalms.*
Goal B: *Analyze the parts and message of Psalm 1.*
Goal C: *Explain how to interpret and use psalms of judgment.*
Goal D: *Analyze ways we can use the Psalms today.*

Key Words

superscription—the writing [heading] above 116 psalms that gives information to better understand the psalm [its author, historical setting, how it was used, and such]

chiasm—parallel poetry in which lines 1 and 2 say the same thing, but the second line inverts the order of thought: the last thought of line 1 is the first thought of line 2. [named after the Greek letter "X" (chi) because of the "X" pattern]

parallelism—referring to two things that are side-by-side, going in the same direction; a main characteristic of Hebrew poetry—two lines of poetry side by side, with the first and second lines expressing the same or opposite thought [thus one line helps give understanding of the other]

synonym—a word that means the same as another word

antithetic—against or opposite; in poetry with antithetic parallelism, the second line is the opposite of the first line in order to give a clear contrast.

synthetic—blended together as a whole; in poetry with synthetic parallelism, all of the lines together give the whole thought or big picture.

Lesson 11
Keys to Interpreting Psalms: Historical Context

Goal: *Interpret a psalm by examining its historical context—including its superscript, author, date, and setting.*

Background

Interpreting a psalm involves examining its historical context—the psalm's superscription, author, date, and setting. Let us look at each of these four things.

A. Superscriptions—writings above the Psalms

Superscriptions are writings (scriptions) above (super) a psalm. Superscriptions (headings) are above 116 of the 150 psalms. In your Bible, you will find these writings between the number of the psalm and verse 1. These writings above the Psalms were not part of the original Psalms. But they are very old. All of them were written before the Septuagint (200 B.C.), which is the Greek translation of the Hebrew Bible.

The writing before a psalm tells us things such as:
- *The author's name* (David, Moses, Hemen, Asaph, Solomon, Hezekiah, and the sons of Korah). For example, the writing above Psalm 47 says, *Of the Sons of Korah.*
- *Type of psalm.* For example, above Psalm 32 is written, *A maskil.* This is a type of poem that contains teachings to think about. Other types of psalms mentioned are: a Song of Ascents, Sabbath, song, prayer, praise.

Q 1 *What are superscriptions, and what is their purpose?*

61

- *Musical terms.* For example, above Psalm 4 is written, *For the director of music. With stringed instruments.* Likewise, the term *Selah* is at the end of 39 psalms. This may be a musical term, or it may be an invitation for those who were worshiping to respond.

- *Type of service.* For example, above Psalm 45 is written, *A wedding song.*

- *Historical notes.* Fourteen superscriptions refer to events in David's life For example, above Psalm 3 is written, *A psalm of David. When he fled from his son Absalom.*

Psalm 142 gives an example of the value of the superscripts or headings. The heading reads, *A maskil* [Hebrew for poem] *of David. When he was in the cave. A prayer.*

The most likely context for Psalm 142 is the cave of Adullam. There, David hid alone from Saul (1 Sam. 22:1-2). He looked around and did not see anyone who was concerned about him (Ps. 142:4). David had gone from being a hero in Israel to a lonely man hiding in a cave. His hiding place was more like a prison than a refuge (Ps. 142: 7). Still, his faith did not waver. He confessed that God was his true refuge (Ps. 142:4), and he expected deliverance. David predicted that he would again praise God in the midst of the righteous (Ps. 142:7).

One of the most common headings is "A Song of Ascents" (Ps. 120–134). Jews sang these Psalms as they were ascending— *going up* to Jerusalem—for one of the holy days (Ps. 122:4; 42:4). They traveled to Jerusalem at least three times a year:

- Spring: Passover and Feast of Unleavened Bread

- Summer: Festival of Weeks (Pentecost)

- Fall: Feast of Atonement and Feast of the Tabernacle

Q 2 ➤ *Who wrote the most psalms?*

Practice singing a song or psalm to God on your way to church! And think about the historical context as you study Psalms 120–134.

B. Authors

The Jews put all the Psalms together into one book. Still, there are five sections, or books of Psalms.

	Book 1: Psalms 1–41	Book 2: Psalms 42–72	Book 3: Psalms 73–89	Book 4: Psalms 90–106	Book 5: Psalms 107–150
Author(s)	Mostly David	Mostly David and sons of Korah	Mostly Asaph	Mostly unknown	Mostly unknown or David

Figure 3.3   Authors of the five books of Psalms[1]

The writings before the Psalms tell us that David wrote 73 psalms. Peter states that David wrote Psalms 16 and 110 (Acts 2:25-35). Hebrews 4:7 also connects David to Psalm 95. Asaph wrote 12 psalms (1 Chron. 15:16-19; 2 Chron. 29:30). Asaph was a Levite with musical and prophetic gifts. The sons of Korah wrote 10 psalms. Solomon wrote 2; Heman 1; Ethan 1; and Moses 1 (Ps. 90).

References in the Bible and in history tell us who helped collect the Psalms into a book. Those who helped were David (1 Chron. 15:16-22), Hezekiah (2 Chron. 29:25-30; Prov. 25:1), and perhaps Ezra (Neh. 11:22; 12:27-36, 45-47).

Q 3 ➤ *When were most of the Psalms written?*

C. Dates

The Psalms were written over a period of 1,000 years—from 1400 to 400 B.C. Psalm 90 is the earliest psalm. Moses wrote it in the 15th century B.C. The latest psalms, such as Psalm 137, come from the 6th to 5th century B.C. Read Psalm 137 and note that it was written just after the captivity in Babylon. The captivity ended in 438 B.C. But most of the psalms were written in the 10th century B.C. As we have noted, King David, 1010-

970 B.C., wrote about half of the psalms. The book of 150 psalms as we know it today was completed during the time of Ezra and Nehemiah (450-400 B.C.).

D. Setting

Many psalms have two settings. The *first* setting is that of the author. For example, David may have been taking care of sheep when he wrote Psalm 23. The *second* setting is the later one—the setting of those who sung the psalm. The people sang many psalms for worship at the temple. Other psalms celebrated special feasts or weddings. We noted that some writings before a psalm tell us why the author wrote. David wrote Psalm 3 while he was fleeing from Absalom (2 Sam. 13:34–18:33). Psalm 18 seems to describe David as he fled from Saul (2 Sam. 21–22). Psalm 30 was for the dedication of the temple (1 Kings 8; 2 Chron. 7). David prayed Psalm 51 as a prayer after he sinned with Bathsheba (2 Sam. 11–12).

Q 4 *How does knowing the setting of Psalm 51 help us understand it?*

Other psalms do not provide any historical details in the headings or superscriptions. But we can discover some of the setting by reading the psalm. Psalm 45 honors a wedding. Psalm 27:1-3 describes how the author had enemies on every side.

Q 5 *Why can a psalm help us, even if we don't know its first setting?*

The people who sang the psalms did not always know the setting of the author. They sang psalms in the temple and in the early church. Often, many years had passed since the psalms were written. Still, people could identify with the feelings of the author. They celebrated the same feasts. They knew the same feelings of despair or joy. People in all cultures, over thousands of years, have rejoiced and cried for similar reasons. So we relate to the Psalms—even when we know little about the historical setting.

Some psalms were part of a Jewish worship ceremony. To understand such psalms, we must see them in their setting or historical context. Psalm 24 was most likely used during a ceremony as the crowd of worshipers followed the king up the hill and through the gates of the temple. The psalm helps the worshipers examine their hearts much as Christians do before taking communion. It also reminds them that the presence of the King of glory—the Lord Almighty—will go before them.

Song Verse	A: The Priest's Statement	Psalm	B: The Peoples' Response (Question)	Psalm
1	*The earth is the LORD's, and everything in it…*	24:1-2	*Who may ascend the hill of the LORD? Who may stand in his holy place?*	24:3
	He who has clean hands and a pure heart…	24:4-6		
2	*Lift up your heads, O you gates; be lifted up, you ancient doors, that the King of glory may come in.*	24:7	*Who is this King of glory?*	24:8a
	The LORD strong and mighty, The LORD mighty in battle.	24:8b		
3	*Lift up your heads, O you gates; lift them up, you ancient doors, that the King of glory may come in.*	24:9	*Who is he, this King of glory?*	24:10a
	The LORD Almighty— he is the King of glory. Selah	24:10b		

Figure 3.4   Psalm 24 is a song with three verses. A priest led the people in this song.

In some psalms, the leader and the people took turns reading. A priest or king spoke first, and the people responded. For example, in Psalm 136 the worship leader makes a statement about God, and the people respond by saying *"His love endures forever."* We see this pattern 26 times in Psalm 136. We can sense the emotion of the crowd growing with each of the 26 verses of the psalm.

Q 6 *In Psalm 136, what words do the people respond to the leader 26 times?*

Song Verse	A: Leader's Statement About God	B: The Peoples' Response	Psalm
1	Give thanks to the Lord, for he is good.	His love endures foreve.	136:1
2	Give thanks to the God of gods.	His love endures forever.	136:2
3	Give thanks to the Lord of lords.	His love endures forever.	136:3

Figure 3.5   In Psalm 136, the people respond after each statement by a leader.

Take time to read through all of Psalm 136. Imagine that a leader is reading each statement about God. Then, worship as you respond with *"His love endures forever."* Lead a group of people to worship God with this psalm. And remember, finding the historical context includes the author, date, and setting of the psalm.

Lesson 11   Keys to Interpreting Psalms: Parallelism, Figurative Language

Goal A: *Identify and give examples of 5 types of parallelism in Hebrew poetry.*
Goal B: *Explain how to interpret figurative language in poetry.*

**Figure 3.6
The Charles Bridge in
Prague, Czech Republic**

Q 7 Why do we call some Hebrew poetry "parallel"?

Q 8 How is parallelism different from the poetry in your culture?

Q 9 In Psalm 19:1 what is parallel to "The heavens"?

A. Recognize two parallel lines as parts of a whole, and use one line to interpret the other.

One of the most beautiful bridges in the world is the Charles Bridge in Prague, Czech Republic. It is 800 years old but is beautiful, because of its perfect design. Every arch is like the other. The parallel arches have the same distance between them. Today, after 8 centuries, we could not build a more beautiful bridge.

The Psalms are old Hebrew poetry, but like the Charles Bridge, they have a beauty that remains. Part of this beauty is because of the parallel thought. Unlike some types of poetry, Hebrew poetry did not usually rhyme words at the end of each line. But a main characteristic of Hebrew poetry is *parallelism. The word *parallel* refers to two things that are side-by-side, like the arches of the Charles Bridge. Also, the two rails of a train track are parallel—both go side by side in the same direction and to the same place. Likewise, the Jewish poets wrote parallel thoughts—two lines of poetry side by side. The first and second lines of poetry expressed the same thought. So we can use one line to help us understand the other. The biblical interpreter should <u>never</u> study one line of a parallelism, without the other. Interpreters must interpret both lines of a parallelism together—as one thought.

How common is this pattern of parallelism? Almost every passage of Hebrew poetry has a parallelism—there are thousands of parallels in the Old Testament and hundreds of in the New Testament. Parallelism is the language of Hebrew poetry.

Five types of parallel thoughts stand out in Hebrew poetry.

1. *Synonyms in parallel lines. Synonyms are different words that mean the same thing. The word *pastor* and the word *shepherd* are synonyms. *Trust* and *believe* are synonyms. When two parallel lines of poetry are synonyms, the second line echoes—repeats—the thoughts of the first line. So we can use the two lines to interpret each other because each clarifies the other. In Figure 3.7, we call the parts of a line of poetry "A" and "B." Notice how the second line repeats line one, in different words. We call this pattern AB, AB.

Parallel Lines	A	B
Line 1:	The heavens	declare the glory of God;
Line 2:	the skies	proclaim the work of his hands.

**Figure 3.7   Psalm 19:1 has parallel lines that are synonyms.
Line 2 echoes line 1.**

Q 10 ➚ *In Psalm 19:2 what is parallel to "Day after day"?*

Q 11 ➘ *Complete Figure 3.8 by filling in the empty boxes.*

Parallel Lines	A	B
Line 1:	Day after day	
Line 2:		

Figure 3.8 Psalm 19:2 has parallel lines that are synonyms. Line 2 repeats the thought of line 1.

Q 12 ➘ *In Figure 3.9, what phrase is the synonym of "voice"?*

Parallel Lines	A	B	C
Line 1:	The seas	have lifted up	O LORD,
Line 2:	The seas	have lifted up	their voice.
Line 3:	The seas	have lifted up	their pounding waves.

Figure 3.9 Psalm 93:3 has three parallel lines that are synonyms. Lines 2 and 3 add to the thought of line 1. Some call this †climactic parallelism—parallelism that builds up to a climax.

Q 13 ➘ *In Psalm 1:1, do lines 1, 2, and 3 all refer to the same man?*

Parallel Lines	A	B	C
Line 1:	Blessed is the man	who does not walk	in the counsel of the wicked
Line 2:	--------------------	or stand	in the way of sinners
Line 3:	--------------------	or sit	in the seat of mockers.

Figure 3.10 Psalm 1:1 has three parallel lines that are synonyms. Lines 2 and 3 refer to A of line 1.

Parallel Lines	A	B
Line 1:	Praise the LORD	
Line 2:	Praise the LORD	from the heavens,
Line 3:	praise him	in the heights above.
Line 4:	Praise him,	all his angels,
Line 5:	praise him,	all his heavenly hosts.
Line 6:	Praise him,	sun and moon,
Line 7:	praise him,	all you shining stars.
Line 8:	Praise him,	you highest heavens.

Figure 3.11 Psalm 148:1-3 has many parallel lines. Some are synonyms, and some add new thoughts.

Q 14 ➘ *In Psalm 148, line _____ is parallel to line 2, line 4 is parallel to line 5, and line _____ is parallel to line 7.*

3

2. Synonyms in parallel lines, in reverse order. In this type of parallel poetry, lines 1 and 2 say the same thing. But the second line changes or inverts the order of thought. We call this pattern AB, BA, because the last thought (B) of line 1 is the first thought of line 2. (This parallel pattern is sometimes called *chiasm after the Greek letter "X." Note the "X" pattern in Figures 3.12 and 3.13.)

Parallel	Part	Part
Line 1:	A: Have mercy on me, O God,	B: according to your unfailing love;
Line 2:	B: according to your great compassion	A: blot out my transgressions.

Figure 3.12 Psalm 51:1 has parallel lines that are synonyms, but line 2 reverses the order of thoughts from A→B to B→A.

Q 15 ➘ *In Psalm 51:1, what thought is parallel to "Have mercy on me"?*

Parallel	Part	Part
	For I know my transgressions, and my sin is always before me (Ps. 51:3).	
Line 1:	A: For I know	B:
Line 2:	B:	A:

Figure 3.13 Psalm 51:3 has parallel lines that are synonyms, but line 2 reverses the order of thoughts from A→B to B→A. Scholars call this form of crossing lines a chiasm, because the pattern looks like the Greek letter X (called Chi and pronounced Ky).

Q 16 ➘ *In Psalm 51:3, fill in the blanks to complete the reverse parallelism.*

3. Contrast in parallel lines. Jewish poets liked to contrast parallel thoughts. The second line was the opposite of the first. When we contrast two things, they both become clearer—such as hot and cold, day and night, love and hate, rich and poor, wet and dry. The second line is the opposite or *antithesis (pronounced an-TI-thi-sis) of the first line. The word *anti* means "against." The Antichrist is against or opposed to Christ. They are opposite in most every way. What is the *antithesis* of strong?

Q 18 ✎ *What 2 things does the Psalmist contrast in Psalm 1:6?*

In Psalm 1:6, notice the contrast (*antithetic parallelism). Sometimes the author tells you the contrast is coming by giving you the word *but* as a clue.

Parallel Lines	Psalm 1:6
Line 1:	*For the Lᴏʀᴅ watches over the way of the righteous,*
Line 2:	*but the way of the wicked will perish.*

Figure 3.14   The parallel lines of Psalm 1:6 are in contrast.

Q 17 ✎ *Complete the contrast of parallel lines in Psalm 37:9 (Figure 3.15).*

Parallel Lines	A	B
For evil men will be cut off, but those who hope in the Lᴏʀᴅ will inherit the land (Ps. 37:9).		
Line 1:	*For evil men,*	*will be cut off,*
Line 2:	*but* _____	_____

Figure 3.15   The parallel lines of Psalm 37:9 are in contrast.

4. Comparison in parallel lines. In this type of parallelism, the first line often begins with *as,* and the second line begins with *so.* This form compares the first and second lines.

Q 19 ✎ *In the parallel lines of Psalm 103:13, what is the comparison?*

Parallel Lines	A	B
Line 1:	**As** *a father has compassion*	*on his children,*
Line 2:	**so** *the Lᴏʀᴅ has compassion*	*on those who fear him.*

Figure 3.16   The parallel lines of Psalm 103:13 are in comparison.

Q 20 ✎ *Complete the comparison of parallel lines in Psalm 125:2 (Figure 3.17).*

Parallel Lines	Psalm 125:2
As the mountains surround Jerusalem, so the Lᴏʀᴅ surrounds his people both now and forevermore (Ps. 125:2).	
Line 1:	*As the mountains surround Jerusalem,*
Line 2:	

Figure 3.17   The parallel lines of Psalm 125:2 are in comparison.

5. Completion in parallel lines. In this type of parallel poetry, one line completes the other. This type of poetry is also called *synthetic parallelism. To *synthesize* means to blend together as a whole. In synthetic poetry, all of the lines together give the whole thought or big picture.

Some call this *step* parallelism—thoughts are revealed step by step. In step parallelism, the second line completes the first line by explaining how, when, who, where, why, and such. In step by step parallelism, the second line may begin with *for, therefore, when,* or *by.* Also, at the beginning of line 2, *you* may add a word like *how, when, where, who,* or *why* to see if it <u>clarifies</u> the relationship between the two lines.

Q 21 ✎ *In Psalm 23:5, what question does line 2 answer?*

Parallel Lines	Psalm 23:5
Line 1:	*You prepare a table before me*
Line 2:	*(Where?) in the presence of my enemies.*

Figure 3.18   In Psalm 23:5, the second line completes the first line.

Q 22 ✎ *In Psalm 106:1, what question does line 2 answer?*

Parallel Lines	Psalm 106:1
Line 1:	*Give thanks to the Lᴏʀᴅ,*
Line 2:	*(Why?)* _____

Figure 3.19   In Psalm 106.1 the second line completes the first line.

Q 23 ✎ *In Psalm 138:3, what question does line 1 answer?*

Parallel Lines	Psalm 138:3
Line 1:	*(When?)* _____
Line 2:	*you made me bold and stout-hearted.*

Figure 3.20   In Psalm 138:3, the second line completes the first line.

The golden rule for interpreting a psalm is to see the connection between parallel lines. A parallel line will either repeat, contrast, or complete a thought. It is an error to separate any parallel line of poetry without seeing its relation to the line with it. It is unwise to seek different meanings in each half of a parallel. Sabio says: "If you appreciate two rails of train track, interpret two lines of parallel poetry together."

Stanzas or strophes. As songs have verses, several parallel lines together form a block of thought called a *stanza or strophe. We may compare these stanzas to the paragraphs in this book. As a paragraph groups several sentences into one block of thought, so the stanza—musical paragraph—groups several parallelisms into one sub-theme. We will study more about stanzas in the next lesson.

Q 24 ✎ *In some Bibles, why is there an extra space after Psalm 139:4?*

You may need to read a psalm several times to see these stanzas—natural blocks of thoughts. You can identify them by changes in content, grammar, literary form, or speaker. Some Bible versions, such as the New International Version, suggest these breaks by putting an **extra space** between the stanzas. If you have an NIV Bible, look at Psalm 139 and note the extra space after verses 4, 6, 10, 12, 16, 18, and 22. These spaces show that one verse of a song ends and another begins.

B. Discern figurative language—its meaning and purpose.

The poetry of the Bible has many comparisons—*word pictures* that help us *see* what the writer means. For example, in Psalm 1, the writer mentions the righteous, and then gives us pictures—comparisons of what the righteous are like (Figure 3.21).

The Righteous	The Wicked
He is like a tree planted by streams of water, which yields its fruit in season and whose leaf does not whither. Whatever he does prospers.	Not so the wicked! They are like chaff that the wind blows away.

Figure 3.21 Psalm 1:3-4 uses figurative language—word pictures that compare and contrast the righteous and the wicked.

How often do we find figurative language in biblical poetry? It is hard to find two verses of poetry together that do not contain a word picture. In chapter 6 of this course, we will study types of figurative language—such as similes and metaphors. Sometimes it is hard to identify each type of figurative language in a passage. Still, you must always seek to understand the author's purpose—what message did he want us to get from the word picture. For example, you may not recognize that Psalm 1:3-4 uses metaphors. But you should be able to discern what the author means by comparing the righteous to a fruitful tree by a river, and the wicked to chaff that the wind blows away.

Figure of Speech	What Is the Meaning?
like a tree planted by streams of water	
like chaff that the wind blows away	

Figure 3.22 Practice interpreting figures of speech in Psalm 1:3-4.

Q 25 ✎ *In your own words, explain what the pictures of Psalm 1:3-4 mean.*

Some modern versions of the Bible remove the figures of speech to clarify meaning. I believe this practice does not help the interpreter. The word pictures are part of the inspired text. If you use a version of the Bible that removes word pictures, you should also study at least one literal translation of the Bible, such as KJV or NASB. The figurative language—the comparisons and word pictures in Scripture—are part of God's revelation. Study them and use them in preaching. In Psalm 1:1, note how much is lost when the pictures of walking, standing, and sitting are removed in the CEV [Contemporary English Version] translation.

Psalm	NIV	CEV

1:1	Blessed is the man
	    who does not **walk** in the counsel of the wicked
	    or **stand** in the way of sinners
	    or **sit** in the seat of mockers.
		God blesses the people
		    who refuse evil advice
		    and won't follow sinners
		    or join in sneering at God.

Figure 3.23   Some modern translations remove figures of speech. This takes away part of the revelation God gave us.

Figures of speech—comparisons and word pictures—are sometimes hard to understand. But they bless readers by causing them to slow down and meditate. At first, reading a psalm may seem confusing. The reader must study each line, analyze the relationship between lines, and ask the Holy Spirit to open his heart and mind. A wise man said, "Sometimes the process is as important as the product." This is true of Bible study. The time and effort a person spends studying God's Word in God's presence are as valuable as the interpretation. Why? Because the time we spend with God is part of our relationship with Him. His anointing on our lives is a result of the time we spend with Him. So take time to study and understand the word comparisons and word pictures in Scripture.

The Psalms express the deep emotions of a writer's soul. As you read a psalm, ask yourself, "What is the mood of the psalmist?" Is it glad, sad, mad, good, or bad? Is he feeling joyful, grateful, doubtful, or fearful? What emotions is he expressing? Watch for phrases that are signs of the writer's mood.

Q 26   *Complete Figure 3.24 by identifying the emotion of the psalmist.*

Mood, Emotion, or Feeling	Sign: Words That Reveal Feelings	Psalm
Loneliness	The darkness is my closest friend.	88:18
	My soul thirsts for God, for the living God. When can I go and meet with God?	42:2
	Why are you downcast, O my soul? Why so disturbed within me?	42:5
	Hide your face from my sins and blot out all my iniquity.	51:9
	Glorify the LORD with me; let us exalt his name together.	34:3

Figure 3.24   Watch for signs in the Psalms—words and phrases that reveal the writer's feelings and mood.

To interpret a psalm well, the reader should read the psalm several times until he or she can summarize the emotions and feelings in less than five words. This process is helpful to understand, appreciate, and interpret the psalm.

The Psalms read more like a spiritual journal or diary than a book of theology. The psalmist often weaves his emotions and circumstances into the psalm. *The psalmist is not just writing about truth—he is living it as he writes.* Remember, the goal of a psalm is not just to communicate truth, but for a writer to express his emotions and touch our emotions—thus leading us in confession, thanksgiving, praise, worship, and prayer. So the interpreter must attempt to sense the mood and recreate the historical setting of the psalmist.

You have studied about the historical context, parallelism, and figurative language of the Psalms. Perhaps all of this makes you feel like the mountain of interpreting Psalms is very steep to climb. You might be asking, "Why did God use so much poetry to communicate His revelation to us?" Because poetry touches our emotions more than any other type of writing in the Bible. One man said that poetry is the emotions of life written down.[2] When we interpret poetry, such as the Psalms, we gain only a partial understanding if we focus only on the doctrine it teaches. To get the most out of poetry, we must pause and meditate—allowing the music of the Spirit to lift us into God's presence.

Keys to Interpreting Psalms—Part 1

Lesson 12

Goal A: *Identify the 3 parts and purposes of a praise psalm—to help you interpret it.*
Goal B: *Use the 6 parts of a lament to help you interpret it.*
Goal C: *Analyze the parts of a thanksgiving psalm to help you interpret it.*

Setting

The Psalms were the hymns of Israel and are powerful tools to strengthen doctrine. Just as believers today sing certain songs at Christmas and Easter, the Jews sang certain psalms at certain times.

- Jews sang Songs of Zion and Songs of Ascent as they went up to worship in Jerusalem.
- At the feasts, Israel sang Psalms of Public Worship that reminded them of the promises God gave to their fathers.
- They sang Royal Psalms to crown a king, celebrate his wedding, or remember the promise that a *"son of David"* would rule forever.
- They sang Lament Psalms to comfort the discouraged.
- They sang Thanksgiving Psalms to worship when a person brought a thanksgiving offering to the Lord.

Figure 3.25 summarizes 13 different types of psalms. In this lesson we will study examples of some of these 13 types of psalms.

Type of Psalm	Psalms
A. Hallelujah or Praise Songs	8, 21, 33–34, 103–106, 111–113, 115–117, 135, 139, 145–150
B. Prayer and Petition Psalms (Including Laments)	4–6, 13, 43, 54, 67, 69–70, 79–80, 85–86, 90, 102, 141–143 Individual laments: 3, 22, 31, 39, 42, 57, 71, 88, 120; Corporate laments: 12, 44 ,80, 94, 137
C. Thanksgiving Songs	18, 30, 34, 41, 66, 92, 100, 106, 116, 118, 124, 126, 136, 138
D. Repentance Psalms	32, 38, 51, 130
E. Historical Songs	78, 105–106, 108, 114, 126, 137
F. Psalms Praising God as King	24, 47, 93, 96–99
G. Songs for Public Gatherings	15, 24, 45, 68, 113–118
H. Psalms of Trust and Devotion	11, 16, 23, 27, 31–32, 40, 46, 56, 62–63, 91, 119, 130–131, 139
I. Songs of Zion	43, 46, 48, 76, 84, 87, 120–134
J. Songs about Creation	8, 19, 29, 33, 65, 104
K. Psalms of Wisdom	1, 34, 37, 73, 112, 119, 128, 133
L. Psalms about the King and Messiah	2, 8, 16, 22, 40–41, 45, 68–69, 72, 89, 102, 110, 118
M. Psalms of Judgment	3. 7, 35, 55, 58, 59, 69, 109, 137, 139:19-22

Figure 3.25   The 13 types of psalms often have a form that is either three parts or five parts.[3]

Background

Some Christians think *emotion in worship* did not exist before the birth of the Church. This is far from true. Worship at the tabernacle and temple was full of emotion—dancing, clapping, and joyful singing with musical instruments.

Q 27 *What instructions are in the headings of Psalms 40 to 80?*

Fifty of the headings in Psalms are to the "chief Musician" or the "director of music." Many of the headings include instructions on how to sing the psalm. For example, the heading of Psalm 45 reads *to the tune of "Lilies."* And the heading of Psalm 54 notes *with stringed instruments*.

The Jews sang the *praise psalms* with great joy. In Psalm 33:1, the psalmist calls the people to rejoice because their praise is beautiful (fitting) to the Lord. In contrast to psalms of repentance, praise psalms focus on the Lord's worthiness. The direction of the praise psalm is away from the psalmist toward God. Psalm 33:3 commands the worshiper to sing *"to the Lord."*

The music with a praise psalm is to be skillful, but not formal. The psalmist wants worshipers to sing the psalm as *"a new song"* (Ps. 33:3).

- *"Sing a new song"* (33:3) is not only a call for new words and new music. *Sing a new song* means to sing to God with new wonder at all God has done for us. The worship of God should never become routine. We should always approach God with rejoicing.
- *"Skillfully"* (33:3) reminds us never to worship with a casual attitude. Musicians are to *play skillfully* because they are playing to the Lord. We must offer Him only our best.
- *"With a shout of joy"* (33:3) refers to our attitudes and emotions. Since God looks into our hearts and examines our attitudes, He requires *genuine* and *sincere* joy in His presence.[4]

A. Praise Psalms magnify the name, majesty, goodness, greatness, and salvation of God (Figure 3.27).

Introduction	Explanation	Conclusion

Figure 3.26   In psalms that have three parts, the middle part is the biggest.

Q 28 ✎ *What is the purpose of the main section or explanation of a praise psalm?*

A praise psalm often has three parts.

- The **Introduction** may state the theme, identify the occasion, set the mood, and call people to praise. The call to praise may mention *who* should praise, and *how* they should praise. For example, the psalmist may ask people to praise God with singing, with musical instruments, with dancing, with clapping, and such.

- The **Explanation** is the middle part of a psalm. It is the largest section—and often has several stanzas (musical paragraphs) or verses of the song. The explanation may include repetition, lists, examples, comparisons, or contrasts. A major purpose of the explanation is to give reasons to praise God. *Reasons* for praising God may include His *acts, attributes,* or *character*.
- The **Conclusion** may be a promise, praise, prayer, exhortation, or summary.

The main task of the interpreter is to find the theme that runs through the parts of a psalm. The theme of Psalm 139 is praise to God **for** knowing and caring for us. Note the three parts of Psalm 139.

Q 29 ✎ *Why does Psalm 139 call us to praise God?*

Example of a praise psalm: Psalm 139

Part	Explanations	Psalm
Introduction (Call to *praise*)	The psalmist praises God—the One who examines his life.	139:1-4
Explanation (*Reasons* to praise— God's attributes and acts)	God knows all about me. God is always with me. God can always find me. God created me for a purpose. God thinks about me always. God's enemies are my enemies.	139:5-6 139:7-10 139:11-12 139:13-16 139:17-18 139:19-22
Conclusion (*Prayer*)	The psalmist invites God to examine and guide his life	139:23-24

Figure 3.27   Psalm 139 is an example of a praise psalm with three parts.

Q 30 ✎ *What Hebrew word means "Praise the Lord"?*

Psalms 146–150. The *Hallel* or *Hallelujah Psalms* is the conclusion of the entire book of Psalms. These five psalms each begin with *Hallelujah*—the Hebrew word for "praise the Lord."

The development section in these psalms is unique. Instead of listing *reasons* to praise, it repeats *commands* to praise. Psalm 148 is a good example.

Q 31 ✎ *In Psalm 148, which groups does the psalmist command to praise the Lord?*

- *First,* Psalm 148 commands the angels to praise (Ps. 148:2).
- *Next,* it commands the heavenly bodies and all nature on earth to praise (Ps. 148:3-6).

- *Finally,* the psalm commands all men and women to praise—from the king and the judges to the old men and children (Ps. 148:11-14).

B. Psalms of Prayer and Petition (especially laments) are a cry to God—with strong, deep feelings.

There are more than 60 lament psalms, which makes it the largest group of psalms. Are you discouraged? Is your church going through hard times? Are you part of a small or large group that is suffering? Use the lament psalms to pray your feelings to God.[5]

In a lament psalm, we may identify six parts or elements (Figure 3.28). Take a moment to read this beautiful psalm. And then we will identify the six elements in it.

> [1]*O Lord, how many are my foes! How many rise up against me!*
> [2]*Many are saying of me, "God will not deliver him." Selah*
> [3]*But you are a shield around me, O Lord;*
> *you bestow glory on me and lift up my head.*
> [4]*To the Lord I cry aloud, and he answers me from his holy hill. Selah*
> [5]*I lie down and sleep; I wake again, because the Lord sustains me.*
> [6]*I will not fear the tens of thousands drawn up against me on every side.*
> [7]*Arise, O Lord! Deliver me, O my God! Strike all my enemies on the jaw;*
> *break the teeth of the wicked.*
> [8]*From the Lord comes deliverance. May your blessing be on your people. Selah*
>
> (Psalm 3:1-8).

Parts or Elements	Explanations	Examples from Psalm 3
Recipient or receiver	The Lord, the One to whom the psalmist cries	[1]*O Lord* (Note that verses 3, 4, 7, and 8 emphasize that the psalmist is crying out to the Lord.)
Complaint	The psalmist pours out the problem to God with deep emotion.	[1]*O Lord, how many are my foes! How many rise up against me!* [2]*Many are saying of me, "God will not deliver him." Selah*
Trust	The psalmist expresses confidence in God, for He alone is able to solve the problem.	[3]*But you are a shield around me, O Lord; you bestow glory on me and lift up my head.* [4]*To the Lord I cry aloud, and he answers me from his holy hill. Selah* [5]*I lie down and sleep; I wake again, because the Lord sustains me.* [6]*I will not fear the tens of thousands drawn up against me on every side.*
Deliverance	The psalmist cries out for God to rescue him from the problem.	[7]*Arise, O Lord! Deliver me, O my God! Strike all my enemies on the jaw; break the teeth of the wicked.*
Assurance	The psalmist affirms faith that God will deliver him. Note that this is parallel to trust in part 3.	[8]*From the Lord comes deliverance.*
Praise	The psalmist glorifies God for His blessings.	[8]*…May your blessing be on your people. Selah*

Figure 3.28   A lament psalm often has six parts or elements (Ps. 3:1-8).[6]

Some of these elements overlap, and are not always in order. An element may appear in several verses. The top scholars do not agree on the number of parts in a psalm, or the various types of psalms. Likewise, scholars differ on which verses go with each part. And some of the parts might be missing (see Psalm 88). Still, analyzing the parts or elements of a psalm is helpful. And studying several psalms of the same type gives us insights. The most important benefit of analyzing the parts of a psalm is *not* for all students to put the verses in the same boxes. Rather, we examine the parts of a psalm to see the psalm more clearly. Analyzing a lament lifts up our eyes to God, the only One who can help us with our problems. Examining a lament guides us to lift our burdens to God, with all of our hearts. And as Paul said, to mix petitions with praise. Seeing the parts of a psalm helps us appreciate the skill, inspiration, and art of the psalmist, who blended facts with feelings. Above all, when you finish analyzing the psalm, take time to pray it, enjoy it, meditate on it—in all of its beauty. As Luther said, there is no emotion

Q 32 *In Psalm 3, what 4 things does the section on trust affirm?*

or experience that humans face that the Psalms do not express. The Psalms teach us to share all our emotions with God—from our valleys, plains, and mountains.

Q 33 ✎ *Complete Figure 3.29 by identifying the verses that go with each part of Psalm 54.*

Parts or Elements	Explanations	Examples From Psalm 54
Recipient or receiver	The Lord, the One to whom the psalmist cries	
Complaint	The psalmist pours out the problem to God with deep emotion.	
Trust	The psalmist expresses confidence in God, for He alone is able to solve the problem.	
Deliverance	The psalmist cries out for God to rescue him from the problem.	
Assurance	The psalmist affirms faith that God will deliver him. (Note that this is parallel to trust in part 3.)	
Praise	The psalmist glorifies God for His blessings.	

Figure 3.29   A lament psalm often has six parts or elements (Ps. 54).[7]

C. Songs of Thanksgiving acknowledge God's help and deliverance of individuals and the nation.

The thanksgiving psalms are a contrast to the lament psalms. In the lament psalm, the psalmist describes his problem, prays for help, affirms trust in God, and praises God for help. In contrast, the thanksgiving psalm recalls the past problem, the past prayer, and the past deliverance. Then he testifies and praises God for His mercy. The lament cries out to God before there is any help. The thanksgiving psalm praises Him for His response.[8] Let us be quick to cry out to God in our distress. But let us also remember to praise Him when He answers our cry.

Read Psalm 138—an example of a thanksgiving psalm. Then study Figure 3.30 that explains and illustrates the five elements of this psalm.

> [1]*I will praise you, O L*ORD*, with all my heart; before the "gods"*
> *I will sing your praise.*
> [2]*I will bow down toward your holy temple and will praise your name*
> *for your love and your faithfulness, for you have exalted*
> *above all things your name and your word.*
> [3]*When I called, you answered me; you made me bold and stouthearted.*
> [4]*May all the kings of the earth praise you, O L*ORD*,*
> *when they hear the words of your mouth.*
> [5]*May they sing of the ways of the L*ORD*, for the glory of the L*ORD *is great.*
> [6]*Though the L*ORD *is on high, he looks upon the lowly,*
> *but the proud he knows from afar.*
> [7]*Though I walk in the midst of trouble, you preserve my life; you stretch out*
> *your hand against the anger of my foes, with your right hand you save me.*
> [8]*The L*ORD *will fulfill* [his purpose] *for me; your love, O L*ORD*, endures forever—*
> *do not abandon the works of your hands* (Ps. 138:1-8).

Q 34 ✎ *In Psalm 138, what does the psalmist affirm in the deliverance section?*

Parts or Elements	Explanations	Examples From Psalm 138
Introduction	The summary of God's help	[1]*I will praise you, O L*ORD*, with all my heart; before the "gods" I will sing your praise.* [2]*I will bow down toward your holy temple and will praise your name for your love and your faithfulness, for you have exalted above all things your name and your word.*
Distress	A problem the psalmist faced	[3]*When I called, you answered me; you made me bold and stout hearted.*
Appeal	The past cry to God for help	[3]*When I called, you answered me; you made me bold and stouthearted.*

Figure 3.30   Continued on next page

Continued from previous page

Deliverance	The solution God gave	[6]*Though the* L[ORD] *is on high, he looks upon the lowly, but the proud he knows from afar* [7]*Though I walk in the midst of trouble, you preserve my life; you stretch out your hand against the anger of my foes, with your right hand you save me*
Testimony	The praise for God's mercy	[4]*May all the kings of the earth praise you, O* L[ORD]*, when they hear the words of your mouth.* [5]*May they sing of the ways of the* L[ORD]*, for the glory of the* L[ORD] *is great.* [8]*The* L[ORD] *will fulfill* [his purpose] *for me; your love, O* L[ORD]*, endures forever—do not abandon the works of your hands.*

Figure 3.30   Psalm 138 is an example of a thanksgiving psalm with five elements or parts.[9]

You should not expect the five parts of a thanksgiving psalm to always be in the same order. But you can expect to find most of the five parts.

Q 35 ✎ *Complete Figure 3.31 by filling in column 3.*

Parts or Elements	Explanations	Examples From Psalm 30
Introduction	The summary of God's help	
Distress	The problem the psalmist faced	
Appeal	The past cry to God for help	
Deliverance	The solution God gave	
Testimony	The praise for God's mercy	

Figure 3.31   Practice identifying the parts of Psalm 30.

In Psalm 30, the psalmist had sinned but thanks God for forgiveness. The lesson he learned was that God judges, but He quickly forgives when we repent. His **anger** does not *last*—but His **favor** *does last*.

Q 36 ✎ *What is the key to interpreting Psalm 30?*

[4]*Sing to the* L[ORD]*, you saints of his; praise his holy name.*
[5]**For his anger lasts only a moment, but his favor lasts a lifetime;**
weeping may remain for a night, but rejoicing comes in the morning (Ps. 30:4-5).

Sometimes we punish ourselves over and over for sins that God has already forgiven. And others too often remind us of our failures. But for those who truly repent, the anger of God lasts only for a moment—while His favor endures forever.

Q 37 ✎ *Do you still condemn yourself for sins that God has forgiven? Explain.*

With the *thanksgiving psalm* a person sometimes made a sacrifice. He invited family and friends to the tabernacle or temple. If there were other worshipers in the temple, they were welcome to join. The psalmist would invite them all to thank God with him as he spoke or sang the poem. The priest offered the animal sacrifice. After it was cooked on the altar, those present ate it. Likewise, today, let us be sure to express our thanks to God, with offerings of thanksgiving and words that glorify God and encourage others to trust Him.

Lesson 13

Keys to Interpreting Psalms—Part 2

Goal A: *Illustrate and explain ways the apostles used the messianic psalms.*
Goal B: *Analyze the parts and message of Psalm 1.*
Goal C: *Explain how to interpret and use psalms of judgment.*
Goal D: *Analyze ways we can use the Psalms today.*

A. Songs about Creation exalt God as Creator of the heavens and the earth.

Creation psalms glorify God above all that He has made (Ps. 29:10). Pagans wrote songs and worshiped their gods as a part of nature.[10] In contrast, Jewish psalms about nature worship God as the One who created and controls creation (Ps. 19:1-5). As a painting glorifies its artist, creation glorifies God.

Q 38 ⬉ Complete Figure 3.32 by filling in column 3.

Psalm 29 traces the path of a mighty storm. It forms in the Mediterranean Sea (29:3) and enters Lebanon with fierce winds—winds which break the huge cedar trees (29:5). As the storm comes into northern Israel, it produces thunder and lightning (29:7-8). During the storm, God sits calmly on His throne, above the flood (29:9). In response to His power and authority, the worshiper cries, *"Glory!"* (29:9).

Part	Explanations	Psalm
Introduction (Call to *praise*)	Call to worship	
Explanation (*Reasons* to praise— God's attributes and acts)	Reasons to praise: The voice of the Lord speaks through the storm.	
Conclusion (*Praise*)	Praise to the Lord	29:10-11

Figure 3.32   Practice examining the parts of Psalm 29.

B. Psalms about the King and Messiah describe experiences of King David or King Solomon.

Q 39 ⬉ What are some ways God speaks through the storm (Ps. 29)?

These *royal psalms* call on God to protect His anointed king. They ask God to give him victory against his enemies (Ps. 20). In response to God's help, the king trusts and praises Him (Ps. 21). Psalm 45 probably records a song from the wedding of one of Israel's kings. Psalms 89 and 132 reflect on God's covenant with King David (2 Sam. 7:1-16).

These psalms referred to kings, such as David, who lived at that time. But the New Testament authors apply many psalms to Jesus. It is good to consider what the author understood about his times, *and* what the Holy Spirit knew about the coming Messiah.

Q 40 ⬈ Explain: Some psalms were fulfilled twice.

Some psalms did not appear to be *messianic, when first written. But New Testament authors quote them in referring to Christ. In this way, these psalms were fulfilled twice—first by an earthly king, and later by the King of kings. Jesus Christ is the great Son of David—whom God promised would rule the nations. Therefore, psalms about the king of Israel find their highest fulfilment in Christ.

Psalms 2 and 110 are messianic psalms. They predict that God will set up His anointed Son as King in *Zion (Ps. 2:6). This King [Jesus] will rule the whole earth. All people will submit to Him or face judgment (Ps. 2:8-12). This prophecy refers to the second coming of Christ. He will come in power to rule the earth and set up His kingdom.

Jews sang the *royal psalms* at special events in the life of Israel's kings. Many of these psalms refer to God's covenant with David. Recall that God promised David that a king in his family would rule forever (2 Sam. 7). Jesus, a son of David, was the King God promised would rule. The temporary kings of Judah and the events in their lives pointed forward to the ministry of the Messiah—the King of kings.

Q 41 ⬉ Complete Figure 3.33 by filling in column 2.

Messianic Psalms	Your Summary of How the New Testament Teaches That Jesus Fulfilled This Psalm	New Testament
2:1-2		Acts 4:25-26
2:7		Acts 13:33; Heb. 1:5; 5:5
2:9		Rev. 2:26-27; 12:5; 19:15
8:2		Matt. 21:16
8:4-6		1 Cor. 15:25-28; Heb. 2:5-10
16:8-11		Acts 2:25-32; 13:34-37
22:1		Matt. 27:46; Mark 15:34
22:7-8		Matt. 27:39, 43; Luke 23:35
22:18		Matt. 27:35; Mark 15:24; Luke 23:34; John 19:23-24

Figure 3.33   Continued on next page

Continued from previous page

22:22		Heb. 2:11-12
40:6-8		Heb. 10:5-10
41:9		John 13:18
45:6-7		Heb. 1:8-9
68:18		Eph. 4:8
69:4		John 15:25
69:9		John 2:17; Rom. 15:3
69:21		Matt. 27:34, 48; John 19:28-30
69:22-23		Rom. 11:9-10
69:25		Acts 1:20
78:2		Matt. 13:35
78:24		John 6:31
97:7		Heb. 1:6
102:25-27		Heb. 1:10-12
110:1		Matt 22:44; Mark 12:36; Luke 20:42; Acts 2:34; Heb. 1:13
110:4		Heb. 5:6; 6:20; 7:17, 21
118:6		Heb. 13:6
118:22-23		Matt. 21:42; Mark 12:10-11; Luke 20:17; Acts 4:11; 1 Pet. 2:7
118:26		Matt. 21:9; 23:39; Mark 11:9; Luke 13:35; 19:38; John 12:13

Figure 3.33   Writers of the New Testament referred to psalms of the Old Testament that Jesus, the Messiah, fulfilled.[11]

C. Songs of Zion (Ps. 120–134)

Zion was another name for Jerusalem. Jews sang psalms of Zion as they went up—*ascended*—to **Jerusalem** for the yearly feasts of Passover, Pentecost, and Tabernacles. Also, they sang Songs of Zion when they thought about Jerusalem, or arrived there.

These types of psalms of Zion have three parts. You must understand the big theme of a psalm in relation to the parts. In Psalm 133,

- The Introduction states the theme: *unity* (Figure 3.34).
- The Explanation illustrates the theme twice.
- The Conclusion looks forward to eternal unity with God.

Q 42 *Name the 3 parts of Psalm 133.*

Q 43 *Explain how each of the 3 parts of Psalm 133 relates to the theme: unity.*

Part	Explanations	Psalm
Introduction	**Theme:** *"How good and pleasant it is when God's people live together in <u>unity</u>!"*	133:1
Explanation	**Two illustrations:** [2]*"It is like precious oil poured on the head, running down on the beard, running down on Aaron's beard, down on the collar of his robe.* [3]*It is as if the dew of [Mount] Hermon were falling on Mount Zion."*	133:2-3a
Conclusion	**Result:** *"For there the LORD bestows [gives] his blessing, even life forevermore."*	133:3b

Figure 3.34   Jews sang Songs of Ascent (Psalms 120–134) as they went up to Zion—which was on hills above the ground around it. They sang Songs of Zion when they thought about Jerusalem, or arrived there.

The *Songs of Ascent* are Psalms 120 to 134. The superscription or heading above each of these psalms is: "A Song of Ascents." Worshipers sang these as they were ascending—going up—to Jerusalem for feasts (Ps. 122:4; 42:4). Some think that Jews sang some of these songs as they climbed up the steps to the temple. As you read these psalms, imagine a group of Jews singing as they traveled toward Jerusalem.

Q 44 *How do we know that Psalms 120–134 are Songs of Ascent to Jerusalem?*

I rejoiced with those who said to me, "Let us go to the house of the LORD!" (Ps. 122:1).

¹*Those who trust in the* L*ORD* *are like Mount Zion, which cannot be shaken but endures forever.* ²*As the mountains surround Jerusalem, so the* L*ORD* *surrounds his people both now and forevermore* (Ps. 125:1-2).

The whole kingdom of Judah became captives in Babylon. In these hard times they did not stop writing about Zion. Even as captives in a foreign land, they longed to worship in the temple at Jerusalem. They prayed that God would send a light and lead them back to Mount Zion. For example, a captured Jew likely wrote Psalms 42 and 43. In the beginning, these two psalms were probably together as one psalm.

> ¹*A*S *THE DEER PANTS FOR STREAMS OF WATER, SO MY SOUL PANTS FOR YOU,* O G*OD.* ²*M*Y *SOUL THIRSTS FOR* G*OD, FOR THE LIVING* G*OD.* W*HEN CAN* I *GO AND MEET WITH* G*OD?*
> (Ps. 42:1-2)
>
> T*HESE THINGS* I *REMEMBER AS* I *POUR OUT MY SOUL: HOW* I *USED TO GO WITH THE MULTITUDE LEADING THE PROCESSION TO THE HOUSE OF* G*OD WITH SHOUTS OF JOY AND THANKSGIVING AMONG THE FESTIVE THRONG* (Ps. 42:4).
>
> S*END FORTH YOUR LIGHT AND YOUR TRUTH,*
> *LET THEM GUIDE ME;*
> *LET THEM BRING ME TO YOUR HOLY MOUNTAIN,*
> *TO THE PLACE WHERE YOU DWELL.*
> (Ps. 43:3)

Figure 3.35   A captive probably wrote Psalms 42 and 43.

D. Psalms of Wisdom and Teaching

These psalms reflect on God's ways and instruct us about righteousness. They are sometimes called the Teaching or *Didactic* Psalms. Wisdom psalms—like the Wisdom Books—contrast blessing and ruin, the righteous and the fool, or discuss the suffering of the righteous. Some of the statements in the wisdom psalms are like proverbs.

Psalm 1 is an example of a wisdom psalm that teaches. It contrasts the righteous and the wicked.

Q 45   *Complete Figure 3.36 by answering the questions contrasting the righteous and the wicked.*

Part	Explanations	Psalm
Introduction	What 3 things do the righteous avoid? What things do the righteous do? What are the righteous like?	1:1-3
Contrast	What are the wicked like? How does the destiny of the wicked differ from that of the righteous?	1:4-5
Conclusion	What summary does the psalmist give?	1:6

Figure 3.36   Practice analyzing the parts and message of Psalm 1.

Psalm 32 teaches about repentance. David is sharing what he learned from his sin. At first, he tried to hide it. This caused him to suffer. He did not have rest day or night (32:3-4). Finally, he confessed his sin. Then God forgave him (32:5). He enjoyed the blessing of having his sin removed (32:1-2). David learned something from this. In this psalm, he urges people to repent as soon as they sin (32:6). They should not be stubborn like mules (32:9).

Q 46 ✎ *Complete Figure 3.37 by filling in the blank column.*

Parts or Elements	Explanations	Summary of Verses in Psalm 32	Psalm 32:
Introduction	The summary of God's forgiveness		1-2
Problem	The guilt the psalmist felt		3-4
Solution	The forgiveness the psalmist found		5
Affirmation	The confidence in God's help		6-7
Instruction	The teaching on obedience and trust		8-10
Appeal	The call for people to praise		11

Figure 3.37   Practice explaining the parts of Psalm 32.

Hidden sin brings great sorrow. But repentance and confession bring joy (Ps. 32:10-11). The New Testament also teaches believers to confess sin and turn away from it. If we repent and confess our sins, God *"is faithful and just and will forgive us our sins and purify us from all unrighteousness"* (1 John 1:9).

Take time to read Psalm 32 and make it your prayer. Ask the Holy Spirit to search your heart. Take time to repent, and turn away from anything in your life that does not please God. Then accept His forgiveness, cleansing, and joy.

E. Psalms of Judgment

These psalms are sometimes called *Imprecatory Psalms. An *imprecation* is a curse. The cry for judgment is most often in psalms of lament. In such passages, the author prays for God to curse or judge the wicked. We saw an example of this in Psalm 3:7 above: *"Arise, O LORD! Deliver me, O my God! Strike all my enemies on the jaw; break the teeth of the wicked."* These passages are not calling for personal revenge. Rather, they show a strong concern for God's name, His justice, and His righteousness. They call on God to lift up the righteous and bring down the wicked.

Q 47 ✎ *Do the Psalms of Judgment seek personal vengeance? Defend your view.*

Many people today are troubled by this kind of psalm. The psalmist often uses hyperbole or over-statement (such as "knock out the teeth") and military metaphors (such as spear and javelin) as he prays for God to punish his enemies. We should not interpret these figures of speech literally. Neither should we use these psalms as an excuse to take personal vengeance.

Both the Old and New Testaments teach us to love God *and* neighbors (Lev. 19:18; Matt. 19:19). We should not seek personal revenge (Deut. 32:35; Rom. 12:19; Heb. 10:30). We should remember that the psalmist leaves vengeance to God, the Righteous Judge (Ps. 3:7).

David wrote most of the psalms of judgment—asking for God to judge his enemies. As a warrior, David used the language of a soldier in hand-to-hand battle. The interpreter should first see these statements in context. A psalm about anger is an **honest reflection of the writer's feelings**. In some passages, the psalmist shows fleshly bitterness early in the psalm. But later in the psalm he returns to faith and trust in God. At other times, he sees his enemies as God's enemies and prays for justice. This reminds us of several passages in the New Testament on the topic of praying for justice and vengeance. Bitterness and desire for personal vengeance are wrong. But the punishment that the New Testament warns is coming upon evildoers is far worse than King David asked for or imagined.

Q 48 ✎ *Is it right to seek personal revenge? Explain.*

Q 49 ✎ *Complete Figure 3.38 on the topic of justice in the New Testament.*

Reference	Your Summaries
Luke 18:1-8	
Rom. 2:8-9	
2 Thess. 1:6-10	
Rev. 6:9-11	

Figure 3.38   Practice summarizing passages in the New Testament on the theme of justice.

Q 50 ✎ *How can psalms of judgment help us release bitterness and anger to God?*

The psalmist *poured out his heart to God* about bitterness and anger over injustice. Anger is a normal human emotion. It arises in all of us from time to time. So let us not deny or repress our anger. Rather, like the psalmist, let us *pray our fiery and bleeding feelings to God.* Let us cast all our cares, concerns, and feelings upon Him—for He cares for us (Ps. 55:22; 1 Pet. 5:7). And let us ask God to forgive our enemies and give them a change of heart, before He pours out eternal wrath—wrath so severe that we pray even our worst enemies and their children will avoid it. James and John once wanted to call down fire from heaven on people who were rude to them. But Jesus rebuked them (Luke 9:54-55). *"For God did not send his Son into the world to condemn the world, but to save the world through him"* (John 3:17). Praying our anger to God and releasing it to Him is a way to obey the command: 26 *" 'In your anger do not sin': Do not let the sun go down while you are still angry, 27and do not give the devil a foothold"* (Eph. 4:26-27). **For as we share our anger with our Father**, we avoid a root of bitterness (Heb. 12:15). We are assured that vengeance belongs to Him. And we are able to exchange our anger and hatred for His love for all mankind.

Juma went on a walk to talk with God. Recently, Jimbo had hurt him deeply, spreading lies about him and smearing his name. As Juma walked he told God about his pain and anger. Juma felt better, telling God what had been happening, although he knew God was already aware of the slander. After a few minutes, the Holy Spirit whispered a question to Juma: "If you could bring Jimbo before My throne right now, what accusations would you bring against him? And what would you like Me to do to him?" Juma walked in silence for several minutes. He thought of how many times the Lord had forgiven him. He remembered the teachings of Jesus about forgiveness. Then he responded to the Lord, "Since you already know everything, I feel no need to bring any accusations against Jimbo. And I would like You to give him the same forgiveness You have given to me." As Juma walked home, he found a new peace in his heart, and a quiet trust in God, the Judge of all men.

Q 51 ⤳ *What are some ways we can use the Psalms today?*

F. Six hermeneutical insights for interpreting and preaching the Psalms

The Psalms are poems and songs that the Lord inspired believers to say, sing, and pray to Him. So how can we believers use the Psalms today? This relates to the second question of hermeneutics. The answer is that we can use the Psalms in the same ways that Israel used them. Here are six ways we can use the Psalms.[12]

Q 52 ✎ *How can we use the Psalms today in worship and prayer?*

1. We can use the Psalms as a guide to praise, worship, and pray.   The Psalms are written with inspiration, skill, and beauty. Few of us can write a beautiful hymn or chorus that believers sing to worship God. Yet we all worship as we sing the songs others in the Church have written. Likewise, we can read, recite, sing, or pray a psalm, and use it to express our highest praise—in words that are better than we could have said without help.

Q 53 ✎ *How can we use the Psalms today to express our emotions? Give an example.*

2. We can let the Psalms guide us to express our emotions to God.   They give us examples of how to express our deepest feelings—from sorrow to joy, from anger to peace, from fear to faith.

3. We can use the Psalms to reflect and meditate on who God is, and what He has done for us. As we read and mediate on the Psalms, they exalt Him as God, Creator, King, Redeemer, Father, Judge, and Missionary. And with each of these seven roles of God, the Psalms magnify His qualities and attributes. For example as God, He is high and holy—altogether righteous. As Creator, He is the One we can worship for making us in His image, and for creating all we need for a joyful life. As Father, He is faithful and loving, ever providing, protecting, and sustaining. The Psalms, perhaps more than any other genre of the Bible, help us to meditate and marvel on who God is, and all that He has done for us.

Q 54 *How can we use the Psalms today for meditation? Illustrate.*

4. We can let the Psalms remind us that life has its ups and downs, its victories and its struggles, its joys and its sorrows. The Psalms balance each other. There are psalms of celebration (Ps. 103), and psalms of humiliation (Ps. 51). There are psalms that describe our security and confidence (Ps. 91). And there are psalms that describe our doubts, fear, and darkness (Ps. 88). So let us remind ourselves that the Psalms are all in one book, bound together. The Psalms assure us that the righteous will dwell in the house of the Lord forever (Ps. 23). But they do not guarantee that life on earth will be free from discouragement, distress, or even death by martyrdom, which the apostles experienced. The Psalms connect us with God in every season and occasion as we travel the road from earth to heaven.

Q 55 *How can we use the Psalms today to remind us of the ups and downs of life? Explain.*

5. We can appreciate the Messianic Psalms that prophesied the coming of Christ, a millennium before He was born. These psalms remind us that God planned our redemption and salvation. They remind us of the high price God paid that we might belong to Him. And they assure us of the glorious future God has ordained for His children.

Q 56 *How can we use the Psalms today to appreciate Christ?*

6. We can use the Psalms to emphasize the contrast in the ways and destinies of the righteous and the wicked. The Wisdom and Teaching Psalms emphasize this contrast. Many refer to Psalm 1 as the front door to the Psalms. It describes the way of the godly, summarizing what they avoid, and what they do. Likewise this psalm contrasts the results of two ways of life. The godly are stable and fruitful, but the ungodly are unstable and doomed—like the chaff that the wind blows away. Peter quoted Psalm 34 to emphasize this contrast:

Q 57 *How can we use the Psalms today to reinforce righteous living?*

> *For the eyes of the Lord are on the righteous and his ears are attentive to their prayer, but the face of the Lord is against those who do evil* (1 Pet. 3:12; Ps. 34:15-16).

We are saved by grace, not works. But the faith that saves is the faith that manifests itself through righteous living (James 2:14-26).

Test Yourself: Circle the letter by the **best** completion to each question or statement.

1. Which may help find the historical context?
a) The superscription
b) The genre
c) The literary context
d) The structure of the psalm

2. How many settings do many psalms have?
a) 1
b) 2
c) 3
d) 4

3. Which is NOT a type of parallelism?
a) Completion
b) Comparison
c) Contrast
d) Congruent

4. What type of parallelism is in Psalm 1?
a) Overstatement
b) Synonymous
c) Completion
d) Congruent

5. A key to interpreting figurative language is
a) knowing the historical context.
b) understanding the background of the recipients.
c) reading through the lens of the New Testament.
d) analyzing comparisons and contrasts.

6. What is the middle part of a praise psalm?
a) The explanation
b) The comparison
c) The exaltation
d) The problem

7. Which is a part of a lament psalm?
a) The introduction
b) The contrast
c) The complaint
d) The resolution

8. Which part of a thanksgiving psalm is "the solution God gave"?
a) The problem
b) The appeal
c) The deliverance
d) The testimony

9. What is the middle part of Psalm 1?
a) The appeal
b) The complaint
c) The comparison
d) The contrast

10. How can psalms of judgment help us?
a) To bring judgment on our enemies
b) To release our anger to God
c) To get personal vengeance
d) To clearly see the problem

Essay Test Topics: Write 50-100 words on each of these goals that you studied in this chapter.

- Interpret a psalm by examining its historical context—including its superscript, author, date, and setting.
- Identify and give examples of 5 types of parallelism in Hebrew poetry.
- Explain how to interpret figurative language in poetry.
- Identify the 3 parts and purposes of a praise psalm—to help you interpret it.
- Use the 6 parts of a lament to help you interpret it.
- Analyze the parts of a thanksgiving psalm to help you interpret it.
- Illustrate and explain ways the apostles used the messianic psalms.
- Analyze the parts and message of Psalm 1.
- Explain how to interpret and use psalms of judgment.
- Analyze ways we can use the Psalms today.

Chapter 4:
Interpreting Wisdom Literature

Introduction

The wisdom literature is found mainly in Job, Proverbs, Ecclesiastes, and Song of Solomon—although proverbs are scattered throughout the Bible. These four books focus little on doctrine, but mostly on truth for the path of life. The Bible writers call this *wisdom*—applying truth or knowledge to daily living. The Wisdom Books treat the most practical issues of life, such as grief, work, marriage, and death.

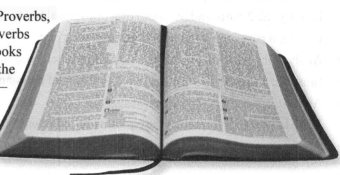

The writer of Ecclesiastes states that he chose his words carefully, to be like *goads* and nails (Eccl. 12:11; see Acts 26:14). His words describe the two purposes of proverbs:

Figure 4.1   Wisdom literature is found mainly in four books of the Bible: Job, Proverbs, Ecclesiastes, and Song of Solomon.

> • As a goad causes an animal to move in a certain direction, a proverb influences our wills.
>
> • As a nail holds a picture on the wall, a proverb holds a truth in our minds.

As people use stones to build a house, biblical writers used proverbs to create much of the Wisdom Books. Each proverb summarizes truth in one short sentence. The proverb presents a great truth in a small package. Proverbs state truth in a general way, without considering exceptions. Like figures of speech, we can misuse proverbs if we do not understand their nature and purpose.

Many preachers do not preach often from the Wisdom Books. We pray that this study will provide great riches for your ministry—a wealth of new material for you to preach and teach.

Lessons:

Proverbs: Their Forms
Goal: *Use the 6 forms of proverbs to interpret them.*

Proverbs: Their Applications

Goal A: *Explain how proverbs teach a truth for one setting that may not apply to other circumstances.*
Goal B: *Defend the idea that proverbs are principles, not promises.*
Goal C: *Illustrate how to interpret a proverb in the context of the whole book of Proverbs.*

Job and Ecclesiastes: Their Interpretations

Goal A: *In Job, explain how knowing the structure of the book helps one interpret its parts.*
Goal B: *In Ecclesiastes, explain 2 signs that affect interpreting.*

Proverbs: Their Forms

Goal: *Use the 6 forms of proverbs to interpret them.*

There are proverbs in many books of the Bible. They are one of the major tools that writers use in the Old and New Testaments. At first, proverbs appear easy to interpret, but later, many proverbs seem hard to understand. Let us consider *six* forms of proverbs. Recognizing the form of a proverb helps us interpret it.

The proverbs have different forms. Discerning the forms makes it easier to interpret the proverbs. Each of these forms is a type of parallelism. You studied these parallel lines in chapter 3 about Psalms—biblical poetry. Recall that *we interpret parallel lines together because one line helps us understand another*. For example, look at Proverbs 20:19. The second line appears to guide us away from a person who talks too much. But compare this "half-thought" of the second line with the first line. What the proverb teaches is that we should avoid people who gossip.

Line 1: *A gossip betrays a confidence;*
Line 2: *so avoid a man who talks too much* (Prov. 20:19).

To interpret a proverb, first compare the lines to see if one line clarifies the other. For example, read line 1 of Proverbs 17:27. This does not mean that a man with knowledge speaks little. Line 2 explains that the proverb is about times of *anger.* So we understand that it means that a wise man *bridles his tongue when he is angry.

Line 1: *A man of knowledge uses words with restraint,*
Line 2: *and a man of understanding is even-tempered* (Prov. 17:27).

In this lesson we will examine six forms of proverbs. Most of these are forms of parallelism that we studied in chapter 3.

A. Some proverbs express the same thought in parallel lines (synonymous lines in a proverb).

In this form, line 2 repeats the idea of line 1—using the same or similar words. Why? Repetition emphasizes a point. Today we have the proverbs in writing. So it is easy for us to review and analyze them. But most of these proverbs were first spoken. Imagine that you are hearing a proverb for the first time, and that you will not have it in writing at all. Hearing the first line a second time gives the listener a better chance of understanding the main truth. As you read Proverbs 6:20, notice how the second line emphasizes the same truth—saying it in a different way.

Parallel Lines:	Proverbs 6:20
Line 1:	My son, keep your father's commands
Line 2:	and do not forsake your mother's teaching.

Figure 4.2   Proverbs 6:20 has parallel lines that express the same thought.

Parallel Lines:	Proverbs 8:8
Line 1:	All the words of my mouth are just:
Line 2:	

Figure 4.3   Proverbs 8:8 has parallel lines that are synonyms.
Line 2 repeats the thought of line 1.

Q 1 *Complete Figure 4.3 by filling in the empty box.*

Q 2 *In Proverbs 3:11 what is the main thought that the author emphasizes twice?*

B. Some proverbs contrast one thought in parallel lines (antithetical lines in a proverb).

Jewish poets liked to emphasize one thought in two lines that are in contrast to each other (Prov. 10:15). The word *but* that begins the second line signals a contrast to line 1.

Sometimes the word *but* does not begin the second line, yet the contrast is still clear. Usually, one line describes the wise person, and the other describes the fool. Often, the results of the actions are also given.

Parallel Lines:	A (Type of Son)	B (Result of Behavior)
Line 1:	*A wise son*	*brings joy to his father,*
Line 2:	*but a foolish son*	[brings] *grief to his mother.*

Figure 4.4   Proverbs 10:1 has parallel lines in contrast.

Note that the main point of Proverbs 10:1 is: Children should behave wisely (their behavior greatly affects their parents). Children should honor and respect the feelings of **both** parents.[1] None of us is an island. What we do affects others. Proverbs such as 10:1 encourage us to consider others and make wise decisions.[2]

Q 3 ✎ *Complete Figure 4.5 by filling in the empty boxes.*

Parallel Lines:	A (Type of Person)	B (Result of Behavior)
Line 1:		
Line 2:		

Figure 4.5   Proverbs 10:16 has parallel lines in contrast.

Q 4 ✎ *Complete Figure 4.6 by filling in the empty boxes.*

Parallel Lines:	A (Type of Person)	B (Behavior)
Line 1:	*Better a poor man*	
Line 2:		

Figure 4.6   Proverbs 19:1 has parallel lines in contrast.

Q 5 ✎ *Complete Figure 4.7 by filling in the empty boxes.*

Parallel Lines:	A (Result)	B (Mental State)
Line 1:		
Line 2:		

Figure 4.7   Proverbs 15:16 has parallel lines in contrast.

Most proverbs state a general truth and do not consider the exceptions. They state that in most cases the wise man prospers and lives a joyful life. In contrast, the fool is poor and has a sad life. But how do we explain life when the fool is wealthy and happy, but the wise man is poor and sad? For example, a righteous believer, like John the Baptist, may suffer in prison—while an evil man, like King Herod, enjoys a feast in his palace? Many of the *better/than* proverbs help us make sense out of these situations—when life seems upside down or backwards. *"Better a **little** with the fear of the Lord, than **great wealth** with turmoil"* (Prov. 15:16). Such proverbs encourage us to walk in wisdom, even when the circumstances are unfriendly. The righteous have an eternal advantage over the wicked—regardless of how things look in this life.

C. Some proverbs compare one thought in parallel lines.

In this type of parallelism, one line is an example and the other line is a comparison. The first line may be a *simile*—a comparison that begins with *like* or *as*. (See examples in Proverbs 25–28). Be sure to keep the emphasis on the main truth.

Figure 4.8   "Like one who seizes a dog by the ears..." (Prov. 26:17).

Parallel Lines:	Proverbs 26:17
Line 1:	
Line 2:	

Figure 4.9   Proverbs 26:17 has parallel lines that compare. Line 2 repeats the thought of line 1.

Q 6 ✎ *Complete Figure 4.9 by filling in the empty boxes.*

Q 7 ✎ *Complete Figure 4.10 by filling in the empty boxes.*

Parallel Lines:	A (Action)	B (Result)
Line 1:	*Remove the dross from silver,*	
Line 2:		

Figure 4.10   Proverbs 25:4-5 has parallel lines in comparison.

D. Some proverbs use parallel lines to complete a thought.

The second line builds on and completes the first line. Sometimes the first line states a *truth*, and the second line states the *reason*.

Q 8 ⬉ *Complete Figure 4.11 by filling in the empty boxes.*

Parallel Lines:	Proverbs 22:9
Line 1:	(Truth)
Line 2:	(Reason)

Figure 4.11 Proverbs 22:9 completes a truth with parallel lines.
The second line explains the reason for the first.

At other times, the first line states a truth, and the second line completes it in a broader way. Always remember to study two parallel lines together, as one thought.

Q 9 ⬉ *Complete Figure 4.12 by filling in the empty boxes.*

Parallel Lines:	Proverbs 16:28
Line 1:	(Truth)
Line 2:	(Completed truth)

Figure 4.12 Proverbs 16:28 completes a truth with parallel lines.
The second line completes the truth of the first.

In Proverbs 16:28, **if** line 2 had said: "And a gossip causes a **feud**," this would be an example of repetition, as we studied in section A above. But in Proverbs 16:28, the second line does not just repeat the first line, it expands it and completes the broader thought. (For more examples see Proverbs 22:17–24:22.)

E. Some proverbs use a group of parallel lines to emphasize one point.

This type of proverb appears often in the "Sayings of Agur" (Prov. 30). It lists several things in a parallel form. These proverbs often use the pattern of "three plus one." Sometimes, the final line is most important to the writer.

[18] *"There are three things that are too amazing for me, four that I do not understand:*

- [19] *the way of an eagle in the sky,*
- *the way of a snake on a rock,*
- *the way of a ship on the high seas,*
- *and the way of a man with a maiden"* (Prov. 30:18-19).

Q 10 ⬉ *In Proverbs 30:18-19, is the fourth line the most important to the author? Explain.*

[16] *There are six things the LORD hates, seven that are detestable to him:* [17] *haughty eyes, a lying tongue, hands that shed innocent blood,* [18] *a heart that devises wicked schemes, feet that are quick to rush into evil,* [19] *a false witness who pours out lies and a man who stirs up dissension among brothers* (Prov. 6:16-19).

Q 11 ⬉ *In Proverbs 6:16-19, do you think the Lord hates the seventh thing more than the other six? Explain.*

Q 12 ⬉ *Complete Figure 4.13 by identifying the form of the proverb.*

Proverbs	Proverbs	Form
22:22-23	[22] *Do not exploit the poor because they are poor and do not crush the needy in court,* [23] *for the LORD will take up their case and will plunder those who plunder them.*	**Completion:** Truth followed by the reason
27:5	*Better is open rebuke than hidden love.*	
25:14	*Like clouds and wind without rain is a man who boasts of gifts he does not give.*	
30:15-16	[15] *"There are three things that are never satisfied, four that never say, 'Enough!':* [16] *the grave, the barren womb, land, which is never satisfied with water, and fire, which never says, 'Enough!'"*	
12:4	*A wife of noble character is her husband's crown, but a disgraceful wife is like decay in his bones.*	

Figure 4.13 Practice identifying the form of a proverb.

F. Some proverbs combine more than one of the forms.

Read Proverbs 3:11-12, and then complete Figure 4.14.

Q 13 Complete Figure 4.14 by filling in the empty boxes.

Parallel Lines:	Proverbs 3:11-12	Form
Line 1:	*My son, do not despise the* Lord's *discipline*	Truth
Line 2:	*and do not resent his rebuke,*	Repetition
Line 3:	*because the* Lord *disciplines those he loves,*	
Line 4:	*as a father the son he delights in.*	

**Figure 4.14   Proverbs 3:11-12 combines three forms in parallel lines—
to emphasize one point.**

Notice that lines 1 and 2 are synonyms—line 2 restates the same thought as line 1. Then, line 3 completes the thought—by stating the reason for the truth of lines 1 and 2. Finally, line 4 *compares* the Lord to an earthly father. So Proverbs 3:11-12 combines three forms of parallel lines.

We have studied forms—the first key for interpreting proverbs.

Lesson 15

Proverbs: Their Application

Goal A: *Explain how proverbs teach a truth for one setting that may not apply to other circumstances.*
Goal B: *Defend the idea that proverbs are principles, not promises.*
Goal C: *Illustrate how to interpret a proverb in the context of the whole book of Proverbs.*

A. Discern the best time to apply each proverb.

Some biblical proverbs seem to conflict with each other. The solution is often to interpret the proverb **on the topic** the writer intends. Study the following example.

Proverbs 26:4—*"Do not answer a fool according to his folly,
or you will be like him yourself."*

Proverbs 26:5—*"Answer a fool according to his folly,
or he will be wise in his own eyes."*

These proverbs were placed side by side to emphasize **timing and context**. Proverbs 26:4 means "Do not stoop down to the level of a fool." There are *times* to remain silent when a fool speaks. But there are *other times* when a wise person must speak to correct foolish words (see Prov. 14:3).

A wise person does not laugh when people are mourning. Likewise, a wise interpreter discerns the best *time* to apply a verse. He discerns that each verse has its *time and place*. Do not bring a hoe to the dinner table, or a casket to a wedding. Discern the time and place to use each proverb.

Q 14 Study the context of Proverbs 6:2. Then explain *when* a person's words are a snare.

B. Read the Proverbs as general principles, not promises.

Proverbs are *not* promises. They are truths that God gave to guide us. The writer of a proverb does *not* prophesy a certain result for obedience. Rather, a proverb states a general truth that applies *most* of the time.

Q 15 Does tithing guarantee prosperity? Explain.

Example: Proverbs 3:9-10

[9]*Honor the* Lord *with your wealth, with the firstfruits of all your crops;*
[10]*then your barns will be filled to overflowing, and your vats will brim over with new wine* (Prov. 3:9-10).

Proverbs 3:9-10 does **not** promise that everyone who tithes will prosper. *Most people* who tithe will prosper. But many factors may affect prosperity—such as a nation's economy, war, famine, earthquakes, fire, thieves, accidents, and bad decisions in business.

I once read a newspaper article about a man who sued his church because the pastor had promised riches, based on tithing (Prov. 3:9-10). The man gave his tithe, yet he lost his job. So he wanted his money back! This man did not discern that proverbs are general principles, not promises!

Example: Proverbs 15:1

A gentle answer turns away wrath, but a harsh word stirs up anger (Prov. 15:1).

Q 16 *Does a soft answer always turn away wrath? Give exceptions.*

A soft answer *usually* turns away wrath, but not always. A drunken husband may beat his wife or children, whether they speak softly or not. An angry boss may act harshly, even when an employee speaks softly. Will the soft words of a thief turn away the wrath of the law? So we see that God gives us proverbs as light for our path, but proverbs do not guarantee results.

Example: Proverbs 13:24

He who spares the rod hates his son, but he who loves him is careful to discipline him (Prov. 13:24).

Q 17 *If a parent does not use the rod on his child, is this always a sign of hate? Explain.*

Some Christian parents have disciplined their children too harshly—thinking that Proverbs 13:24 requires constant use of the rod. There are times to apply Proverbs 13:24. But the rod is not the only way to discipline a child. God disciplines all of us without using a rod. Parents may discipline their children with words, or by taking away privileges. Other Scriptures warn fathers not to be harsh with children (Eph. 6:4).

We have looked at three examples showing that Biblical proverbs state general principles about life. But these proverbs were never written as promises. The principle that the proverb teaches is always true, but there are exceptions. As always, the goal of the interpreter is to determine the principle that the writer meant to teach us.

Example: Proverbs 22:6

Train a child in the way he should go, and when he is old he will not turn from it (Prov. 22:6).

Q 18 *Does raising a child in a godly manner guarantee the child's salvation? Explain.*

Does this proverb teach that a parent has complete control over the salvation of a child? No! The writer never intended this. As Joshua reminded Israel, each person has a free will, and must choose whom to serve (Josh. 24:15). Proverb 22:6 states what happens most of the time. It guides parents to raise their children as the Bible teaches. The role of parents is important in training a child. Statistics teach us that most people who serve God today met Him at an early age. Still, exceptions to this general principle may occur. Parents may be righteous, yet have a child who rebels (Ezek. 18:5-13). God is the most righteous Father of all, yet many of His children have rebelled.

C. Interpret a proverb in the context of the whole book of Proverbs.

A book like Proverbs often jumps from one thought to another. Still, even in Proverbs, the writer scattered many proverbs on the same topic. So, in the context of the whole book of Proverbs, we understand what he teaches on various topics and themes.[3]

Group all the proverbs on a certain subject and compare them. Often, you will see a pattern of thought. Or, the meaning of a proverb may become clear in the light of another one on the same topic. A quick look at a concordance reveals 19 proverbs that mention friend or friends. Studying all of these proverbs will give balance and clarity to your *wisdom* about friendship.

Practice. Remember that earlier we emphasized interpreting a text in the light of other passages on the same topic, in the same book. We want you to practice interpreting a proverb by studying what the book says on the topic of that proverb. Proverbs 18:21 is a verse that has confused many believers.

The tongue has the power of life and death, and those who love it will eat its fruit (Prov. 18:21).

Many miss the meaning of this verse because they do not interpret it in the light of other verses in Proverbs. They claim that we have whatever we confess, and avoid the things we are silent about. These confused believers think that everything depends on what we say. They tell us that we can be sick only if we say we are sick. And that we become wealthy by claiming to be rich.

We want to understand God's Word to us, and we want to say what the Scripture says. But it is important to know the meaning of Scripture—not just the words of Scripture. Proverbs has many verses about the tongue. Looking at these verses together will give us the book's whole message about the tongue.

Q 19 ⬉ *Complete Figure 4.15 on life and death in the tongue.*

Proverbs	Life in the Tongue	Death in the Tongue	Proverbs
1:8	Life is in the instruction of parents.	The tongues of sinners lead some to death.	1:10-19
3:1-2			5:3-5
6:20-23			6:24
8:32-35			11:9, 13
10:20-21			12:13
12:17-19			12:22
14:25a			14:25b
15:4a			15:4b
15:22			21:6
15:31			26:28

**Figure 4.15   Together, verses in Proverbs help us to understand how
"The tongue has the power of life and death" (Prov. 18:21).**

Some proverbs may seem to approve sinful practices. But a wise interpreter discerns that proverbs may describe behavior that God does not approve. Again, this emphasizes comparing what the entire book of Proverbs says about a topic. Figure 4.16 gives you practice in using one proverb to understand another.

Q 20 ⬉ *Complete Figure 4.16 on interpreting hard proverbs.*

Proverbs	Proverb A	Proverb B	Proverbs
14:20	*The poor are shunned even by their neighbors, but the rich have many friends.*		14:21
17:8	*A bribe is a charm to the one who gives it; wherever he turns, he succeeds.*		17:23
26:22	*The words of a gossip are like choice morsels; they go down to a man's inmost parts.*		26:20

Figure 4.16   If a proverb is hard to understand, interpret it in the light of other proverbs on the same topic.

In Figure 4.16, verses under Proverb A may appear to approve favoring the rich, bribing authorities, and gossiping about others. But other proverbs and other passages in the Bible teach us that favoritism, bribes, and gossip are wrong. The key to interpreting a hard proverb is comparing it to other proverbs on the same topic. Remember, the Bible cannot contradict itself—so any interpretation must agree with the rest of Scripture.

We have studied four keys for interpreting proverbs. We trust that these keys will help you interpret proverbs throughout the Bible—in the Wisdom Literature, and also in many passages of the New Testament. Jesus used many proverbs. Likewise, there are many proverbs in the Epistles. Knowing the value of proverbs and the principles to interpret them will bring insight on hundreds of biblical passages.

Lesson 16 Job and Ecclesiastes

Goal A: *In Job, explain how knowing the structure of the book helps one interpret its parts.*

Goal B: *In Ecclesiastes, explain 2 signs that affect interpreting.*

Setting

We have already studied the most popular Wisdom Book, Proverbs. The other three books called "Wisdom Literature" are Job, Ecclesiastes, and Song of Solomon.

Q 21 ↗ *Name the 4 Wisdom Books.*

- **Job** tells the story of a man who loses his wealth, family, and position—but still serves God to the end of his life.

- **Ecclesiastes** reads like a personal testimony of a man who gains everything on earth, but does not serve God most of his life.

- **Song of Solomon** records the comments of a young couple as they reflect on their meeting, courtship, and marriage. Their memories become the lyrics that Israelites sang at weddings, for generations.

Each of these three Wisdom Books has some challenges for the interpreter. Here in *Hermeneutics 2* we will take time to focus on Job and Ecclesiastes.

A. Job: The story of a man who would not give up on God

Topic	Job
Prologue: The Setting of Job's Trials	1–2
I. Job's Lament Over His Trials	3
II. Talks Between Job and His Three Friends	4–27
III. Wisdom: Its Location, Value, and Meaning	28
IV. Job's Claim That He Is Innocent	29–31
V. Elihu's Four Speeches to Defend God	32–37
VI. God Answers Job	38:1–42:6
Epilogue: Job Is Restored	42:7-17

Figure 4.17   Outline of Job 1–42

Speaker	Cycle 1 (Job 4–14)	Cycle 2 (Job 15–21)	Cycle 3 (Job 22–26)
Eliphaz	4–5	15	22
Job	6–7	16–17	23–24
Bildad	8	18	25
Job	9–10	19	26
Zophar	11	20	
Job	12–14	21	

Figure 4.18   To interpret Job, you should note the pattern of speaking between Job and his friends (Job 4–26).[4]

The story of Job is like a drama with several acts or parts. You can almost see it happening.

The beginning takes place in heaven. God presents Job as a model of righteousness and agrees for Satan to test him (Job 1–2). As a result, Job loses his family, wealth, and health.

Next we see Job surrounded by four *"friends."* In three cycles, they take turns accusing Job—and Job defends himself after each one speaks (Figure 4.18). When these older friends fail to humble Job, a youth named Elihu proudly begins to speak. Then God is no longer silent—He speaks from heaven. In the end, Job is restored and makes a sacrifice for his "self-righteous" friends.

Two parts of Job confuse most interpreters. Let us look at each of these parts.

1. The Prologue (Job 1–2).   Many readers struggle to interpret these first two chapters of Job. Here are some common questions believers ask:

Q 22 ↗ *Can Satan enter heaven and talk with God about believers? Explain.*

We must remember one of the basic rules of interpretation: Do not base a doctrine or teaching on one event or one verse. We cannot say—from this one passage—that Satan can enter heaven often. Job 1–2 only tells us about one time that God talked with Satan. So we *cannot* use this one event, told in a poetic manner, to conclude that God and Satan talk from time to time. All we can say from this event is that God and Satan *once* talked about a righteous man named Job. We know that the word *Satan* means "accuser," and that he is the accuser of believers.

> *Then I heard a loud voice in heaven say: "Now have come the salvation and the power and the kingdom of our God, and the authority of his Christ. For the accuser of our brothers, who accuses them before our God day and night, has been hurled down* (Rev. 12:10).

Revelation 12:10 tells us that Satan accuses believers day and night before God. Still, we know that all of us are *before* God. Our Father in heaven sees everything. So we are not sure how close Satan comes to God when he accuses us. God is omnipresent—He can be all places at the same time. But Satan, like other angels and humans, can only be one place at a time. Since Satan is busy on earth, perhaps he accuses believers on earth. Also, Revelation 12:10 says nothing about God responding when Satan accuses us. So we must admit that we know little about communication between Satan and God. And we must be silent when the Scriptures are silent.

2. The statements of Job's friends.   Readers may ask these common questions, especially about Job 4–27:

Q 23 ↗ *Did Job's friends speak the truth? Explain.*

We need to keep in mind that Job's friends used proverbs to condemn Job. Proverbs, as you have learned, are principles that apply *most* of the time—but do not include the exceptions. Job's friends did not realize that it is possible to be righteous but still suffer loss, sickness, and poverty. So Job's three friends made many errors. God Himself rebuked Job's three friends for their folly.

> [7]*After the* LORD *had said these things to Job, he said to Eliphaz the Temanite, "I am angry with you and your two friends,* **because you have not spoken of me what is right***, as my servant Job has.* [8]*So now take seven bulls and seven rams and go to my servant Job and sacrifice a burnt offering for yourselves. My servant Job will pray for you, and I will accept his prayer and not deal with you according to* **your folly. You have not spoken of me what is right***, as my servant Job has."* [9]*So Eliphaz the Temanite, Bildad the Shuhite and Zophar the Naamathite did what the* LORD *told them; and the* LORD *accepted Job's prayer* (Job 42:7-9).

Q 24 ↗ *Why are the words of Job's friends in the Bible? Explain.*

The Bible records the wisdom and the foolishness of people. It records foolish acts, such as the sins of Adam and Eve, Cain, Noah, Gideon, Samson, and the idolatry of the Israelites. And Scripture records foolish statements such as Satan's words, *"A man will give all he has for his own life"* (Job 2:4). There is much that we can learn from the mistakes of others, so God has included these errors in the Bible.

In Job, the words of Job's friends are an important part of the story. They are like steps leading up to the place where God reveals Himself (Job 38:1–42:6). The words of Job's friends give us the complete picture of Job's trial. They prepare the reader for God's response from heaven. Job's wife and friends speak what many people think. In response to their foolish ideas, God reveals Himself in His own words.

Q 25 ↖ *What value do the words of Job's friends have for us today?*

Today, the book of Job has great value for the righteous person who suffers. The story of Job does not simply teach—it encourages. For generations, believers who suffer have found comfort in this book. The questions of Job's friends are the same questions that many believers have. Likewise, the words of Job strengthen believers to remain faithful during pain and sorrow. God's response at the end of the book of Job brings hope to us. It gives a broader purpose to our suffering. So to interpret the book of Job, do not dig for gold in every verse. Recognize the folly of Job's friends, and see the big message of the book: **God is faithful.** He knows our trials, and He is worthy of our trust at all times.

B. Ecclesiastes: The story of a man who lived most of his life rebelling against God

I remember attending a meeting when I was a young man. The speaker was once a member of a gang. He gave his testimony about the grace of God. *First,* he told of his great sins and how that way of life robbed him of happiness, hope, and purpose. *Second,* he told how he was converted and his attitude changed. *Third,* he warned all of us youth not to waste our lives as he had done—but to serve God from that moment on.

Likewise, Ecclesiastes is the testimony of a great man who rebelled against God. He traveled on a godless road, looking for happiness and meaning in life. As an old man, he counseled all to begin serving God during youth, and to honor Him throughout life—knowing that God is our Judge.

Remember the testimony of the ex-gang member that I mentioned? If you had walked into the service in the middle of his sermon, you might have heard him describing a robbery. Without the context of the entire message, his words would have seemed strange for a church service. In the same way, the book of Ecclesiastes has *some thoughts from Solomon's rebellious, worldly years, and other thoughts from his last days.* How can we tell the difference between the two types of verses? Let us consider two types of **signs** that will help us interpret.

Sign 1: Words such as **meaningless, under the sun, vanity,** and **chasing the wind** *point toward* a worldly view. Verses that include these words describe life when Solomon was living in rebellion.

Q 26 Which words are a sign that Solomon is referring to his rebellious years?

Solomon emphasizes the theme of Ecclesiastes several times: *"**Meaningless! Meaningless!" says the Teacher. "Utterly meaningless! Everything is meaningless"*** (Eccl. 1:2; 12:8). Solomon learned that life without God is empty, useless, and meaningless. He was the most foolish wise man who ever lived (Eccl. 4:13)! The word *meaningless* occurs **35 times** in this book!

In Ecclesiastes 1:2 some translations put **meaningless** for the Hebrew phrase *"Vanity of vanities"* (See NASB or the NRSV). But in Hebrew, the original phrase of Solomon, *"vanity of vanities,"* meant: the <u>greatest</u> of vanities. For example, the *Holy of Holies* is the *holiest* place in the temple. The *Song of Songs* is the *greatest* song. The *King of kings* is the *greatest* King. And the *vanity of vanities* is the *most meaningless,* most empty thing of all—living without God.[5]

Q 27 What does the Hebrew phrase "vanity of vanities" mean? Explain.

Likewise, consider the phrase *"**under the sun**"* (Eccl. 1:3). This phrase occurs **29 times** in Ecclesiastes! *Under the sun* is a contrast to *above the sun.* In Ecclesiastes, those living *under the sun* are those who focus only on this world. Life for them is meaningless. Those who want to find meaning in life must look to God. Life *under the sun*—life without God— is a waste of time; an empty, futile, meaningless life. A person can have too much to live *with,* yet too little to live *for.*

Q 28 What contrast helps us explain "under the sun"? Explain.

The words *"**chasing after the wind**"* occur **nine times** in the book (Eccl. 1:14, 17; 2:11, 17, 26; 4:4, 6, 16; 6:9). Seeking things first and God last is like chasing after the wind. In his years of rebellion, Solomon was chasing the wind. As Augustine, an African preacher said, "The heart is restless until it finds its rest in God."[6]

Read the three passages that follow. Notice the signs that point toward a worldly point of view. These verses illustrate what life was like for Solomon when he lived in rebellion.

Q 29 ✎ *In Ecclesiastes 2:17-18, which words are signs of a worldly point of view, from a rebel?*

¹⁷*So I hated life, because the work that is done **under the sun** was grievous to me. All of it is **meaningless**, a **chasing after the wind**. ¹⁸I hated all the things I had toiled for **under the sun**, because I must leave them to the one who comes after me* (Eccl. 2:17-18).

¹⁸*I also thought, "As for men, God tests them so that they may see that they are like the animals. ¹⁹Man's fate is like that of the animals; the same fate awaits them both: As one dies, so dies the other. All have the same breath; man has no advantage over the animal. **Everything is meaningless**. ²⁰All go to the same place; all come from dust, and to dust all return. ²¹Who knows if the spirit of man rises upward and if the spirit of the animal goes down into the earth?"* (Eccl. 3:18-21).

Q 30 ✎ *Explain the attitude of Ecclesiastes 6:1-2.*

¹*I have seen another evil **under the sun**, and it weighs heavily on men: ²God gives a man wealth, possessions and honor, so that he lacks nothing his heart desires, but God does not enable him to enjoy them, and a stranger enjoys them instead. This is **meaningless**, a grievous evil* (Eccl. 6:1-2).

Q 31 ➚ *In Ecclesiastes, which words are like a sign that points toward a godly view?*

Sign 2: Words like **God, Creator**, and **eternity** usually *point toward* a godly view. Words like this show that Solomon was writing as an old man, counseling us to honor God.

¹¹*...He has also set **eternity** in the hearts of men; yet they cannot fathom what God had done from **beginning to end**. ¹²I know that there is nothing better for men than to be happy and do **<u>good</u>** while they live. ¹³That everyone may eat and drink, and find satisfaction in all his toil—this is the **gift of God**. ¹⁴I know that everything **God** does will endure forever; nothing can be added to it and nothing taken from it. **God** does it so that men will revere him* (Eccl. 3:11-14).

*Remember your **Creator** in the days of your youth, before the days of trouble come and the years approach when you will say, "I find no pleasure in them"* (Eccl. 12:1).

Test Yourself: Circle the letter by the **best** completion to each question or statement.

1. What form is this?
My son, keep your father's commands
and do not forsake your mother's teaching.
a) Synonymous
b) Contrast
c) Comparison
d) Completion

2. What form is this?
Like one who seizes a dog by the ears
is a passer-by who meddles in a quarrel not his own.
a) Synonymous
b) Contrast
c) Comparison
d) Completion

3. What form is this?
A generous man will himself be blessed,
for he shares his food with the poor.
a) Synonymous
b) Contrast
c) Comparison
d) Completion

4. What form is this?
A wise son bring joy to his father,
but a foolish son grief to his mother.
a) Synonymous
b) Contrast
c) Comparison
d) Completion

5. What form is this?
All the words of my mouth are just;
none of them is crooked or perverse.
a) Synonymous
b) Contrast
c) Comparison
d) Completion

6. When two proverbs give opposite advice,
a) interpret them with the book of Proverbs.
b) discern one is a principle, the other a promise.
c) decide which one is right.
d) discern the right time for each.

7. Does tithing guarantee prosperity?
a) Yes
b) No
c) Sometimes
d) Rarely

8. A proverb with which to interpret a topic scattered through the whole book is:
a) Trust in the Lord with all your heart.
b) The Lord detests all the proud.
c) Life and death is in the power of the tongue.
d) A gentle answer turns away wrath.

9. What helps us interpret sayings of Job's friends?
a) Job's responses to his friends
b) The wisdom of Proverbs
c) The trouble Job encounters
d) The latter part of the book of Job

10. What word helps us interpret Ecclesiastes?
a) Meaningless
b) Time
c) Possessions
d) Pleasure

 Essay Test Topics: Write 50-100 words on each of these goals that you studied in this chapter.

- Use the 6 forms of proverbs to interpret them.
- Explain how proverbs teach a truth for one setting that may not apply to other circumstances.
- Defend the idea that proverbs are principles, not promises.
- Illustrate how to interpret a proverb in the context of the whole book of Proverbs.
- In Job, explain how knowing the structure of the book helps one interpret its parts.
- In Ecclesiastes, explain 2 signs that affect interpreting.

Chapter 5:
Interpreting Prophecy

Introduction

"What were they going to do?" This was the pressing question on the minds of all the Jewish elders. They had been working on the temple without authorization when the Persian governor appeared with his soldiers. The angry governor asked for a list of all Jews who were working on the temple. We can imagine the Jews asking, "What do we do while we wait for the king's response?" It would be at least a year before King Darius could raise an army and return to slaughter them. Should they use the time to build a fortress? Should they train an army? In this dark moment of indecision, Zechariah came forward with a fresh word from God. God showed him a vision of the lampstand in the temple, and an angel explained its meaning:

> [6]..."This is the word of the LORD to Zerubbabel: 'Not by might nor by power, but by my Spirit,' says the LORD Almighty. What are you, O mighty mountain? Before Zerubbabel you will become level ground. Then he will bring out the capstone to shouts of 'God bless it! God bless it!'" (Zech. 4:6-7).

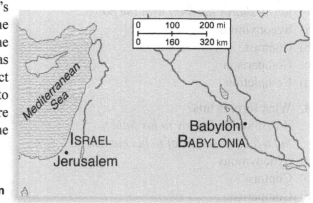

Figure 5.1
A lampstand of the temple

Zerubbabel and the people understood the angel's message. They determined to keep working on the temple until the king issued a response (Ezra 5:5). The message came back months later—and the report was favorable (Ezra 6:6-12). The king paid for the project from the royal treasury. The elders were faithful to continue working. They did not even stop to prepare for war. Zerubbabel's prophecy played a key role in the rebuilding of the temple.

Figure 5.2
Map showing Israel in relation to Babylon

Lessons:

Interpreting the Prophets—Part 1
Goal A: *Summarize the background that Genesis through 1 Kings gives for the 16 prophets.*
Goal B: *Identify the 3 kingdoms that ruled Israel during the times of the major and minor prophets.*
Goal C: *Analyze the common standards of the 16 prophets, and the 300-year period in which they lived.*
Goal D: *Summarize the character, anointing, and authority of the prophets.*

Interpreting the Prophets—Part 2
Goal A: *Contrast and illustrate forthtelling and foretelling in the ministry of the prophets.*
Goal B: *Analyze the 2 roads of blessings and curses that run through the Old Testament and the New Testament. Illustrate this with a drawing.*
Goal C: *Explain ways that believers today should minister as the prophets did.*

 Key Words

the Prophets—usually refers to the 16 prophets who wrote 17 books of the Old Testament from 760-460 B.C.

covenant—an agreement from God to man that promised blessings for obedience and curses for disobedience. The old covenant was an agreement that governed the relationship between God and Israel. The new covenant, after Christ, governs the relationship between God and individuals.

forthtelling—speaking forth the Word of God to the people nearby

foretelling—speaking about the future, as in prophecy

Lesson 17

Interpreting the Prophets—Part 1

Goal A: *Summarize the background that Genesis through 1 Kings gives for the 16 prophets.*
Goal B. *Identify the 3 kingdoms that ruled Israel during the times of the major and minor prophets.*
Goal C: *Analyze the common standards of the 16 prophets, and the 300-year period in which they lived.*
Goal D: *Summarize the character, anointing, and authority of the prophets*

Congratulations! You have studied *Hermeneutics 2* through the Law, Historical Books, Poetry, and Wisdom Literature. Now, we will focus on interpreting the 16 prophets who wrote.

It is important to know when each prophet lived and ministered. Isaiah is the first prophetic book in the Old Testament. Micah is number eleven. And yet Isaiah and Micah lived at the same time. Both ministered to the kings of Judah. These two prophets worked side by side. So why are Isaiah and Micah not listed beside each other in the Bible? Isaiah, Jeremiah, and Ezekiel are long books. Each of them was written on a scroll by itself. But the 12 Minor Prophets were all together on one scroll. As the scrolls were replaced by books, long books like Isaiah, Jeremiah, and Ezekiel were placed together. Likewise, since the 12 Minor Prophets (shorter books) were all on one scroll, they were placed together in the Bible.

Q 1 ⌐ In the Bible, are the prophets listed in the order in which they lived? Explain.

The 16 writing prophets of the Old Testament, Isaiah through Malachi, ministered from about 760 to 460 B.C. During these 300 years, three major kingdoms affected the history of Israel and Judah. These three powers or kingdoms were *Assyria, Babylon, and Persia.

Q 2 ⌐ When did the 16 writing prophets of the Old Testament minister?

- Assyria conquered Israel in 722 B.C.
- Babylon conquered Judah in 586 B.C.
- Persia conquered the Medes in 550 B.C. This happened when Cyrus, King of Persia, attacked his father-in-law Astyages, King of Media. Then, in 539 B.C. the Persians conquered Babylon without a fight! That was the night when Daniel interpreted the handwriting on the wall (Dan. 5:1-31).

We will use these three kingdoms to group the prophets (Figure 5.3). This will help you understand the context of their messages. First, let us consider three questions about the prophets.

Q 3 ⌐ What is an easy way to group the prophets? Explain.

A. What background does Genesis through 1 Kings give for the 16 prophets?

- **Genesis** tells about a *covenant that God made with Abraham. God's purpose was to raise up a nation that would tell the world about Him. God promised to bless all the nations of the earth through the seed of Abraham.

Q 4 ⌐ For what purpose did God raise up Abraham?

- **Exodus** tells about a Pharaoh who did not know or like Joseph. Under this Pharaoh, the Israelites began to serve as slaves. They were strangers and mistreated for 400 years (Gen. 15:14; Acts 7:6; Gal. 3:17). God raised up Moses to lead them out of Egypt. The Lord established His covenant with Israel at Sinai. He used Israel to prepare the world for the promised Messiah.

- **Leviticus** lists the offerings and laws required for Israel to relate to a holy God—especially Leviticus 26.

Q 5 ➢ *What problem does Numbers reveal about Israel?*

- **Numbers** is the story of the great rebellion. Israel was marching toward the Promised Land. But they feared the giants and lost their faith in God. So God refused to fulfill the promise He had given to them. Instead, only their children would inherit the land. During this time, God supplied their needs. They ate God's manna, but continued to worship idols (Acts 7:40-41).

- **Deuteronomy** summarizes the Law and the choices. Moses prophesied that Israel would choose to be blessed or cursed (See Deut. 28–30). Then God buried Moses. As the Pentateuch closes, we see Joshua becoming the new leader.

- **Joshua** tells the story of how Israel conquered Canaan. God parted the Jordan River and led Israel from victory to victory. They divided the land among the 12 tribes. Still, Israel did not fully obey the Word of God. They allowed some of God's enemies to remain in Canaan. This led to continued fighting and Jews marrying pagans in the land.

- **Judges** emphasizes the cycle of Israel: sin, slavery, repentance, and deliverance. This was a dark period in the history of Israel. The tribe of Benjamin was almost completely destroyed. *"In those days Israel had no king; everyone did as he saw fit"* (Judges 21:25).

- **Ruth** is a story that is like a candle in the dark time of the judges. It is like a prophecy that says that God loves all people. Even those of Moab, like Ruth, can find a place in God's family. And this foreign female became a relative of the Messiah, who would die for Jews and Gentiles. He would act as their kinsman-redeemer.

- **1 and 2 Samuel** show us a nation moving from judges to a king. Samuel was a judge, a prophet, and a priest. He served the nation of Israel faithfully for 40 years. He anointed both Saul and David as kings. David was promised a son, through whom God's eternal kingdom would come.

- **1 Kings 1–11** covers the reign of Solomon. His many wives turned his heart away from God. God judged him by dividing the Kingdom of Israel. The Lord took ten tribes away from Solomon and the house of David. Only Judah and Benjamin remained. As 1 Kings closes, the Northern Kingdom is traveling away from God. Not one of their 20 kings loved God. And of the 16 writing prophets, only 3 ministered in the Northern Kingdom. We have traced the history of Israel from Genesis through 1 Kings. This gives us a good background to survey the 16 writing prophets.

> THE HISTORICAL CONTEXT IS ALWAYS NECESSARY FOR THE INTERPRETER.

The historical context is always necessary for the interpreter. For example, Jeremiah wrote 70 years before Zerubbabel's crisis of rebuilding the temple. Jeremiah warned: *"Do not trust in deceptive words and say, 'This is the temple of the LORD, the temple of the LORD, the temple of the LORD!'"* (Jer. 7:4). The phrase *"temple of the LORD"* by itself sounds biblical. But it reflects a false belief. The false prophets of Jeremiah's day preached that the people were safe as long as Solomon's Temple stood. They claimed that God would never allow enemies to destroy His temple. Jeremiah disagreed. He warned that without national repentance, the temple would not stand or save them. In a short time, his prophecy came true. King Nebuchadnezzar took the people as slaves to Babylon—and the temple was in ruins.

Q 6 ➢ *Which 3 kingdoms ruled Israel when the 16 prophets wrote?*

Every interpreter of the Bible should identify the historical background of a prophetic book. As we noted in *Hermeneutics 1,* students studied all of these backgrounds in the Faith & Action books *Survey of the Old Testament* and *Survey of the New Testament.* Also, it is easy to review the historical background by using a study Bible. Or if you look up the prophetic book in a Bible dictionary, it summarizes the historical background. Figure. 5.3 gives an overview of three kingdoms that ruled the Jews, and the period of each prophet.

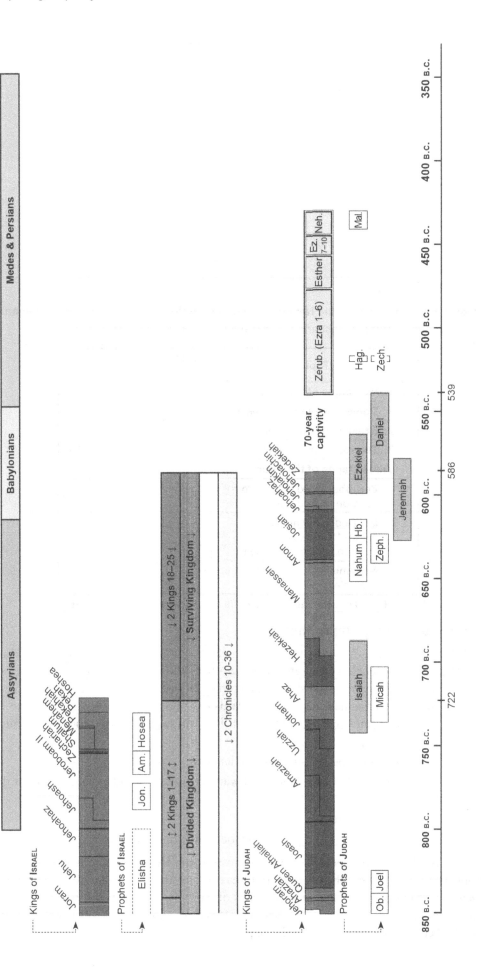

Figure 5.3 Kings and prophets of the Old Testament (through Malachi) (Gray shading shows wicked kings.) The captivity was partial before it became total. That is, the captivity occurred in three stages, as Figure 5.6 explains.

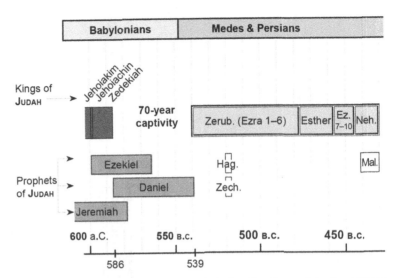

Figure 5.4   Ezra, Esther, and Nehemiah lived during the time of the last Old Testament prophets Haggai, Zechariah, and Malachi. (■ shading shows wicked kings.)

Topic	Date (B.C.)	Scripture
A. Three stages of the exile		
1. **Daniel** and others are taken.	605	Dan. 1:1-7
2. **Ezekiel** and 10,000 are taken.	597	2 Kings 24:14
3. **The rest** of Judah is taken.	586	2 Kings 25:11-21
B. Three stages of the return		
1. **Zerubbabel** led 50,000 from Babylon to Jerusalem.⁺	538	Ezra 2
2. **Ezra** led 1,700 men and 5,000–10,000 women and children back to Jerusalem.	457	Ezra 8:1-14, 18-21
3. **Nehemiah** led a group back to Jerusalem.	444	Neh. 2:1-10

Figure 5.5   Three stages of the exile and three stages of the return[1]

B. Were there only 16 prophets?

When we say ***the Prophets,*** we usually mean the 16 prophets who wrote from 760–460 B.C. Bible teachers often refer to these 16 as the *classical prophets*. The word *classical* refers to certain standards or characteristics. These prophets are called *classical* because their ministries had the same standards or similar things. First of all, these 16 prophets wrote their messages. In addition, all 16 of these prophets did four things much of the time:[2]

Q 7 ➢ *What are 5 things that all of the classical prophets did?*

- They spoke to all the people, not just the leaders.
- They declared that God was angry, and warned of coming judgment because of the people's sins.
- They called people to repent.
- They encouraged people and promised God's salvation for those who obeyed.

Q 8 ➢ *Name 3 men who were called prophets before Isaiah.*

The 16 classical prophets were God's messengers. But they were neither the only prophets nor the first prophets. The Scriptures refer to Abraham (Gen. 20:7) and Moses (Deut. 18:15) as prophets. Judges 6:8 speaks of a prophet. Elijah and Elisha were well-known prophets (1 Kings 17–19). Samuel started a school for the prophets (1 Sam. 19:20). Acts 2:29-30 refers to David as a prophet.

This brings us to a related topic. Not all who prophesied lived in the role or office of a prophet. Some examples are: Enoch, the seventh from Adam (Jude 14), Noah (Gen. 9:25-27), Joseph (Gen. 37:6-7), and Jacob (Gen. 49:10). The Holy Spirit enabled people like these to prophesy, although they were not known as prophets.

Q 9 *Should we call everyone who prophesies a prophet? Explain.*

Likewise, in the New Testament there were only a few apostles and prophets. God used these to lay the foundation of the Church (Eph. 2:20).[2] But it was God's will for all believers to be filled with the Holy Spirit and to prophesy (Joel 2:28; Acts 2:14-21, 38-39; 1 Cor. 14:1, 24, 31, 39). This is a major theme of Luke and Acts. God's will is to fill believers with the Holy Spirit so that they can share God's message with people, do supernatural works (healings and miracles), and speak supernatural words (tongues and prophecy).[3] Why? So that we can be witnesses of Jesus. Paul echoed this same prayer: *"Be eager to prophesy, and do not forbid speaking in tongues"* (1 Cor. 14:39).

Q 10 *Does God want all believers to prophesy? Explain.*

God inspired Moses to pray, *"I wish that all the LORD's people were prophets and that the LORD would put his Spirit on them!"* (Num. 11:29). This prayer has come true for millions today. They are known as Pentecostals and Charismatics. Filled with the Spirit, they pray for the sick and are bold witnesses for Jesus. They are like Jesus, who was *"a prophet, powerful in word and deed"* (Luke 24:19). The Spirit of the Lord who was upon Jesus is upon them. He has anointed them to preach the good news to the poor. He has sent them to proclaim freedom for the prisoners, new sight for the blind, release for the oppressed, and the year of the Lord's favor (Luke 4:18-19; Isa. 61:1-2).

Q 11 *What is the key to being lifted up by God (Heb. 1:9)?*

C. What do we know about the character, anointing, and authority of the prophets?[4]

> PROPHETS WERE RIGHTEOUS.

First, the prophets were righteous. God's Spirit on them caused them to love what was right. The Spirit of the Lord is always associated with righteousness. Read Isaiah 11:2, 5.

Q 12 *What should believers hate and love (Amos 5:15; Rom. 12:9)?*

Application. The prophets loved God and hated sin (Mic. 3:8). Likewise, all believers today should love what is right and hate what is wrong. Some today think that they can love God and love the sinful things of the world. These are deceived. No person can love God and love evil (1 John 2:15).

Fellowship with the Father requires us to love what He loves, and hate what He hates (Rev. 2:6). Let God's Spirit shepherd your emotions and thoughts. Sometimes a feeling or thought is like a sheep that goes astray. By the Spirit, we must quickly bring that thought back to submit to the Shepherd (2 Cor. 10:5). If you are drawn to love what is wrong, *"resist the devil, and he will flee from you"* (James 4:7). Do your part. Depend on the Spirit. *"Those who are led by the Spirit of God are sons of God"* (Rom. 8:14). Hate evil, but love good (Amos 5:15).

> PROPHETS WERE CALLED BY GOD, ANOINTED, AND EMPOWERED TO CALL OUT TO PEOPLE.

Second, the prophets were called by God, anointed, and empowered to call out to people (Num. 11:16-17; Isa. 61:1-2; Mic. 3:8). Thus, a prophet spoke for God to others. The relationship between Moses and Aaron shows the role of a prophet. Moses spoke to Aaron and put words in his mouth. Then Aaron spoke to the people for Moses. Moses was like God to Aaron, giving him a message; and Aaron was like a mouth for Moses. Likewise, the prophets were a mouth for God (Exod. 4:15-16; 7:1-2). The most common Hebrew word for prophet is *nabi.* It occurs more than 300 times in the Old Testament. The word may come from the verb "to proclaim" or "call." A prophet is one whom God calls to proclaim His Word to men.[5] The prophets did not choose themselves (Compare

Heb. 5:4). Rather, God chose and called them. The call of God came to the prophets in different ways. If you want to be inspired, take time to read what God told the prophets when He called them (Isa. 6:1-13; Jer. 1:4-19; Ezek. 1:1–3:15; Amos 7:14-15). The call from God to be a prophet came with courage and power to call out to the people. God spoke to people through the prophets (Heb. 1:1). People often referred to a prophet as *a man of God*. The Shunammite called the prophet *"a holy man of God"* (2 Kings 4:9).

Application. Pastors, evangelists, and missionaries today should have a sense of God's call. As one wise man said, "If you can live without preaching, do it." Like the prophets, pastors must feel compelled to proclaim God's Word. In the same way, all believers today should recognize that God has called us from the darkness to the light. We should be known for our holy living. Sinners should link believers with God.

Q 13 *How did the prophets receive their messages?*

> PROPHETS
> RECEIVED THEIR
> MESSAGES FROM
> GOD.

Third, the prophets received their messages from God. We have looked at the Hebrew word *nabi*. It is always translated as *prophet* in the Bible, and may be based on the word *call*. There were two other Hebrew words for a prophet. The Hebrew word *roeh* is a form of the verb *to see*. This word is always translated as *seer,* that is, *one who sees* the spiritual things of God. There are several verses in which God asks the seers, *"What do you see?"* (Jer. 1:11; Amos 8:2). Another Hebrew word, *hozeh,* is also a form of the verb *see*. Our Bibles translate *hozeh* as *seer* or *prophet*. Thus a prophet was one called by God to call to the people. The prophets, by the Spirit of Christ in them, saw or perceived the things of God (1 Pet. 1:11).

Q 14 *How does God speak to you?*

The prophets *saw* and *heard* the things of God in various ways. Sometimes God spoke through dreams, as He did to Joseph (Gen. 37). Often He spoke through visions (Isa. 6:1; Ezek. 1:1; Dan. 7). At times, He spoke through Scripture (Dan. 9:2). Once in a while, God spoke out loud, as we do (1 Sam. 3). But most of the time, God probably spoke to the prophets through the inner voice of the Spirit (Jer. 1; Hos. 1; Joel 1). So the 16 prophets who wrote Scripture received their messages from God in various ways.

Q 15 *Summarize what 2 Peter 1:20-21 says in relation to the 16 prophets.*

The prophets spoke for God. They often began their messages with words like *"thus says the Lord,"* *"declares the Lord,"* *"an oracle of the Lord,"* or *"the Lord God came to me and said."* These phrases revealed the authority behind the words of the prophets. They urged the hearers to listen carefully.

Lesson 18

Interpreting the Prophets—Part 2

Goal A: *Contrast and illustrate forthtelling and foretelling in the ministry of the prophets.*

Goal B: *Analyze the 2 roads of blessings and curses that run through the Old Testament and the New Testament. Illustrate this with a drawing.*

Goal C: *Explain ways that believers today should minister like the prophets.*

 When the resurrected Christ walked with the two on the road to Emmaus, He explained those things written about Him in the Scriptures. Perhaps Jesus explained some of the prophecies in Figure 5.6.

Prophecy About Christ	Old Testament	New Testament
His virgin birth	Isa. 7:14	Matt. 1:23
His birthplace	Mic. 5:2	Matt 2:1, 6
His triumphal entry	Zech. 9:9	Matt. 21:7-9
His agony in Gethsemane	Isa. 50:4-9	John 18:22; 19:3
His piercing	Zech. 12:!0	John 19:34, 37

Figure 5.6   Continued on next page

Continued from previous page

| His suffering for us | Isa. 53 | 1 Pet. 2:21-25 |
| His second coming | Dan. 7:13 | Luke 21.27 |

Figure 5.6   Writers of the New Testament recorded many prophecies that Jesus fulfilled.

Like the two disciples on the road to Emmaus, most of us would, without some help, find it difficult to understand how Jesus fulfilled the prophecies. But now we have the New Testament, which explains many of these prophecies from the Old Testament. So we can take time to understand and meditate on the prophecies and their fulfillment.

D. In what sense were the prophets forthtellers and foretellers?

> **PROPHETS WERE**
> *FORTHTELLERS.*

Prophesying is what the prophets did when they spoke for God to the people. When we say the prophets were **forthtellers*, we mean that they <u>spoke forth</u> the Word of God to the people among whom they lived. An interpreter speaks what he hears another person say. Likewise, the prophets spoke what God said to them. The prophets were a mouth and a voice for God. Amos spoke (prophesied) about the *social injustice, idolatry, and immorality* in Israel. Hosea prophesied against *Israel's worship of Baal.* Israel was *unfaithful to the Lord,* her husband. The prophets emphasized that God demands *justice, righteousness, and holy living.* They prophesied (spoke about) God and His *changeless character.* They reminded Israel of God's *grace and great acts.* He had delivered them from Egypt (Amos 2:10-11; 3:1-2; 9:7). They spoke of God's covenant love for His people (Jer. 11:1-13). They urged the people to *worship God alone* (Jer. 10:1-16).

Q 16 ⬉ *Summarize the forthtelling in Micah 6:8.*

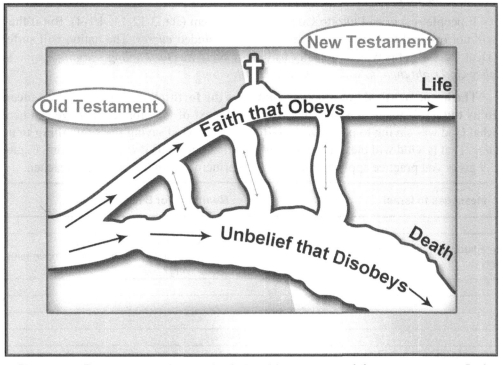

Q 17 ⬉ *Do you think the roads of blessings and curses continue through the New Testament? Defend your answer.*

Figure 5.7   Two roads run through both the old covenant and the new covenant. God will bless those whose faith expresses itself in obedience to Him, and He will curse those whose unbelief expresses itself in disobedience to Him (Matt. 7:13-14, 21-23, 24-27).

Q 18 ⬈ *What was the old covenant? Who created it? What was it based upon?*

The old covenant was an agreement from God that governed the relationship between God and Israel. The covenant had laws for Israel to obey. The covenant stated positive and negative realities. God would *bless* the Israelites if they obeyed the Law, or He would

Q 19 ⬈ *What 2 realities did the old covenant proclaim (Lev. 26; Deut. 27–30)?*

Q 20 ☜ *How does the background of Leviticus 26 and Deuteronomy 27–30 help you interpret the prophets?*

curse them if they disobeyed. In other words, God did not just *give* Israel the Law—He promised to enforce it.[6] **The ministry of the prophets was to remind Israel what the Law required, and what God would do in response to their behavior** (Figure 5.8).

Old Testament	Blessings for Obeying the Law	Curses for Disobeying the Law	Old Testament
Lev. 26:1-13	Life, health, land, prosperity, abundant crops, respect, safety, and relationship with God	Death, disease, drought, lack, danger, destruction, fear, defeat, exile, poverty, disgrace, and separation from God	Lev. 26:14-39
Deut. 4:32-40			Deut. 4:15-28
Deut. 28:1-14			Deut.27:14-26; 28:15-68

Figure 5.8   To interpret the Prophets, remember that most of what they said related to blessings and curses that came as a result of obedience or disobedience (Deut. 27–30).

As you read the Prophets, look for a simple pattern:

1) The prophet rebukes Israel for sin, or reminds Israel of God's love;
2) The prophet warns about a curse, or promises a blessing—depending on Israel's behavior.

Q 21 ➚ *Why do we have so many writings from the short, 300-year period of the prophets?*

The 16 prophets all wrote in a narrow period of biblical history—just 300 years from Amos (760 B.C.) to Malachi (460 B.C.). And most of their writings were rebukes and warnings about coming judgment because of Israel's sin. God had them *write* for two reasons. *First,* to warn Israel of coming judgment—and future hope if repentance followed punishment. *Second,* to show future generations that God will surely **bless** those who express *faith* through obedience, and **curse** those who express *unbelief* through rebellion.

If people *repent* and turn to God, He *blesses* them (Jer. 3:12-14; 4:1-4). But if they will not respond to God's grace, the covenant included *curses*. The nation will suffer (Deut. 27–28). This type of ministry by the prophets was *forthtelling—urging people to obey God right then, to walk on the road of blessings.*

Q 22 ☜ *What messages do the prophets have for us today?*

The hermeneutical question is, What does the forthtelling of the prophets mean to us today? If we understand the historical context of the prophet, then we can hear what God was saying to people *then*. **Often,** we hear God saying **the same thing to us** *now*. That is, God will bless us if we obey Him, but punish us if we disobey Him. Figure 5.9 gives you practice applying the truths and principles that the prophets preached.

Q 23 ☜ *Fill in the blanks and answer the questions of Figure 5.9.*

Old Testament	Messages to Israel	Meanings for Believers Today
Isa. 26:3-4		
Amos 2:4-16	In what ways were Israel and Judah unfaithful to God and the covenant?	How is our destiny united with our lifestyle? What does James say to those who claim to have faith without righteous living?
Amos 9:11-15		
Hos. 8:14		
Mic. 6:8		
Jer. 29:11-13		
Hos. 13:3 Hos. 13:7-9	Because of Israel's unfaithfulness to God, what 4 things would they be like? Which 3 animals represented the way God would respond to them?	
Ezek. 9:4		
Jer. 4:1-2		
Mal. 2:13-16		
Mal. 3:7		

Figure 5.9   Practice applying the messages of the Prophets to believers today.

Under the old covenant, through the prophets, God called Israel and Judah to a **balance** of *right belief* **and** *right living. Under the new covenant*, God requires this same **balance** between *right belief* **and** *right* living. For the just will *live by faith* (Hab. 2:4; Rom. 1:17; Gal. 3:11; Heb. 10:38). What God wanted from Israel and Judah was faith in Him and obedience to the Law. And what God wants from people today is faith in Christ and obedience to His teachings. Reading the Prophets is a constant reminder that God not only provides a covenant, He enforces it. For those who believe in Christ and obey His teachings (loving God and our neighbors), **the final, eternal result will be blessings**. This obedience is possible as we walk in the light of Scripture, depend on God, resist the devil and lusts of the flesh, abide in Christ, and live filled with the Spirit. But for those who express their unbelief through self-will and disobedience, the eternal result will be curses.[7] Figure 5.10 gives you practice summarizing passages on the **balance** God requires between *right belief* and *right living—this is an emphasis of both covenants.* Under the new covenant, God requires a balance between right belief and right living. But He writes His Law in our hearts, washes our sins away by the blood of the Lamb, gives us easy access to His presence and His word, shares His nature and power with us through the Holy Spirit (2 Pet. 1:4), and forgives us when we confess and turn from our sins (1 John 1:7-9).

Q 24 *Fill in the second column of Figure 5.10.*

New Testament	Your Summaries on the Balance of Right Belief and Right Practice
Matt. 5:13	
Matt. 5:14-16	
Matt. 7:12	
Matt. 7:21-23	
Matt. 7:24-27	
Matt. 22:37-40	
Matt. 25:31-46	
Matt. 28:19-20	
Rom. 8:4	
Rom. 8:12-14	
Rom. 13:8-10	
1 Cor. 5:7	
1 Cor. 6:9-11	
Eph. 2:8-10	
Col. 3:17	
Tit. 2:11-14	
James 1:27	
James 2:18	
1 Pet. 3:12	
Rev. 19:18	

Figure 5.10 Practice identifying passages in both covenants, showing that God requires a balance between right belief and right living.

[31] *"When the Son of Man comes in his glory, and all the angels with him, he will sit on his throne in heavenly glory.* [32]*All the nations will be gathered before him, and he will separate the people one from another as a shepherd separates the sheep from the goats.* [33]*He will put the sheep on his right and the goats on his left.* [34]*Then the King will say to those on his right, 'Come, you who are **blessed** by my Father; take your inheritance, the kingdom prepared for you since the creation of the world.* [35]*For I was hungry and you gave me something to eat, I was thirsty and you gave me something to drink, I was a stranger and you invited me in,* [36]*I needed clothes and you clothed me, I was sick and you looked after me, I was in prison and you came to visit me.'* ....[41]*Then he will say to those on his left, 'Depart*

Q 25 *In Matthew 25:31-43, whom does Jesus bless, and whom does He curse?*

*from me, you who are **cursed**, into the eternal fire prepared for the devil and his angels.* [42]*For I was hungry and you gave me nothing to eat, I was thirsty and you gave me nothing to drink,* [43]*I was a stranger and you did not invite me in, I needed clothes and you did not clothe me, I was sick and in prison and you did not look after me"* (Matt. 25:31-36, 41-43).

As you seek to interpret the Prophets, remember that Jesus summarized all 16 of them *and* the Law in one verse: *"So in everything, do to others what you would have them do to you, for this sums up the Law and the Prophets"* (Matt. 7:12). [Some English readers might like to hear this truth sung as: *Lifesong* by Casting Crowns https://www.youtube.com/watch?v=vaia32TsPq0]

Q 26 ✎ *Are most of the prophecies that were foretold still future? Explain.*

> **PROPHETS WERE**
> *FORETELLERS.*

As **foretellers,* the prophets spoke about the future. The prophets brought bad news and good news. They warned of future judgment and called people to repent. They promised God's help to those who obeyed. There are many examples of foretelling to strengthen the message of responsibility to the covenant (Lev. 26; Deut. 27–30). Many of the judgments that the prophets foretold were fulfilled within a few decades as Assyria and Babylon conquered Israel.

Q 27 ↗ *Why do some stumble over prophecy about the future?*

Note that Isaiah *prophesied* about Cyrus and called him by name 150 years before his decree in 538 B.C. Those who lack faith find prophecy hard to believe. Why? Because they depend on the natural and not on the supernatural. Even some who write about the Bible deny prophecies like that of Isaiah. They do not believe that God enabled Isaiah to write about Cyrus 150 years ahead of time. But those of us with faith believe the Bible, though we do not understand everything in it! We believe that God knows the beginning from the end. And we believe that God enabled Isaiah to write about the Messiah 800 years before He was born in Bethlehem (Isa. 53).

E. What methods and styles did the prophets use?

> **PROPHETS**
> **USED VARIOUS**
> **METHODS AND**
> **STYLES.**

No two preachers today preach exactly the same. Likewise, the prophets used different methods.

- Isaiah sang a song that was a parable (Isa. 5).
- Jeremiah wrote Lamentations. This book includes five sad poems about Judah.
- Prophets often used drama. At God's instructions, Jeremiah made a yoke and wore it as he prophesied (Jer. 27). Likewise, Ezekiel often acted out his messages as a drama. Once he drew on a clay tablet and built a ramp to it (Ezek. 4). Another time he cut off his hair and then struck a third of it, burned a third, and scattered a third, saving only a few hairs (Ezek. 5).
- Sometimes the prophets used stories or parables to tell the truth. Ezekiel told about two sisters (Israel and Judah) who committed adultery (Ezek. 23). Another time, he brought his message through a parable about a cooking pot (Ezek. 24).

Q 28 ✎ *Summarize the comparisons in Amos 5:24 and Isaiah 53:6-7.*

- Sometimes the prophets used comparisons.

Q 29 ✎ *Explain the contrast in Isaiah 1:3.*

- Other times, they used contrasts.
- At other times, the prophets used questions.
- Many times the prophets shared their messages by telling of the visions they saw (Dan. 7:2-3).

So we see that God enabled the prophets to make their messages clear and interesting.

In contrast, messages by some preachers today are often boring. Some people who come to church fall asleep. One proverb summarizes this problem: "that knife is as dull as a sermon!" *"My brothers, this should not be"* (James 3:10)! Do not kill the Word of

Q 30 ✎ *In Habakkuk 1:2-3, who asked, "Why do you tolerate wrong?" Was it Habakkuk or God?*

Life by the way you share it! Preacher or teacher, study the methods of the prophets. Learn to use stories, drama, songs, proverbs, pictures, comparisons, and contrasts to share your message. The God who helped the prophets will help you be creative as you seek Him.

Q 31 ➤ *What can preachers today learn from the methods of the prophets?*

F. Hermeneutical concerns: Interpret the themes of the Prophets through the writings of the New Testament.

The Prophets emphasize *three* common themes.[8]

First, the writing prophets emphasized the responsibilities of the covenant. They believed that God is loving, gracious, and faithful. They knew that God is unchanging, holy, righteous, and just. They testified that God is merciful, patient, and compassionate. He is a God who wants a relationship with people, and takes the first step toward us. He is the One who redeemed His people from Egypt. There was never any question as to whether God wanted to bless His people. Still, to receive God's blessings and favor, **the Israelites needed to keep *their part* of the covenant**. The covenant promised blessings for obedience and curses for disobedience. The Israelites needed to fulfill their responsibilities if they wanted God to bless them. Their part was to obey His Word. As we noted above, the period from 760 to 460 B.C. was the last three centuries of the Northern and Southern Kingdoms. Because of their disobedience, God was not able to bless them in the way He desired. The Northern Kingdom of 10 tribes disappeared after Assyria conquered them in 722 B.C. As Hosea prophesied, they became like smoke (Hos. 13:3). And today we refer to the Northern Kingdom as the *lost tribes of Israel*. The Southern Kingdom had some good years of serving God, some good kings, and some good revivals. So their kingdom lasted about 150 years longer, until 586 B.C. But overall, these last 300 years remind us of the words of Jesus as He wept over Jerusalem:

Q 32 ➤ *Upon what human response did the blessings of the covenant depend?*

Q 33 ➤ *Why has the glory of Israel's earthly kingdom been lost for over 2500 years?*

> [37]*"O Jerusalem, Jerusalem, you who kill the prophets and stone those sent to you, how often I have longed to gather your children together, as a hen gathers her chicks under her wings, but you were not willing.* [38]*Look, your house is left to you desolate.* [39]*For I tell you, you will not see me again until you say, 'Blessed is he who comes in the name of the Lord'"* (Matt. 23:37-39).

By the time of Jesus, the kingdom of the Jews had crumbled. The glorious days of David and Solomon were gone. Jesus, the Son of David, came announcing that the Kingdom of God was at hand—in a new way. He shifted the focus from an earthly land and enemies of flesh. Christ's concern was not to overthrow the bondage of the Romans. He emphasized freedom from the slavery of sin! He stressed God's love, mercy, forgiveness, and redemption. He came to be the Lamb of God that takes away the sins of the world (John 1:29). In Christ, God came close to the people He created. He lived in flesh, experienced life as we do, and died to redeem us. By His Spirit, God comes to live in believers, the new temple. All of this became a part of the gospel. Still, the apostles are faithful to emphasize that our only proper response to God's love is obedience. And the faith that saves is the faith that expresses itself in a life that pleases God. In Figure 5.10 you practiced summarizing verses that stress the balance between right belief and right living.

Q 34 ➤ *In what way did the ministry of Jesus relate to a kingdom?*

Q 35 ➤ *What response continues to be necessary for us to enjoy the blessings of God?*

Second, the prophets emphasized the theme of the **Day of the Lord**. At times, God seemed distant. Yet the prophets often predicted that God was coming. The *Day of the Lord* refers to those times when God reveals Himself—bringing sudden judgment or blessing. At times, this theme of the Day of the Lord was about the present, the *even now*. At other times, it was *eschatological*—about the future, the *not yet*. To sinners, the Day of Judgment is a day to fear. But to those whom God has forgiven and redeemed, the Day of the Lord is a day to rejoice.

Q 36 ➤ *Is the Day of the Lord sad or glad? Explain.*

Q 37 ✎ *What does the prophet's theme of the Day of the Lord mean to us today?*

The prophets remind us to live now in light of the Day of the Lord. Some, like Esau, live only for the moment. Others lose love and hope because sin increases (Matt. 24:12). But those who live by faith keep one eye on the future. Justice and other blessings we want do not always come to us in this life. Sometimes the wicked prosper and the righteous suffer. But as Paul reminds us:

> [6]*God is just: He will pay back trouble to those who trouble you* [7]*and give relief to you who are troubled, and to us as well. This will happen when the Lord Jesus is revealed from heaven in blazing fire with his powerful angels* (2 Thess. 1:6-7).

So as we interpret the Prophets and all of Scripture, let us, like the apostles, remember that the Day of the Lord is coming. The Kingdom is *already* here, and we are in it—but the Kingdom has *not yet* come fully, because the King has *not yet* returned. All of the blessings and promises of the New Testament will come fully when the Day of the Lord arrives.

Q 38 ✎ *How does the anointing of the prophets and Christ relate to us today?*

Third, the prophets emphasized the theme of the *Messiah. With this theme of the Messiah came an emphasis on hope, forgiveness, and restoration—to those who repent, call on the name of the Lord, and return to a life of faith in God.

The word *Messiah* comes from a Hebrew word that means "anointed one." In the New Testament, the Anointed One is called *the Christ.* In the Old Testament, the prophets anointed kings with oil (1 Sam. 10:1; 16:3, 13; 24:6; 2 Sam. 1:14). This showed that God was setting the kings apart for a special service. In the New Testament, God anointed the Messiah or Christ with the Holy Spirit. Jesus was already God's Son when the Spirit came down on Him in the form of a dove at His baptism (Luke 3:21-22). The dove showed that the anointing of the Holy Spirit came upon Him as He began His ministry. Read Luke 4:18-19.

Q 39 ✎ *Does God want believers to prophesy today? Explain and illustrate.*

Application.   The second question of hermeneutics leads us to ask: What does a passage mean to us today?

Too often, teachers and writers comment on the anointing of the prophets and the Messiah and then stop. When they teach on the anointing, they are always facing the past. This is incomplete hermeneutics. God's desire is to pour out His Spirit on all believers **today**. Then we can continue to speak God's message, and do supernatural deeds for God, as the prophets and the Messiah did. The Spirit inspired both Moses and Paul to express God's desire that all of God's people prophesy. God wants believers to be filled with the Spirit. He wants us to speak forth the message of the Bible with wisdom, boldness, and compassion. He wants us to talk about future blessings to those who live by faith. And He wants us to warn about future curses and punishment for those who disobey and ignore the will of God. God wants all believers to be anointed by the Spirt and to prophesy in these ways.

Q 40 ✎ *Do you think Peter was prophesying to the crowd on the Day of Pentecost?*

Q 41 ✎ *Do you think Stephen was prophesying in his message of Acts 7?*

Q 42 ✎ *What does prophetic forthtelling emphasize today about being in a covenant with God?*

Recall that the main work of the prophets was *forthtelling.* It was emphasizing the blessings and curses of the covenant. Likewise today, prophesying should be mostly *forthtelling.* It should emphasize that God's blessings come on those whose faith expresses itself in obedience. But His wrath comes on those whose unbelief expresses itself through self-will and disobedience.

Q 43 ✎ *Complete Figure 5.11 by summarizing passages about ministering as prophets today—being God's messengers.*

Bible	Your Summaries
Num. 11:29	
Joel 2:28	
Acts 2:17, 38-39	
Acts 19:6	
1 Cor. 1:7	

Figure 5.11   Continued on next page

Continued from previous page

| 1 Cor. 14:5 | |
| 1 Cor. 14:39 | |

Figure 5.11   Practice summarizing passages that teach it is God's desire for all of His people to be filled with the Spirit and to be His messengers, like the prophets.

Through the anointing that God pours out on each believer, all of the blessings and gifts of the Spirit flow through the Church today (1 Cor. 12–14). The anointing of the Spirit did not die with the apostles. God will provide it until Jesus, our Savior and Messiah, returns (1 John 2:27).

"Therefore you do not lack any spiritual gift as you eagerly wait for our Lord Jesus Christ to be revealed" (1 Cor. 1:7). Luke explains that as God anointed Jesus the Messiah, He wants to anoint all of His sons and daughters for ministry. *First,* we must become God's children. *Then,* after we have been forgiven and are born again, God desires to anoint us for service. This is a big theme in Luke and Acts. Notice that whenever Luke writes about the Holy Spirit, in either of his books, he always writes about the Spirit anointing sons, not sinners. Writers such as John emphasize that the Spirit convicts sinners of sin (John 16:8). But God led Luke to emphasize that the Holy Spirit anoints believers to serve, just as He anointed Jesus to serve. Believers fulfill the role of prophets today as the Spirit anoints us to speak God's message to our generation. An example of the anointing theme in Luke is:

"But you will receive power when the Holy Spirit comes on you; and you will be my witnesses in Jerusalem, and in all Judea and Samaria, and to the ends of the earth" (Acts 1:8).

Notice that the apostles and the others of the 120 were already God's sons or daughters. Still, they needed the Spirit to anoint them to witness.

The prophets emphasized the theme of the Messiah or Anointed One. And the prophet Joel prophesied of a time when God's anointing would increase. Then, God's desire would be to pour out His anointing on all of His children as He did on His Only Son (Joel 2:28-32). This began to be fulfilled on the Day of Pentecost (Acts 2:1-21). And it continues to be fulfilled in these last days as believers seek this anointing. Today, there are over 500 million Pentecostals and Charismatics who have received this anointing to witness and serve.[9] We believers prophesy today, as the Spirit anoints us to share God's message of love, forgiveness, and blessings as God's children—as we turn from evil and live by faith in Christ.

CAUTION

God *inspired* the apostles to write Scripture. Sometimes the Spirit led them to interpret passages in ways that surprise us. For example, Matthew applies to Christ the words, *"Out of Egypt I called my son"* (Matt. 2:15; Hos. 11:1). If we study these words in Hosea, without Matthew's comment, we would think these words refer only to the Exodus. Through *inspiration,* Matthew sees a parallel meaning. Israel went into Egypt as a small nation. Later, God led the nation out of Egypt. Likewise Jesus, God's Son, went to Egypt as an infant. Later, after King Herod died, God led Jesus out of Egypt. We believe the Spirit inspired Matthew to interpret and apply Hosea's passage to Christ. But today, the canon of Scripture is closed. And we do not claim the same authority of inspiration for believers that we recognize in the apostles. It is an error for anyone to claim insight by *illumination,* an insight contrary to what apostles wrote by *inspiration.* The Spirit does indeed guide preachers and teachers today. But let us beware of any teachings that contradict the *inspired* words of the prophets and apostles.[10] It is well for us to be guided by Paul's words, *"Do not go beyond what is written"* in Scripture (1 Cor. 4:6).

Q 45 ↖ *Is it prophesying today when anointed believers share the gospel of the new covenant with others? Explain.*

Q 44 ↖ *How did the messages of Peter and Stephen fulfill what Joel predicted (Joel 2:28)? Is this anointed speaking what Joel was talking about? Explain.*

Q 46 ↖ *How do you respond to new doctrines today that contradict the Scriptures? Explain.*

Test Yourself: Circle the letter by the **best** completion to each question or statement.

1. What does Genesis contribute to the background of the Prophets?
a) The story of the flood
b) The rise of Pharaoh
c) The call and life of Abraham
d) The source of their messages

2. Which kingdom ruled at the time of Isaiah?
a) Egyptian
b) Assyrian
c) Babylonian
d) Medo-Persian

3. What was common for all 16 prophets?
a) Acceptance by the people
b) Warning the people
c) Healing the sick
d) Restoration of the people

4. What was NOT common during the 300 years of the prophets?
a) Revival
b) Idolatry
c) Immorality
d) Instability

5. What did the prophets hate?
a) Israel's enemies
b) Ungodly kings
c) Sin
d) Satan

6. An example of forthtelling is:
a) Where there is no ox, the stall is clean.
b) I behold him, but not now.
c) All that a man has he will give for his life.
d) You have mistreated the wife of your youth.

7. Which reference is on blessings and curses?
a) Leviticus 15–16
b) Ezekiel 36–38
c) Deuteronomy 28–30
d) Isaiah 22–23

8. How were people saved under the Old Testament?
a) By keeping the Law
b) By faith expressed in obedience
c) By the sacrifices of the priests
d) By following Jewish traditions

9. What did Deuteronomy 4 promise?
a) Poverty for the disobedient
b) The coming of the Messiah
c) Redemption for the nation
d) Justice for the oppressed

10. What is the key to ministering today like the prophets?
a) Foretelling the future
b) Forthtelling the gospel
c) Emphasizing repentance and grace
d) Being filled with the Spirit

 Essay Test Topics: Write 50-100 words on each of these goals that you studied in this chapter.

• Summarize the background that Genesis through 1 Kings gives for the 16 prophets.

• Identify the 3 kingdoms that ruled Israel during the times of the prophets.

• Analyze the common standards of the 16 prophets, and the 300-year period in which they lived.

• Summarize the character, anointing, and authority of the prophets.

• Contrast and illustrate forthtelling and foretelling in the ministry of the prophets.

• Analyze the 2 roads of blessings and curses that run through the Old Testament and the New Testament. Illustrate this with a drawing.

• Explain ways that believers today should minister as the prophets did.

Unit Two:
Interpreting the Genres of the New Testament

Figure: Unit 2 The Gospels are a combination of stories *about* Jesus and teachings *of* Jesus. The rock in this picture has five fossils embedded in it. Likewise, Matthew's Gospel has five teachings of Jesus surrounded by historical narrative (stories).

Chapter 6 coaches you to interpret the Gospels.
- *Define "kingdom of God," and compare the revelation of God's kingdom to three phases of light.*
- *Compare the "already" and "not yet" aspects of the kingdom on five topics.*
- *Explain the Gospels as combinations of stories about Jesus and teachings of Jesus. Draw a diagram of Matthew 1–28 to illustrate this.*
- *Analyze the role of ethics in the Kingdom, and the reasons for various views on ethics.*

Chapter 7 gives you practice to interpret Acts.
- *Summarize the relationship of history and theology in Luke's writings.*
- *Compare and contrast what Luke, John, and Paul emphasize about the Spirit.*
- *Contrast descriptive and prescriptive aspects of a passage in Acts, related to church expansion. Support your positions with parallel passages.*

D.
APOCALYPTIC
REVELATION

HOUSE OF
NEW TESTAMENT BOOKS

B. 13 LETTERS FROM PAUL

TITUS
1&2
TIMOTHY
1&2
THESSALONIANS

PHILEMON
COLOSSIANS
PHILIPPIANS
EPHESIANS

GALATIANS
1&2
CORINTHIANS
ROMANS

End Pastoral Times

Prison

Salvation

False Teachers

Suffering

2 PETER
1,2&3
JOHN
JUDE

1 PETER
JAMES
HEBREWS

C. 8 LETTERS FOR ALL

A. 5 HISTORICAL BOOKS

MATT. | MARK | LUKE | JOHN | ACTS

Chapter 8 guides you to interpret the Epistles.
- *Review the historical and cultural background of your passage.*
- *Research parallel passages using the six circles of literary context.*
- *Examine word usage and relationships of your passage.*
- *Discern literal and figurative language to interpret a passage in the Epistles.*

Chapter 9 helps you interpret Apocalyptic Passages.
- *Illustrate how the historical context and the biblical authors help us interpret apocalyptic writings.*
- *Identify at least ten characters in Revelation. Summarize their roles.*
- *Compare parallel passages to discern the big story of apocalyptic passages.*
- *Identify five contrasts in Revelation that help you interpret apocalyptic passages.*

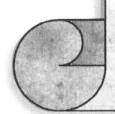

Chapter 6:
Interpreting the Gospels

Introduction

Figure 6.1 shows that Matthew's Gospel, like the other Gospels, is a combination of stories about Jesus, and teachings of Jesus. To interpret the stories about Jesus, such as Matthew 1–4 and 8–10, we need to follow the rules for interpreting historical narrative, which you studied in chapter 1 of this book (Review Figure 1.3, Seven Guidelines for Interpreting Biblical Stories.).

In contrast to stories about Jesus, the Gospels also contain teachings of Jesus, like Matthew 5–7. Matthew's Gospel contains five sections of teachings (See Figures 6.2 and 6.10). Interpreting the teachings of Jesus is like interpreting the Epistles. In *Hermeneutics 1,* you studied a lot about interpreting Epistles (Review Figure 1.2). Here in chapter 6 we will give you examples and practice to interpret the teachings of Jesus. We will especially focus on Jesus' teachings about ethics—values and behavior in His kingdom. Before we consider stories and teachings of the Gospels, let us review the kingdom of God, which provides a framework for interpreting the Gospels.

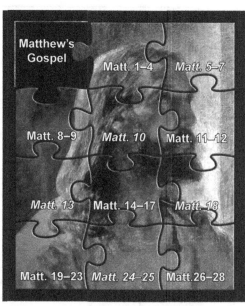

Figure 6.1   Small stories (like Matt. 1–4) and teachings (like Matt. 5–7 that are in *italics*) make up Matthew's Gospel—his story of Jesus.

Lessons:

Interpreting the Kingdom of God in the Gospels—Part 1
Goal A: *Define the kingdom of God.*
Goal B: *Explain why the kingdom of God is sometimes called the kingdom of heaven.*
Goal C: *Contrast God's rule on earth and in heaven.*
Goal D: *Compare the revelation of God's kingdom to three phases of sunlight.*

Interpreting the Kingdom of God in the Gospels—Part 2
Goal A: *Explain: The kingdom of God has "already" come, but has "not yet" fully come.*
Goal B: *Compare the "already" and "not yet" aspects of the Kingdom on 5 topics.*
Goal C: *Identify present and future aspects of passages in the Gospels.*

Interpreting the Gospels: Teachings and Historical Narrative—Part 1
Goal A: *Explain the Gospels as a combination of stories about Jesus and teaching of Jesus. Draw a diagram of Matthew to illustrate this.*
Goal B: *Analyze the biblical role of ethics in the Kingdom.*
Goal C: *Demonstrate the skill of interpreting the Gospels in the light of the Epistles.*

Interpreting the Gospels: Teachings and Historical Narrative—Part 2
Goal A: *Analyze the reasons for various views on ethics.*
Goal B: *Analyze the parts of a story to help identify the main point.*
Goal C: *Answer 3 key questions on the author's points and applications of a given Gospel story.*

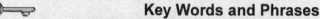
🗝 Key Words and Phrases 🗝

kingdom of God—the realm over which God rules; although this is everywhere, His kingdom is more vibrant in the lives of those who are in relationship with Jesus Christ and where God's will is being obeyed. [At Creation, God's kingdom was present; at the coming of Jesus, the kingdom of God came into history; when Jesus returns, the Kingdom will be fully realized.]

already but not yet—the new age of the Kingdom has *already* begun at the coming of Jesus, but it is *not yet* complete until He returns (Figures 6.5 and 6.8).

ethics of the kingdom—God's standards of behavior for us to live by now, in this present age; the commands of Jesus in the Gospels guide the ethics or behavior of believers in the Kingdom (Figure 6.11).

historical narrative—stories about Jesus as recorded in the Gospels

---

Lesson 19

Interpreting the Kingdom of God in the Gospels—Part 1

Goal A: *Define the kingdom of God.*
Goal B: *Explain why the kingdom of God is sometimes called the kingdom of heaven.*
Goal C: *Contrast God's rule on earth and in heaven.*
Goal D: *Compare the revelation of God's kingdom to three phases of sunlight.*

To interpret the Gospels, we must understand the *kingdom of God in relation to the ministry and teachings of Jesus. In this lesson we will enable you to answer four questions about the kingdom of God:

- What is the kingdom of God?
- How are the kingdom of God and the kingdom of heaven related?
- Does God's kingdom include heaven and earth?
- How is the growth of God's kingdom like three phases of sunlight?

A. The kingdom of God includes His rule and His realm.

For there to be a kingdom there must be two things: a *king* who rules and a *place* he rules.[1] The kingdom of God is the realm or region in which He rules. God rules everywhere, so there is a sense in which His kingdom is everywhere. Yet God's rule is not the same in all places. Jesus taught us to pray: *"Your **kingdom** come, your will be done **on earth as it is in heaven**"* (Matt. 6:10). This prayer reminds us that God's will is being done more perfectly in heaven than on earth. We will discuss *the will of God* more fully in the next lesson, under section B, point 2.

Q 1 ⟋ Define the kingdom of God.

Q 2 ⟍ Does God rule perfectly in all places? Explain.

B. How are the kingdom of God and the kingdom of heaven related?

A careful study of the New Testament reveals that the *kingdom of God and the kingdom of heaven* are the same kingdom. It was common in the days of Jesus for Jews to substitute the word *heaven* for God. The name of God was so sacred to Jews that they did not use it often. So Matthew—since he wrote mostly to Jews—often used the phrase *kingdom of heaven*. In contrast, Mark and Luke—since they wrote to Gentiles—usually use the term *kingdom of God*. Note that "heaven" and "God" are *synonyms—they mean the same thing in the following passages:

Q 3 ⟋ Why is the kingdom of God sometimes called the kingdom of heaven?

Matthew	Kingdom of Heaven	Kingdom of God	Mark	Luke
8:11	*"I say to you that many will come from the east and the west, and will take their places at the feast with Abraham, Isaac and Jacob in the **kingdom of heaven**."*	*"People will come from east and west and north and south, and will take their places at the feast in the **kingdom of God**."*		13:29
11:11	*"I tell you the truth: Among those born of women there has not risen anyone greater than John the Baptist; yet he who is least in the **kingdom of heaven** is greater than he."*	*"I tell you, among those born of women there is no one greater than John; yet the one who is least in the **kingdom of God** is greater than he."*		7:28

Figure 6.2   Continued on next page

111

Continued from previous page

13:11	He replied, "The knowledge of the secrets of the **kingdom of heaven** has been given to you, but not to them."	He told them, "The secret of the **kingdom of God** has been given to you. But to those on the outside everything is said in parables."	4:11	See 8:10
13:31	He told them another parable: "The **kingdom of heaven** is like a mustard seed, which a man took and planted in his field."	[30]Again he said, "What shall we say the **kingdom of God** is like, or what parable shall we use to describe it? [31]It is like a mustard seed, which is the smallest seed you plant in the ground."	4:30-31	See 13:18-19

Figure 6.2   The words *kingdom of heaven* and *kingdom of God* refer to the same kingdom.

There are many other parallel passages in the New Testament that show that the *kingdom of heaven* and the *kingdom of God* are simply different names for the same kingdom.

C. God is the Ruler of heaven and earth.

There are several truths related to the issue of where God reigns.

Q 4 Did the rule or kingdom of God have a beginning? Explain.

1. God has always ruled.   His decree created the earth—He spoke and it was so. His rule set boundaries for the oceans. He ordained the relationships between the sun, moon, and earth. He ordered man, birds, animals, and fish to be fruitful and multiply. From Genesis through Malachi, we see God ruling the earth. As Paul wrote,

[24]*"The God who made the world and everything in it is the Lord of heaven and earth ... [26]From one man he made every nation of men, that they should inhabit the whole earth; and he determined the times set for them and the exact places where they should live"* (Acts 17:24, 26).

Q 5 How is God's rule unlike a dictator's rule?

2. God has not ruled like a dictator, who allows no choices.   He permits angels and humans to rebel. One day He will rule with a rod of iron (Rev. 12:5). Then, He will judge all who have rebelled against Him. But until the final judgment, God chooses to give some freedom to humans, angels, and demons.

Q 6 How is God's kingdom related to Satan's kingdom?

3. God's kingdom and Satan's kingdom are at war.   The Almighty allows Satan to be a lesser ruler over earth (John 12:31; 14:30; Eph. 2:2; 6:12; 1 John 5:19). For a discussion of Satan's kingdom and spiritual warfare, see *The Full Life Study Bible* on Ephesians 6:11; also read the article on "Power Over Demons and Satan," Mark 3:27; and the article on "The Kingdom of God," Matthew 12:28.

4. Sometimes, God acts—takes action—as a king and brings justice.   When Adam and Eve fell into sin, God stepped in. As King of all, He punished them for their sins. Still, He showed mercy and promised a Redeemer (Gen. 3:15). At times, God reminds us that He is in control and reigning on earth. He sent a flood to destroy evil, and angels to destroy Sodom and Gomorrah. He delivered Israel from Egypt. He used Israel to punish the Canaanites. Later He used the Assyrians and Babylonians to punish Israel. There is much evidence to show that God's kingdom has always included the earth.

Q 7 Give an example of an event in your life that showed God's rule.

Q 8 Under the old covenant, why could the King not have close relationships with people?

5. Under the old covenant, God's rule or kingdom lacked the personal relationships He desired.   The kingdom of God—His ruling over people and places—was like a shadow, haze, or dim sunlight in Old Testament times. The King could not have the personal relationship He desired when the Law was on stone. People could not come close to Him because of their sins and sinfulness. Even the high priest could not come near to God often. The curtain was always there to keep people away from God. So Jesus told Nicodemus that all must be born again to see the kingdom of God (John 3:3). That is, to see (know, understand, and experience) the personal rule of God over our lives, we need a new heart.

D. Through Jesus, the kingdom of God came in a clear, personal, powerful way.

The kingdom of God is like a shining light, growing brighter on the earth. The Old Testament prophets announced the Kingdom, and were a part of the earliest phase or revelation. Even the great prophet, John the Baptist, was a part of the early phase of the Kingdom. Reflect on Jesus' words about John:

> [11] *"I tell you the truth: Among those born of women there has not risen anyone greater than John the Baptist;* **yet he who is least in the kingdom of heaven is greater than he.** [12]*From the days of John the Baptist until now,* **the kingdom of heaven has been forcefully advancing,** *and forceful men lay hold of it.* [13]*For all the Prophets and the Law prophesied until John.* [14]*And if you are willing to accept it, he is the Elijah who was to come.* [15]*He who has ears, let him hear"* (Matt. 11:11-15).

John the Baptist looked at the fullness of the kingdom of God as a person presses his face to the window glass to look inside a house. John Wesley comments, "The least true Christian believer has a more perfect knowledge of Jesus Christ, of His redemption and Kingdom, than John the Baptist had, who died before the full manifestation of the gospel."[2] John recognized Jesus, but we know Him personally.

Q 9 *In what sense are believers under the new covenant greater than John the Baptist?*

John came preparing the way for Jesus and preaching, *"Repent, for the kingdom of heaven is* **near***"* (Matt. 3:2). Early in His ministry, Jesus told the people, *"Repent, for the kingdom of heaven is* **near***"* (Matt. 4:17). Those who bow to Jesus to rule their lives receive the King and His kingdom. Thus they inherit the righteousness, joy, and peace of the kingdom of God (Rom. 14:17).

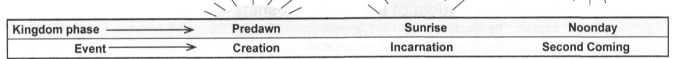

Kingdom phase ⟶	Predawn	Sunrise	Noonday
Event ⟶	Creation	Incarnation	Second Coming

Figure 6.3   The earthly revelation of the Kingdom is like three phases of sunlight.

- **Predawn.** From the beginning of earth, God's kingdom was present, like the light that comes before dawn.

- **Sunrise.** At the coming of Jesus to earth, God's kingdom came like a sunrise. The Kingdom came when the King came.[3] In the person and mission of Jesus, the kingdom of God came into history.

Q 10 *Compare the revelation of the kingdom of God to 3 phases of sunlight.*

- **Noonday.** At some time in the future, Jesus will return. Then the kingdom of God will come like the sun shines at the full light of day.

Signs, wonders, healings, miracles, and deliverance show that the kingdom (ruling) of God is present. As Jesus said,

> [25] *"Every kingdom divided against itself will be ruined, and every city or household divided against itself will not stand.* [26]*If Satan drives out Satan, he is divided against himself. How then can* <u>his kingdom</u> *stand?* [27]*And if I drive out demons by Beelzebub, by whom do your people drive them out? So then, they will be your judges.* [28]**But if I drive out demons by the Spirit of God, then the kingdom of God has come upon you***"* (Matt. 12:25-28).

In spite of signs of the kingdom of God, many Jews refused to accept Jesus as the King. He spoke tragic words about many Jews in relation to the kingdom of God.

Q 11 *How is a healing or deliverance a sign that God's kingdom is present?*

> [11] *"I say to you that many will come from the east and the west, and will take their places at the feast with Abraham, Isaac and Jacob* **in the kingdom of heaven***.* [12]*But the* **subjects of the kingdom** *[unbelieving Jews] will be thrown outside, into the darkness, where there will be weeping and gnashing of teeth"* (Matt. 8:11-12).

Q 12 ✗ *Will Abraham, Isaac, and Jacob be in the kingdom of God? Explain.*

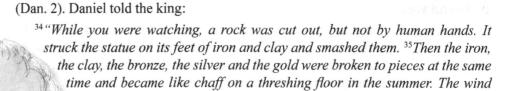

**Figure 6.4
Nebuchadnezzar's dream**

Q 13 ✗ *When did the rock that Nebuchadnezzar saw strike the earth?*

Daniel's interpretation of Nebuchadnezzar's dream relates to the kingdom of God (Dan. 2). Daniel told the king:

> 34 *"While you were watching, a rock was cut out, but not by human hands. It struck the statue on its feet of iron and clay and smashed them.* 35 *Then the iron, the clay, the bronze, the silver and the gold were broken to pieces at the same time and became like chaff on a threshing floor in the summer. The wind swept them away without leaving a trace.* **But the rock that struck the statue became a huge mountain and filled the whole earth.** 36 *This was the dream, and now we will interpret it to the king"* (Dan. 2:34-36).

> 44 *"In the time of those kings, the God of heaven will set up a kingdom that will never be destroyed, nor will it be left to another people. It will crush all those kingdoms and bring them to an end, but it will itself endure forever.* 45 *This is the meaning of the vision of the rock cut out of a mountain, but not by human hands—a rock that broke the iron, the bronze, the clay, the silver and the gold to pieces. The great God has shown the king what will take place in the future. The dream is true and the interpretation is trustworthy"* (Dan. 2:44-45).

The rock that Nebuchadnezzar saw struck the earth when Jesus was born. Since that time His kingdom has been growing like a mustard seed. When Jesus returns, God's kingdom will fill the whole earth.

Jesus died to redeem us through His blood. Now, He invites all to accept Him as King over our lives. His desire is to live in people—not in a tent. Under the new covenant, God writes His Law on our hearts and puts His Spirit within us. We delight in pleasing Him. We enjoy His presence within as He rules over our lives in His kingdom.

Lesson 20

Interpreting the Kingdom of God in the Gospels—Part 2

Goal A: *Explain: The kingdom of God has "already" come, but has "not yet" fully come.*
Goal B: *Compare the "already" and "not yet" aspects of the Kingdom on 5 topics.*
Goal C: *Identify present and future aspects of passages in the Gospels.*

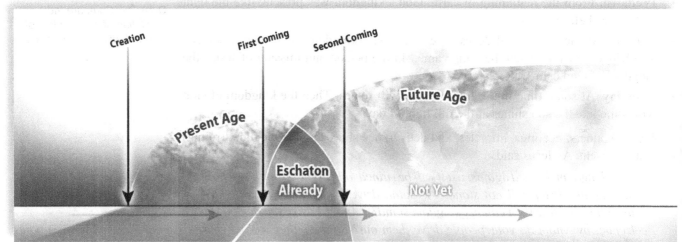

Figure 6.5 **Believers live in the *eschaton*—the end of the present age, and the beginning of the future age. The glorious future age of the kingdom of God has already begun—but it is not yet fully here.**

Q 14 ✗ *What does the Greek word "eschaton" mean?*

Q 15 ✗ *What did the Jews expect the Kingdom to look like when it came?*

A. The *"already" and *"not yet" aspects of the kingdom of God

The New Testament is written from an eschatological view. The Greek word *eschaton* means "the end." *Eschatology is about the end—when God brings this age to a close. Most Jews at the time of Jesus were looking for the end of the age. The Romans had conquered the Jews and were ruling over them when Christ was born. The hand of Rome was heavy upon the Jews. But the Israelites eagerly awaited a new, glorious day—a time that would surpass the glory of Solomon's kingdom. Scripture promised that a son of David would reign on the throne forever. Many Jews were watching for the birth of this Messiah—the Savior of Israel. At the birth of John the Baptist, Zechariah was filled with the Spirit. He prophesied about Christ, the *"rising sun"* from heaven (Luke 1:78), and rejoiced for *"salvation from our enemies and from the hand of all who hate us"* (Luke 1:71). When Simeon and Anna saw the baby Jesus, they rejoiced to see the *"glory to your people Israel"* (Luke 2:32) and *"the redemption of Jerusalem"* (Luke 2:38). Full of the Spirit, these Jewish believers knew that the *eschaton* had come. They believed this was the time when God would deliver them from the Romans. And He would close the curtain on sickness, injustice, sin, and Satan. He would begin the new age of His glorious rule on earth.

Q 16 ⟋ *What did the Kingdom look like when King Jesus came to earth the first time?*

The Jewish Hope—the *Eschaton*	
Present Age (The time of Satan's rule)	**Future Age** (The time of God's rule)
Characteristics: Sin, sickness, suffering, poverty, persecution, and demon possession	**Characteristics:** Righteousness, health, rejoicing, prosperity, freedom, being filled with the Spirit

Figure 6.6   The Jews looked forward to the end of the present age and the beginning of a new glorious age. The Gospel writers use the phrases *this age* and *the age to come* to describe the two phases of God working out His plan (Mark 10:30).[4]

The future age is the age of the Messiah. This is the time when the kingdom of God (the rule of the King) will come to earth.

Q 17 ⟋ *Complete Figure 6.7, summarizing prophecies about the glorious future age.*

Reference	Characteristics of the Glorious Future Age of God's Kingdom
Isa. 2:2-4	
Isa. 11:4-5	
Isa. 11:6-9	
Isa. 40:3-5	
Jer. 31:31-34	
Joel 2:28-30	
Zech. 13:1	

Figure 6.7   Practice identifying characteristics of the future age.[5]

John the Baptist announced that the coming of the *eschaton* was near. God was ready to separate the grain from the chaff. John preached that it was time to make earth ready for the King. It was time for *"all mankind* to *see God's salvation"* (Luke 3:6; Isa. 40:5). Then John baptized Jesus and guided everyone toward Him. Imagine the eschatological excitement of those days.

Jesus came and announced that the promised Kingdom was at hand through His ministry (Mark 1:14-15; Luke 17:20-21). Jesus cast out demons and said, *"If I drive out demons by the Spirit of God, then the kingdom of God has come upon you"* (Matt. 12:28). He healed the sick, worked miracles, and accepted sinners. His ministry was evidence that the end had come (Matt. 11:2-6; Luke 11:20; 15:1-2). Everyone kept watching Jesus to see if He was the One to come, or if they should look for someone else. Was He really the Messiah who would end trouble on earth and bring in the new age? Multitudes were following Him and shouting His praises in the streets of Jerusalem. Then suddenly, He was crucified—and their hopes died when Jesus died.[6]

Q 18 ⟋ *How did the ministry of Jesus excite the Jews and raise expectations that the Kingdom had come in all its glory?*

Then on the third day Jesus arose from the grave! Hope resurrected with Him! His followers thought the time had surely come for Jesus to *"restore the kingdom to Israel"* (Acts 1:6). But instead, Jesus commissioned His followers to go into all the world and make disciples among all nations. He ascended to the Father, and poured out the Holy Spirit to enable us.

Q 19 ⟋ *What task did Jesus direct His followers to do until He returns?*

Q 20 *What are tensions between the "already" and "not yet" aspects of the Kingdom?*

Believers began to understand that even though the new age had begun, it would not be complete until Jesus came again. The Kingdom would not come in its fullness until the King returned. As Peter preached in Acts 3, Jesus had come to bring the beginning of the end. Believers began to understand that through the death, resurrection, and ascension of Jesus—and the fullness of the Spirit—the blessings of the future age had already begun. The new age of the Kingdom had *already* begun, but it was *not yet* complete.

The first Christians learned to live between the times—at the end of one age and the beginning of another. They became truly eschatological. At communion, they celebrated the Lord's death *"until he comes"* (1 Cor. 11:26).

- *Already,* their sins were forgiven. But they were *not yet* perfect.
- *Already,* they had victory over death, *yet* they must still die.
- *Already,* the Spirit gave them power over demons. *Yet* they lived in a world where Satan still attacked them and stirred up persecution.
- *Already,* they had escaped condemnation. *Yet* they must face a future judgment (2 Cor. 5:10).

Living now in God's kingdom means living under His rule and Lordship. In Christ, God has forgiven our sins, and adopted us. As children in His kingdom, we are committed to His ethics—His standards of behavior for us to live by now, in this present age. So we pray that His kingdom and kingship come—first in our lives, and then in all the earth.[7]

Q 21 *Are those who daily rebel against God in His kingdom—that is, under His rule?*

Q 22 *Has the kingdom or rule of God come fully? Explain.*

We have said that the kingdom of God is the realm over which the King reigns. The kingdom of God came like a sunrise when Jesus came to earth. His kingdom has already begun, but it is not yet complete on the earth. The noonday phase of God's kingdom will come when Jesus comes again. Likewise, you have *already* started studying hermeneutics, but you have *not yet* completed your study. Figure 6.8 compares the *already* and *not yet* aspects of the kingdom of God on several topics.

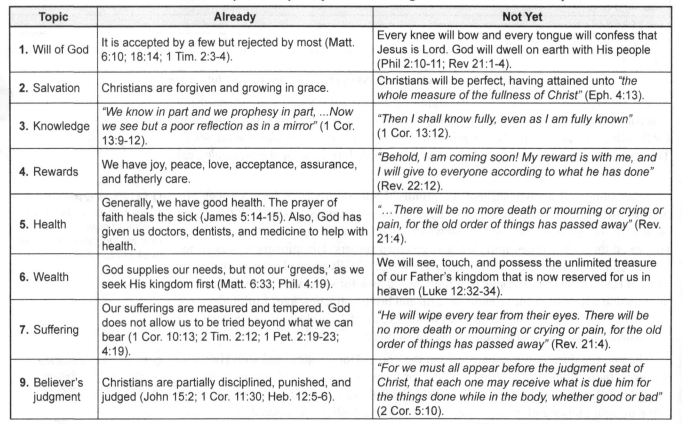

Topic	Already	Not Yet
1. Will of God	It is accepted by a few but rejected by most (Matt. 6:10; 18:14; 1 Tim. 2:3-4).	Every knee will bow and every tongue will confess that Jesus is Lord. God will dwell on earth with His people (Phil 2:10-11; Rev 21:1-4).
2. Salvation	Christians are forgiven and growing in grace.	Christians will be perfect, having attained unto *"the whole measure of the fullness of Christ"* (Eph. 4:13).
3. Knowledge	*"We know in part and we prophesy in part, ...Now we see but a poor reflection as in a mirror"* (1 Cor. 13:9-12).	*"Then I shall know fully, even as I am fully known"* (1 Cor. 13:12).
4. Rewards	We have joy, peace, love, acceptance, assurance, and fatherly care.	*"Behold, I am coming soon! My reward is with me, and I will give to everyone according to what he has done"* (Rev. 22:12).
5. Health	Generally, we have good health. The prayer of faith heals the sick (James 5:14-15). Also, God has given us doctors, dentists, and medicine to help with health.	*"...There will be no more death or mourning or crying or pain, for the old order of things has passed away"* (Rev. 21:4).
6. Wealth	God supplies our needs, but not our 'greeds,' as we seek His kingdom first (Matt. 6:33; Phil. 4:19).	We will see, touch, and possess the unlimited treasure of our Father's kingdom that is now reserved for us in heaven (Luke 12:32-34).
7. Suffering	Our sufferings are measured and tempered. God does not allow us to be tried beyond what we can bear (1 Cor. 10:13; 2 Tim. 2:12; 1 Pet. 2:19-23; 4:19).	*"He will wipe every tear from their eyes. There will be no more death or mourning or crying or pain, for the old order of things has passed away"* (Rev. 21:4).
9. Believer's judgment	Christians are partially disciplined, punished, and judged (John 15:2; 1 Cor. 11:30; Heb. 12:5-6).	*"For we must all appear before the judgment seat of Christ, that each one may receive what is due him for the things done while in the body, whether good or bad"* (2 Cor. 5:10).

Figure 6.8   Continued on next page

Continued from previous page

10. Sinner's judgment	Sinners receive a portion of the wages of sin. They are separated from fellowship with God and suffer some results of their evil acts (Eph. 2:1; 1 Tim. 5:24).	The dead will be raised, and every sinner will be judged according to what he has done. Each one whose name is not written in the book of life will be cast into the lake of fire (Rev. 20:12; 21:8, 27).
11. Satan's judgment	Satan has been thrown out of the highest heaven. Believers rejoice in partial victory over him (Luke 10:18-19).	The devil will be thrown into the lake of fire and *"will be tormented day and night for ever and ever"* (Rev. 20:10).

Figure 6.8 *Already* and *not yet* aspects of the kingdom of God

B. Identify present and future aspects of the Kingdom in passages of the Gospels.

We have studied about the *already* and *not yet* aspects of the kingdom of God. This knowledge will help you interpret many passages in the Gospels. Now it is time for you to practice interpreting. Note how identifying present and future aspects of a passage relates to Mathewson's second question: How does this passage relate to the salvation process or continuum? In other words, in a passage of a Gospel ask: In this passage, how much of God's rule, kingdom, and will do we already see, and how much is still in the future?

Q 23 ✎ *Complete Figure 6.9, filling in the blanks of each column.*

Matthew	Already	Not Yet
3:2-12	God judges those who do not repent, and even now sin brings sad results.	
5:3	The poor in spirit—those who live depending on God—enjoy being in God's kingdom, under His rule.	
5:10	Those in Christ who are persecuted for righteousness are in God's kingdom.	
5:19-20	We enter the Kingdom now as children of God in Christ. We practice obeying His commands and pleasing Him, through the power of the Spirit. We keep the spirit of the Law that Jesus taught in six illustrations of Matthew 5:21-48.	
6:10	His kingdom and rule come into our lives as we pray and walk in the Spirit, not the flesh (Rom. 8:4; Gal. 5:16).	
7:1-5	The righteous pay more attention to their own faults than the faults of others, and thus receive God's mercy.	
7:21-23	True believers live the way God wants and wills us to live. But sinners are lawless, refusing to submit to the rule and Lordship of Christ.	
8:10-12	Already there are many Gentiles who believe in Christ and are entering the kingdom of God.	
10:14-15	Some accept and some reject God's messengers.	
10:32-33	Some confess Jesus, and some deny Him.	
13:24-30	Believers and unbelievers live side by side, and the difference is plain.	
13:31-32	The kingdom of God has grown a lot.	
13:33	The rule of God in our lives has increased.	
13:44-46	The wise surrender all to Christ to receive the Kingdom.	
18:1-4	Followers of Christ discern that humility is necessary in walking toward the heavenly kingdom.	
18:15-20	God has given guidelines for relating to other believers.	
19:30–20:16	The gospel is offered to the poor, lower levels of society.	
25:1-13	The wedding is announced and the invitations are being given. Some have made plans to attend.	

Figure 6.9 Continued on next page

Continued from previous page

25:14-30	The Master has given us responsibilities as His stewards. He has gone on a long journey.	
25:31-46	The sheep are acting like sheep, and the goats are behaving like goats.	

Figure 6.9   Practice identifying *already* and *not yet* aspects of the kingdom in passages of Matthew.

Lesson 21

Interpreting the Gospels: Teachings and Historical Narrative—Part 1

Goal A: *Explain the Gospels as combination of stories about Jesus and teaching of Jesus. Draw a diagram of Matthew to illustrate this.*

Goal B: *Analyze the biblical role of ethics in the Kingdom.*

Goal C: *Demonstrate the skill of interpreting the Gospels in the light of the Epistles.*

Q 24 ⟋ *Why are there four Gospels?*

Setting

One of the first questions about the Gospels is: Why are there four of them? It is true that they are all about the life and teachings of Christ. Yet each writer wrote for a different group of believes. *Mark* was probably the first Gospel. It was written for believers everywhere. Later, Matthew wrote his Gospel, especially for Jews. And Luke wrote, especially for Gentiles. Mark, Matthew, and Luke are called the Synoptic Gospels. *Synoptic* means "one view" or "the same view." In contrast, John organizes his Gospel in a way that is different from the Synoptic Gospels. (For a thorough discussion on the structure, purposes, and themes of John see the *Faith & Action* courses *Survey of the New Testament* and *Gospel of John.*) As we interpret a Gospel, it is important to analyze how a passage relates to the purpose of an author and the community of believers to whom he wrote. For like the Epistles, each Gospel was written for the needs of a group of believers.

Q 25 ⟋ *The material in the Gospels is either _____ about Jesus, or _____ of Jesus; either His _____ or His _____.*

The Holy Spirit led the writers of the Gospels to adapt the story of Jesus to their listeners. In this sense, they serve as a hermeneutical model for us. For as we share the message of Jesus today, we must apply the life and teachings of Jesus in relevant ways.[8]

Narrative

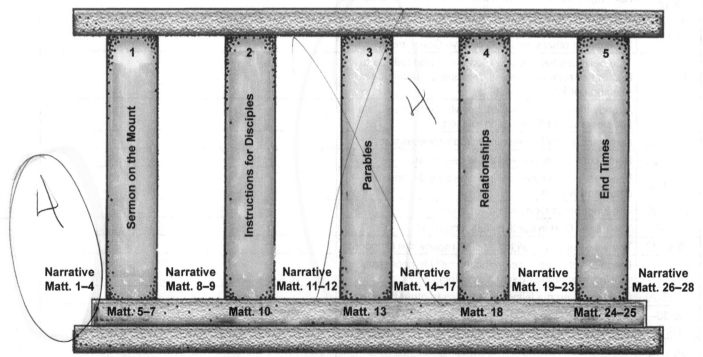

Figure 6.10   Gospels, such as Matthew, are a combination of historical stories *about* Jesus (narrative) and teachings *of* Jesus. Almost any passage in the Gospels is either about the *works* or *words* of Jesus.

Figure 6.10 (continued)   Matthew organizes his Gospel around five pillars of the teachings of Jesus. And between the pillars, he puts narrative. (After each pillar or section of teaching, Matthew transitions with a sentence that begins with: *When Jesus had finished these...* See Matt. 8:1, 11:1, 13:53; 19:1: 26:1). Thus he alerts us that he is shifting from teachings to narrative.

We will examine the **teachings of Jesus** *first*, since they are more direct. To interpret the teachings of Jesus, we follow the same guidelines as interpreting the Epistles, since they are also teachings.[9]

A. Five interpretations of the role of *ethics in the Kingdom

There are many commands (imperatives) of Jesus in the Gospels. These commands guide the ethics or behavior of believers in the Kingdom. Many of the commands of Jesus are in the context of teaching on the Law of the Old Testament. More than any other topic of the Gospels, there is confusion and disagreement on the relationship of salvation to the commands of Christ. Figure 6.11 summarizes five different interpretations of the meaning of Christ's commands.[10] Read the five views, and then we will briefly discuss each of them.

Q 26 ⬉ What context is the source of Jesus' teaching?

Q 27 ⬈ According to some, who walks the low road to heaven, and who walks the high road?

Interpretation of Christ's Commands	Summary of Interpretation
1. Low road and high road	On the **lower road** to heaven, all believers can and must obey the Ten Commandments, other commands of Jesus such as the *love commandment* (Mark 12:28-34) and the *Golden Rule* (Matt. 7:12). On the **higher road** pastors and leaders obey all the commands of Christ, including denial of self (Matt. 16:24-25), surrender of all possessions (Luke 12:33), denial of marriage (Matt. 19:11-12), and hate of family (Luke 14:26).
2. Road to heaven on earth	As all believers obey Christ's teachings now, this transforms society and expands the kingdom of God on earth—bringing love, peace, and justice.
3. Road to the cross	The teachings are impossible for believers to live on earth. Their purpose is to bring despair and guilt that lead us to kneel at the cross.
4. Inward attitudes—rather than a road	The teachings of Jesus are about being, rather than doing. God is more concerned about attitude than actions. Christ cares mainly about your heart, not your hands and feet. Ideals versus real behavior (ethereal)
5. Road of love in response to Christ (the biblical view)	The commands of Christ are for all believers in the Kingdom to obey. We are saved by grace, and our works add nothing to our position of being God's children. Our obedience is a response to God's love and forgiveness.

Figure 6.11   Five ways of interpreting the commands of Christ in relation to salvation

Comments on the five interpretations of Christ's commands:

1. High and low roads.   Some refer to this high/low theory as the *Roman Catholic* interpretation. But we see this same view among some Protestants. We may find it among Wesleyans who distinguish the justified from the fully sanctified; among those who claim Jesus as Savior, but not Lord; common Christians versus those living a victorious life. This view is attractive, for it makes salvation available on a low shelf and at a cheap price. It lists a few commands, but excludes the hardest ones.

Q 28 ⬉ How would you respond to someone who said there are two roads to heaven?

But the Bible does not offer us two different roads to heaven. There is only one gospel, one road to heaven, one gate into God's kingdom. The qualifications for being a pastor or a deacon are higher than qualifications for church membership. But pastors, deacons, and church members all travel the same road to heaven (1 Tim. 3). There are not two levels in teachings, such as the Sermon on the Mount. Matthew 5–7 presents the ethics of the Kingdom—not to sinners, but to all disciples (followers of Jesus). Being a Christian means being a disciple—a student and follower of Christ. God gave the Law to the Israelites *after* He redeemed them from slavery in Egypt. And Jesus preached the Sermon on the Mount to His disciples (Matt. 5:1-2). Words like *anyone* and *whoever* are for all, not just a minority on a high road to heaven, with a superior commitment (Mark 8:34-35; Matt. 16:24-25).

Q 29 ⬉ Complete the summaries in Figure 6.12.

Reference	Your Summaries
Matt. 5:1-2	
Matt. 16:24-25	

Figure 6.12   Practice showing that there is one gospel for all.

Q 30 ⟋ *Is the purpose of Christ's commands to make the earth good enough for Him to return? Explain.*

2. Road to heaven on earth.   This view claims that the purpose of Christ's commands is to transform the earth into a paradise. A few have taught this as *the mustard seed conspiracy.* But due to the increasing sin and corruption on earth, we do not hear this view much. Jesus did not say the earth would get better and better until the whole world welcomed Him to return and sit on a throne. No! He said sin would increase so much that the love of most would turn cold as winter (Matt. 24:12). (See also 2 Tim. 3:13; Rev. 12:9).

Q 31 ⟍ *Does the purpose of the Law end when it leads us to the cross? Defend your response.*

3. Road to the cross.   Luther taught that Law is like a mirror, a hammer, and a guide. As a mirror, the Law shows us our sinfulness. As a hammer, it pounds us with guilt. And as a guide, it leads us to Christ. The Law and commands of God may indeed do these three things for sinners. Paul does say the Law leads us to Christ (Gal. 3:24). But after Jesus saves us from our sins, the commands of Christ show us what pleases God and the way God expects us to live (recall Figure 5.7 about the two roads that run through both covenants). As Romans 8:4 explains, the righteous requirements of the Law are fully met in us as we avoid walking in the flesh, and walk in the Spirit. The purpose of Christ's commands do not end at the foot of the cross. There is Law in God's kingdom, and He puts it in our minds and writes it on our hearts (Jer. 31:33-34; Heb. 8:10)!

Q 32 ⟋ *Why are our actions as important as our attitudes?*

4. Inward attitudes rather than a road.   Liberals made this view popular some years ago. They make an unbiblical contrast between the heart and the hands. They claim that *if* we agree to do right in our hearts, God is less concerned about our actions. It is true that God searches the heart. But it is also true that God cares about our behavior! More than half of all of the Gospels and the Epistles is about our behavior!

Q 33 ⟍ *Complete the summaries in Figure 6.13.*

Reference	Your Summaries
Matt. 7:12	
Matt. 7:24-27	

Figure 6.13   Practice showing that a pure heart and righteous living go hand in hand.

Q 34 ⟍ *What is the biblical relationship between faith and obedience?*

5. Road of love in *response* to Christ.   The commands of Jesus are to those He has already saved from sin. Our obedience is the *proof* of our gratitude (John 14:15, 21, 23-24). A life of love and obedience is our only reasonable response to Christ's love for us (Rom. 12:1-2). And our love expresses itself by obeying His commands.

Pastor, you will get what you preach. Take the teachings and commands of Jesus seriously. Preach these to your people. Impress on them that to be in the Kingdom, we must be under the rule of the King. Jesus is the King of the kingdom of heaven. Before He ascended, the last thing the King told us to do was to make disciples, ***"teaching them to obey everything I have commanded you"*** (Matt. 28:18-20). Obeying the commands of Jesus is not an option (Matt. 7:12, 24-27). Emphasize that those who love Jesus obey Him, and most of your sheep will practice obeying the teachings of Jesus.

Q 35 ⟋ *How does Paul help us understand to whom we should give?*

If you need help interpreting and applying the commands of Christ, ask the apostles. Paul, John, Peter, James, and Jude wrote letters that interpret and apply the Gospels. For example, a difficult saying of Jesus is: *"Give to the one who asks you, and do not turn away from the one who wants to borrow from you"* (Matt. 5:42). Every pastor faces a stream of requests—people asking for free food, money, or a loan. Likewise, your church members face similar requests. Balancing this command of Christ with a teaching of Paul is helpful. The apostle was teaching about the problem of idleness. He insisted that believers must be willing to work. And if they refused to work, they should not eat free food from other believers (2 Thess. 3:6-10). Likewise, Paul gave guidelines for helping widows (1 Tim. 5:9-10). Comparing the teachings of Paul and Christ, we understand that Jesus does not expect us to give to the idle, the lazy, or those who have family members who can help them.

Another difficult saying of Jesus is: [38]*"You have heard that it was said, 'Eye for eye, and tooth for tooth.'* [39]*But I tell you, Do not resist an evil person. If someone strikes you on the right cheek, turn to him the other also"* (Matt. 5:38-39). The main point of Jesus is do not retaliate—do not hit back when someone strikes you. This is an ethic of Christ's kingdom; it is a standard of behavior that Jesus expects us to follow. We must not return blow for blow or insult for insult. Paul emphasizes this same teaching by saying:

> [17]*Do not repay anyone evil for evil. Be careful to do what is right in the eyes of everybody.* [18]*If it is possible, as far as it depends on you, live at peace with everyone.* [19]*Do not take revenge, my friends, but leave room for God's wrath, for it is written: "It is mine to avenge; I will repay," says the Lord.* [20]*On the contrary: "If your enemy is hungry, feed him; if he is thirsty, give him something to drink. In doing this, you will heap burning coals on his head."* [21]*Do not be overcome by evil, but overcome evil with good* (Rom. 12:17-21).

Today, if we lived by an eye for an eye and a tooth for a tooth, we would all be blind by 15 and toothless at 30.

To interpret and reinforce the commands of Christ, look for parallel passages in the Epistles. Several of the apostles wrote epistles to help us interpret and apply Gospels.

Q 37 ✎ *Complete the summaries in Figure 6.14.*

Reference	Gospel Teaching	Teaching in the Epistles	Reference
Matt. 5:10-12			1 Pet. 2:19-21
Matt. 5:21-22			James 1:19-21
Matt. 5:31-32			1 Cor. 7:15
Matt. 18:21-35			Eph. 4:32–5:1
Matt. 19:16-26			1 Tim. 6:17-19

Figure 6.14   Practice using the Epistles to interpret, emphasize, and apply the Gospels.

Q 36 ⤢ *How does Paul help us understand Christ's teaching on turning the other cheek?*

Lesson 22

Interpreting the Gospels: Teachings and Historical Narrative—Part 2

Goal A: *Analyze the reasons for various views on ethics.*
Goal B: *Analyze the parts of a story to help identify the main point.*
Goal C: *Answer 3 key questions on the author's points and applications of a given gospel story.*

A. Reasons for various interpretations on the role of ethics in the Kingdom

The authors, contributors, and reviewers of this course believe that obeying the teachings of Christ is a response of love that expresses our gratitude and faith in Christ. But why are there so many interpretations on the purpose of Christ's commands?

1. Fee says that most of the interpretations on the purpose of Christ's commands are "hermeneutical *ploys*."   That is, these interpretations are crafty schemes to "get around" obeying the commands (imperatives) of Christ—God's standards of behavior in His kingdom. Fee says most of these *hermeneutical ploys* arose because the imperatives (commands) seem like law—law that is impossible to obey. And Christian life in the New Testament is based on grace, not law. Fee explains that it is a misunderstanding to see Christ's commands as a requirement to enter or remain in the Kingdom.

Q 38 ⤢ *What is a ploy? Why do people use ploys?*

Q 39 ⤢ *Why have people looked for salvation without obeying the commands of Christ?*

Q 40 ↖ *Does salvation depend on perfect obedience to Christ's commands? Defend your answer.*

Q 41 ↗ *If Christ's commands are not a ladder to heaven, why do we try to keep them?*

Our salvation does not depend on perfect obedience to the commands of Christ. Forgiveness, redemption, adoption, righteous standing, and justification are all aspects of our salvation—the free gift of God to those who repent and receive Jesus as Savior and Lord. The commands of Christ describe how we should live *because* of what Christ has done for us. *"We love* [him] *because he first loved us"* (1 John 4:19). Obeying the commands is not a ladder to climb into the Kingdom, or a wall to keep people from leaving the Kingdom. Obeying the commands of Christ is the response of love to Christ. Obedience is the proof and expression of love for God. Obedience is the outward sign of new life within us. Thus John records that Jesus said (**four times**) that those who love Him obey His commands:

- *"If you love me, you will obey what I command"* (John 14:15).
- *"Whoever has my commands and obeys them, he is the one who loves me"* (John 14:21).
- *"If anyone loves me, he will obey my teaching"* (John 14:23).
- *"He who does not love me will not obey my teaching"* (John 14:24).

Later, John continues to emphasize the same truth (**four more times**):

³*We know that we have come to know him if we obey his commands.* ⁴*The man who says, "I know him," but does not do what he commands is a liar, and the truth is not in him.* ⁵*But if anyone obeys his word, God's love is truly made complete in him. This is how we know we are in him:* ⁶*Whoever claims to live in him must walk as Jesus did* (1 John 2:3-6).

These are just a few of the times John insists that those who love Christ obey His commands. As much as John emphasizes this truth, there are still many who misinterpret it. Would it have made any difference if John had emphasized this truth *100* times?

Q 42 ↗ *Was Saul of Tarsus sincere as he persecuted Christians?*

Q 43 ↖ *What was necessary for the conversion of Saul, who was both intellectual, relational, and spiritual?*

2. Another reason for various views on the purpose of Christ's commands is that *sincere people come to conclusions in different ways*. There are three factors that shape decisions and conclusions: intellect, relationships, and spiritual experience. (For an entire chapter on this subject see the *Faith & Action* text *Cross-Cultural Communications,* chapter 3.) Let us look at some examples.

LOGIC
FACTS
BRAIN POWER
INTELLECT
RESEARCH
REASON

Intellect influences some people more than others. Some societies, especially the West, have an intellectual approach to life. These tend to be guided most by logic, facts, and inductive or deductive reasoning. Those who are mainly intellectual are guided by the writings and conclusions of intellectuals they know and respect. Popular books, radio preachers, and TV preachers influence millions. In a lesser way, the intellectuals value relationships and spiritual experience. What influenced Saul of Tarsus to reject Jesus and persecute Christians? How did Saul come to the conclusion that Jesus was a false messiah? Saul did not arrive at this conclusion via a hermeneutical ploy. His intellect assured him that he was being faithful to Moses and the Prophets. His relationship with fellow Jews, Jewish forefathers, and Jewish traditions testified that his beliefs and actions were righteous. Saul is an example of one who truly believed he was serving God by killing followers of Jesus (John 16:2). Such people are sincere, but wrong. For Saul, it took a personal encounter with Jesus Christ to change his interpretation.

Q 44 ↗ *Why did some who believed in Jesus refuse to take a stand for Him (John 12:42-43)?*

Q 45 ↗ *Why do most people attend a church that affirms their lifestyle?*

Relationships guide the conclusions and behavior of many. These are influenced most by family, friends, community, and tradition. To a lesser degree they value intellect and spiritual factors. Consider John's words about many who saw the truth, but would not confess it:

> [42]*Yet at the same time many even among the leaders believed in him. But because of the Pharisees they would not confess their faith for fear they would be put out of the synagogue;* [43]*for they loved praise from men more than praise from God* (John 12:42-43).

Some cling to false interpretations because following a biblical path would lead them away from friends, family, and their favorite place of worship.

Spiritual experience helps shape the interpretations and theology of most believers. Even if believers are mainly intellectual or relational, spiritual experience is a powerful factor. There are some who have an intellectual belief in Christ and the Scriptures, but fall short of saving faith. Demons believe in God, and shudder (James 2:19). Likewise some have a faith that does not affect their behavior or ethics. James calls this useless faith—as useless as a body without the spirit of life in it (James 2:26). In contrast, all true believers are spiritual, because to enter the Kingdom we must be born again. But the spiritual experience of believers differs. Some accept Christ, but do not experience being filled with the Spirit. These lack the

FAMILY
FRIENDS
COMMUNITY

RELATIONAL

FEELINGS
TESTIMONIALS
TRADITION

Figure 6.15 Intellect, relationships, and spiritual experience represent three main factors that affect people's conclusions.

HOLY SCRIPTURE
MEDITATION
RIGHTEOUSNESS

SPIRITUAL

SUBMISSION
POWER

power that God intends for us to have, to be the master of our fleshly desires. Those who lack spiritual power tend to walk in the flesh, rather than in the Spirit. Thus it is their common experience to fail to keep God's commands. As a result, they embrace a theology and a church that mirrors and affirms their spiritual experience. Otherwise, they would live in tension, guilt, and disharmony. So their experience becomes their standard, and their hermeneutic. They interpret the purpose of Christ's commands in a way that is self-affirming. Still, spiritual light may come to those in this group by living side by side with a believer who is filled with the Spirit, and models victorious living over sin.

Q 46 ↖ *What can turn a fleshly Christian toward victorious living?*

We have considered some reasons why Christians have various interpretations on the purpose of Christ's commands. It is easy to criticize others. But criticism is as useless as faith without righteous living. Criticizing others does not persuade them. It only ignites hostilities, and causes people to defend themselves. It is impossible to know the motives of people, or the reasons why people believe as they do. So let us make it our aim to be understanding—listen more than we talk, and speak the truth in love. Most of all, let us be living examples that it is both possible and joyful to obey the commands of Christ. It is better to light a candle than to curse the darkness.

Q 47 ↖ *How can we influence others to obey the commands of Christ?*

B. What shall we do when we do not fully obey the commands of Christ?

Let us have the courage to believe and proclaim that it is God's will for us to obey His commands. Here are some guidelines to follow as we seek to obey.

Q 48 ↗ *How does our Heavenly Father respond if we fall or go astray?*

1. Let us emphasize that we are saved by grace, not by works. None of us is perfect. And our salvation is *not* based on perfection. We are accepted in the Beloved

(Eph. 1:5-7). We are children in the family of God, because Jesus paid the penalty for our sins. So let us not be examples of the doctrine of *eternal insecurity*—feeling that one sin separates us from God. Let us remind ourselves that God does not reject His children because of one sin. He will discipline us if we practice sin. But an earthly father does not kick a child out of the family for one failure. If a child falls, a loving parent helps the child to stand. If a child disobeys, a loving parent will discipline the child to improve his attitude and behavior. How much more does God reach out to help us if we fall or go astray!

2. Let us hate sin, beware of it, and overcome it.   Sin is terrible; it destroys faith and drags people to hell. It is an offense and insult to God, our Father. It is a reproach and a stain on the Church. Sin is a stumbling block to the lost. Sin is dangerous, because it hardens (Heb. 3:13). Sins are like links of a chain—one leads to another, and another. So as Jesus taught, let us take sin seriously (Matt. 5:29-30). If something is causing us to sin, let us deal with it. If a friendship is leading us into sin, let us separate from it. If Internet or television is leading us to sin, let us raise our standards, seek accountability, and replace the temptation with something wholesome. Let us resist sin and Satan, and seek more of the Holy Spirit in our lives (James 4:7). As we seek to obey the commands of Christ, let us beware of a casual attitude toward sinning.

Q 49 ⟋ *If you break a commandment, which direction should you turn?*

3. When we sin, let us run toward Jesus, not away from Him.   Peter had his insights and his blunders. One of his worst statements was: *"Go away from me, Lord; I am a sinful man!"* (Luke 5:8). Jesus did not come to earth to get away from sinners; He came to save us from the penalty and the power of sin. So when we sin, let us repent at once and move *toward* Jesus for forgiveness and deliverance. His name is Jesus, *Savior*, because He came to save us from our sins (Matt. 1:21). Dare to run to Him in the power of His name. Even if you have seven demons, He will drive them out (Luke 8:2).

Q 50 ⟋ *How should we respond to a believer who gets entangled in a sin (Gal. 6:1)?*

Q 51 ⟍ *What should we do to restore a believer who falls?*

4. Let us remember that growing in grace is a process.   A baby must learn to crawl, and then walk. In time it learns to run. Throughout life it will fall from time to time. But normal people may live for years without falling. Likewise, as we grow in Christ, we mature from strength to strength. If we see a brother or sister sinning, let us pray for that person (1 John 5:16). *"Brothers, if someone is caught* [entangled] *in a sin, you who are spiritual should restore him gently. But watch yourself, or you also may be tempted"* (Gal. 6:1). From Galatians 6:1 we see a contrast between spiritual believers and those entangled in sin. Mature believers have learned to walk in the Spirit, not the flesh. Still, let us not condemn, but gently restore those who get tangled in sin. And let us walk in humility, and be watchful. For the key to freedom from sin is to live alert, watchful, weaned from the world, filled with the Word and the Spirit. Let he who stands take heed, lest he fall—as the Israelites fell short of the Promised Land, in the wilderness (1 Cor. 10:12).

Q 52 ⟍ *Summarize 5 statements in 1 John 2:1-6 by completing Figure 6.16.*

1 John	Statement	Summaries
2:1a	Declaration	It is God's will that _____.
2:1b-2	Affirmation	
2:3-4	Explanation	
2:5	Progression	Our love for God **progresses** to completion and maturity as we obey His commands.
2:6	Conclusion	

Figure 6.16   **Practice explaining that growing in grace is a process.**

[1]My dear children, I write this to you so that you will not sin. But if anybody does sin, we have one who speaks to the Father in our defense—Jesus Christ, the Righteous One. [2]He is the atoning sacrifice for our sins, and not only for ours but also for the sins of the whole world. [3]We know that we have come to know him if

we obey his commands. [4]The man who says, "I know him," but does not do what he commands is a liar, and the truth is not in him. [5]But if anyone obeys his word, God's love [love of God] is truly made complete in him. This is how we know we are in him: [6]Whoever claims to live in him must walk as Jesus did (1 John 2:1-6).

C. Practice interpreting narrative passages of Matthew's Gospel.

The Gospels are a combination of *historical narrative (stories about Jesus) and teachings of Jesus (review Figure 6.10). In this lesson we will guide you to practice interpreting sections of the Gospel of Matthew that are historical narrative—biblical stories about Jesus. In previous lessons of this chapter you analyzed passages in Matthew to discover the *already* and *not yet* aspects of the gospel. We will continue to study in Matthew, to make it easier for you to review the historical, cultural, and literary contexts (Figure 1.1). Sometimes you may not be able to answer all of the questions in Figure 1.1. Still, do your best, and find a friend to help. As you seek to answers these questions, they will help you interpret your passage well. Also, please take a few minutes to review the guidelines for interpreting a historical narrative (Figure 1.3).

As our first example, let us discover the author's point in the historical story of Matthew 8:1-4, the healing of a leper. Note the literary context. This story is the first in a group of miracles (Matt. 8–9), just after Matthew's first teaching pillar (Matt. 5–7).

Analyze the plot of a story to discern the author's point.

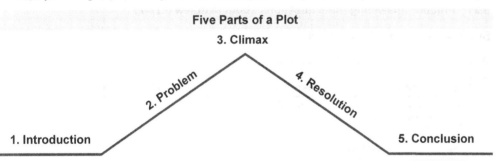

Five Parts of a Plot

3. Climax

2. Problem

4. Resolution

1. Introduction

5. Conclusion

Figure 6.17 *Plot* describes the structure of a story. It shows the arrangement of events and actions within a story. Many stories have five parts in the plot

Part of the Story	Questions to Help You Get the Main Point	Matthew
1. Introduction	What happened when Jesus was on the mountain? Who was with Jesus?	8:1
2. Problem	What was the problem?	8:2
3. Climax	What was the quick response of Jesus?	8:3a
4. Solution	How did Jesus solve the problem?	8:3b
5. Conclusion	Why do you think Jesus sent the healed man to the priest?	8:4

Figure 6.18 The parts of a story: Jesus heals a leper (Matt. 8:1-4)

Q 53 Analyze the plot of Matthew 8:1-4 by answering the questions in the middle column of Figure 6.18.

Three Questions	Answers
1. What is God telling us about Himself?	In the Gospels, miracle stories, such as the healing of the leper, show us the power of God's kingdom is breaking through in the ministry of Jesus.[11] Also, in this story, God shows us His compassion for human needs.
2. How does this little story relate to the big story of salvation?	In the healing of the leper, we see that the Savior and Messiah has come to earth. He is the One who heals the diseases of body, soul, and spirit. He is *willing* to help all who come to Him in faith.
3. What does God want us to be and do?	God wants us to recognize that He is willing to help us; so bring our needs as we kneel to Him in faith.

Figure 6.19 Illustration of answering three questions about the healing of the leper (Matt. 8:1-4)

Student practice: Matthew 8:23-27

Q 54 ↖ *Analyze the plot of Matthew 8:23-27 by completing Figure 6.20.*

Part of the Story	Questions to Help You Get the Main Point	Matthew
1. Introduction	Who was in the boat?	
2. Problem	What was the problem?	
3. Climax	What was the turning point?	
4. Solution	How did Jesus solve the problem?	
5. Conclusion	What affect did the miracle have on the disciples?	

Figure 6.20   The parts of a story: Jesus calms the storm (Matt. 8:23-27)

Q 55 ↖ *Fill in column 2 of Figure 6.21.*

Three Questions	Answers
1. What is God telling us about Himself?	
2. How does this little story relate to the big story of salvation?	
3. What does God want us to be and do?	

Figure 6.21   Practice answering three questions about Matthew 8:23-27.

Student Practice: Matthew 9:9-13

Q 56 ↖ *Analyze the plot of Matthew 9:9-13 by completing Figure 6.22.*

Part of the Story	Questions to Help You Get the Main Point	Matthew
1. Introduction	Who was in the booth?	
2. Problem	What was the problem?	9:10
3. Climax	What was the turning point?	
4. Solution	How did Jesus resolve the tension?	9:12
5. Conclusion	What affect did the miracle have on the disciples?	

Figure 6.22   The parts of a story: Jesus calls Matthew (Matt. 9:9-13)

Q 57 ↖ *Fill in column 2 of Figure 6.22.*

Three Questions	Answers
1. What is God telling us about Himself?	
2. How does this little story relate to the big story of salvation?	
3. What does God want us to be and do?	

Figure 6.23   Practice answering three questions about Matthew 9:9-13.

Test Yourself: Circle the letter by the ***best*** completion to each question or statement.

1. Where is the kingdom of God strongest today?
a) In heaven
b) On earth
c) In sinners
d) In saints

2. At the Incarnation, the kingdom of God came to earth like
a) predawn.
b) sunrise.
c) noon.
d) sunset.

3. What aspect of the Kingdom has not yet fully come?
a) Forgiveness
b) Adoption
c) Election
d) Salvation

4. Which of these contains stories about Jesus?
a) Matthew 4
b) Matthew 6
c) Matthew 13
d) Matthew 24

5. Which road is the correct response to ethics in the Kingdom?
a) The low road to heaven
b) The road to heaven on earth
c) The road to the cross
d) The road of love

6. Which statement illustrates the *already* but *not yet* truth?
a) You must be born again.
b) I give you power over demons.
c) Neither do I condemn you.
d) It is finished.

7. Which writer helps us interpret Christ's teachings on an eye for an eye?
a) Luke
b) John
c) Paul
d) James

8. How does Fee describe views on ethics that do not agree with his view?
a) Options
b) Divergent
c) Errors
d) Ploys

9. How many parts do most stories have?
a) 3
b) 4
c) 5
d) 6

10. The final question to ask about a story is:
a) What is God telling us about Himself?
b) What does God want us to be and do?
c) How does this story relate to the gospel?
d) What will I do with the truth of this story?

 Essay Test Topics: Write 50-100 words on each of these goals that you studied in this chapter.

- Define the kingdom of God.
- Explain why the kingdom of God is sometimes called the kingdom of heaven.
- Contrast God's rule on earth and in heaven.
- Compare the revelation of God's kingdom to 3 phases of sunlight.
- Explain: The kingdom of God has "already" come, but has "not yet" fully come.
- Compare the "already" and "not yet" aspects of the Kingdom on 5 topics.
- Identify present and future aspects of passages in the Gospels.
- Explain the Gospels as a combination of stories about Jesus and teaching of Jesus. Draw a diagram of Matthew to illustrate this.
- Analyze the biblical role of ethics in the Kingdom.
- Demonstrate the skill of interpreting the Gospels in the light of the Epistles.
- Analyze the reasons for various views on ethics.
- Analyze the parts of a story to help identify the main point.
- Answer 3 key questions on the author's points and applications of a given Gospel story.

Chapter 7:
Interpreting Acts

Introduction

⁶So when they met together, they asked him, "Lord, are you at this time going to restore the kingdom to Israel?" ⁷He said to them: "It is not for you to know the times or dates the Father has set by his own authority. ⁸But you will receive power when the Holy Spirit comes on you; and you will be my witnesses in Jerusalem, and in all Judea and Samaria, and to the ends of the earth." ⁹After he said this, he was taken up before their very eyes, and a cloud hid him from their sight (Acts 1:6-9).

Q 1 ↖ *Should Acts be used as a basis for doctrine? Defend your response.*

Figure 7.1   The Ascension (Acts 1:6-9)

Like the other gospel writers, Luke was a historian and a theologian. *One of Luke's purposes for Acts is to give believers a guide for faith and practice.* Acts gives us guidance for what the Church should know, believe, and do. Some argue that we should not use Acts as a guide because it is history. But recall that Luke did not write a complete history; he wrote a selective history. Paul used history for the purpose of teaching.[1] He reviewed the history of Abraham to teach that we are justified by faith (Rom. 4).[2] Likewise, Luke used history to teach certain theological themes.[3] He chose a few stories and events for special purposes. Luke emphasized what the early church believed. And He emphasized godly ways believers lived, and the powerful witnessing they did. Why is it helpful to study about the faith, character, and deeds of these early believers? Because these first believers were under the same covenant we are under!

The Church in Acts teaches us to believe in such things as:

- The Scriptures, salvation through faith in Jesus, praying, sharing, and fellowship;
- The work of the Holy Spirit in glorifying Jesus; the return of Jesus;
- Knowing and worshiping God;
- Righteous living, witnessing, signs and wonders, being filled with the Spirit;
- Speaking in tongues, prophesying, and valuing other spiritual gifts;
- Solving Church growth problems, evangelizing, and discipling new believers;
- God's power; His presence during persecution; His love for all nations.

Luke did not know how long the Church would remain on earth. But one of his purposes was to teach future believers. The power and principles of Acts are for the Church until Jesus returns.[4]

Lessons:

Acts: Luke—Both Historian and Theologian

Goal A: *Summarize the relationship of history and theology in Luke's writings.*
Goal B: *Compare and contrast what Luke, John, and Paul emphasize about the Spirit.*
Goal C: *Explain and illustrate the Lucan purpose of being filled with the Spirit.*

Discerning Descriptive and Prescriptive Aspects of Historical Narrative

Goal A: *Contrast descriptive and prescriptive aspects of a passage.*
Goal B: *Identify prescriptive aspects of passages in Acts, related to church expansion.*
Goal C: *Explain the need to confirm prescriptive aspects with parallel passages. Illustrate.*
Goal D: *Show from Acts that Luke intended to emphasize being filled with the Spirit.*

descriptive aspects of a story—those parts that give us details of the narrative—answering questions that begin with *when, where, who, what, why,* and *how;* [providing the setting, characters, and action of the story]

prescriptive aspects of a story—those parts that tell us what we should *believe, discern, be,* and *do;* refers to the interpretation of the narrative; must be able to be stated as principles that can be found in parallel passages of Scripture

 Lesson 23

Acts: Luke—Both Historian and Theologian

Goal A: *Summarize the relationship of history and theology in Luke's writings.*
Goal B: *Compare and contrast what Luke, John, and Paul emphasize about the Spirit.*
Goal C: *Explain and illustrate the Lucan purpose of being filled with the Spirit.*

Background and overview of Luke's purposes, emphasis, and theology in Acts

Luke was not an apostle, but he was a traveling companion of Paul. We know this from the word *we* that Luke uses in narrating Acts (16:10; 20:5; 21:18; 27:1; and 28:16). Paul refers to Luke as a *dear friend* and *doctor* (Col. 4:14). Luke's two-volume set, Luke/Acts, spans 60 years—from the birth of Christ to Paul's preaching in Rome. Together, Luke and Acts are over 30 percent of the New Testament.

To interpret Luke well, we must understand him as a writer of both *history* and *theology. We can only understand Luke as a historian as we understand him as a theologian.*[5] In other words, Luke did not write history as an end in itself. His purpose was not *only* to give us facts about what Jesus continued to do by the power of the Holy Spirit through the early church. Rather, the Holy Spirit led Luke to use history as a servant of theology. In Acts, we recognize that Luke chose a few key events from **30 years** of history. Imagine how many *thousands* of events Luke could have written about from a period of 30 years. But he chose a few historical events for key theological purposes (See Figure 7.2). Therefore, we may also say that *we can only understand Luke as a theologian as we understand him as a historian.*[6] Luke made sure his theology was based on reliable history of Jesus and the early church.

Five Purposes of Acts
1. Acts serves as a bridge between the Gospels and Paul's letters.
2. Acts traces the growth of the Church.
3. Acts explains and defends the Church.
4. Acts serves as a guide for faith and practice.
5. Acts emphasizes that the Holy Spirit is the key to being witnesses for Jesus—and the salvation He provides for all people.

Figure 7.2   We can identify at least five purposes for which Luke wrote Acts.

As Luke was both historian and theologian, so were the other Gospel writers. Both Matthew and John were apostles who traveled with Jesus. They listened to Him, observed Him, and ministered with Him for over 3 years. Matthew and John heard the teachings of Jesus and saw His miracles. Yet their Gospels are quite different from each other. Matthew wrote primarily to the Jews, emphasizing that Jesus was the Messiah. He begins with a Jewish genealogy of Jesus, and his Gospel includes nine more references to the Old Testament Scriptures than the other Synoptic Gospels. In contrast, John wrote to emphasize Jesus as Son of God. He begins, not with a genealogy, but with *"In the beginning was the Word, and the Word was with God, and the Word was God"* (John

Q 2 *How do we know that Luke traveled with Paul?*

Q 3 *How much of the New Testament did Luke write?*

Q 4 *Explain: We can only understand Luke as a historian as we understand him as a theologian.*

Q 5 *What are 5 reasons why Luke wrote Acts?*

Q 6 *How did Matthew, John, and Luke each adapt what they knew for different purposes? Illustrate.*

1:1). Likewise, from all the miracles of Jesus, John emphasizes only seven. The Spirit led Matthew and John to write for their readers and their purposes. Likewise, the Spirit led Luke to select from history those facts and teachings that served God's purposes for him to write.

Only in Luke	Luke	Only in Luke	Luke
The songs of Elizabeth, Mary, Zechariah, and Simeon	1:39-80	Comparison: planning of the tower-builder	14:28-30
The shepherds and angels at the birth of Christ	2:8-20	Further comparison: planning of king going to war	14:31-33
Jesus presented in the temple; Anna and Simeon	2:21-40	The parable of the lost coin	15:8-10
Jesus in the temple at age twelve	2:41-52	The parable of the lost son	15:11-32
Jesus raises the dead son of the widow of Nain	7:11-17	Parable of the clever manager	16:1-15
Jesus rebukes the anger of James and John	9:51-56	Account of the rich man and Lazarus	16:19-31
Plow illustration on discipleship	9:61-62	Illustration about the master and servant	17:7-10
The seventy-two sent ahead of Jesus	10:1-12	The healing of the ten lepers	17:11-19
Return and report of the seventy-two	10:17-20	Reply concerning the kingdom of God	17:20-21
Parable of the Good Samaritan	10:25-37	Parable of the persistent widow	18:1-8
Martha, Martha	10:38-42	Parable of the Pharisee and the publican	18:9-14
Parable of the persistent friend	11:5-10	Jericho: conversion of Zacchaeus	19:1-10
Parable of the rich fool	12:13-21	Parable of ten pounds and servants	19:11-27
Reply about those slain by Pilate	13:1-5	The Savior weeps over Jerusalem	19:41-44
Parable of the fruitless fig tree	13:6-9	Healing of the ear of the servant of the high priest	22:51
Woman loosed from a crippling spirit	13:10-17	Repentance of the thief on the cross	23:32-43
Reply to Pharisees about Herod	13:31-33	On the road to Emmaus	24:13-35
Sabbath cure of a sick man	14:1-6	Emphasis to wait for the Holy Spirit baptism	24:49
Parable about feasts and guests	14:7-14	The ascension of Jesus up to heaven	24:50-53
Parable of the great feast	14:15-24		

Figure 7.3   There are more than 45 teachings and events found only in Luke.

In this first lesson, let us review three things that Luke emphasizes.

Q 7 ✎ *What one theme does Luke emphasize about the Spirit?*

A. Luke emphasizes one ministry of the Holy Spirit—one role or purpose.

In his Gospel and in Acts, Luke emphasizes only one ministry of the Holy Spirit. He stresses the Pentecostal dimension of the Holy Spirit—the Spirit empowers believers to serve as witnesses of Jesus and the salvation He provides for all people.[7] Use a concordance to examine Luke's references to the Spirit in Acts. Over 50 times Luke emphasizes that the Spirit empowers us to serves as witnesses of Jesus and the salvation He makes possible.

Q 8 ✎ *Concerning the Holy Spirit, how does Luke's emphasis differ from the emphases of John and Paul?*

Luke, John, and Paul emphasize different ministries of the Holy Spirit (Figure 7.4). These three writers all emphasize that the Holy Spirit gives us power to serve. In Luke's Gospel, the entire ministry of Jesus is because the Spirit is upon Him (Luke 4:18-19). John adds the Spirit's role in salvation. Paul includes what Luke and John teach. And he adds the Spirit's role in helping us live a holy life to serve. Thus, Luke emphasizes one role of the Spirit, John emphasizes two roles of the Spirit, and Paul tells of three.

Writer	Ministry of the Holy Spirit	Selected Scriptures
Luke	1) Service (The Spirit enables us to witness about salvation for all people through Jesus.)	1) Luke 1:15-17, 39-56, 67-80; 2:25-38; 3:21-22; 4:18-19; 11:5-13; 24:45-49 (And all references to the Spirit in Acts)
John	1) Service 2) Salvation (The Spirit draws us to Christ and then helps us travel on the road to heaven.)	1) John 1:32; 7:37-39; 14:12-31; 15:26; 20:21-22 2) John 3:5-8; 16:8-11; 1 John 2:20
Paul	1) Service 2) Salvation 3) Sanctification (The Spirit enables us to live a holy life that pleases God.)	1) Rom. 15:19 2) Rom. 8:23; 1 Cor. 6:11; 12:13; 2 Cor. 1:22; Titus 3:5 3) Rom. 8:1-17; Gal. 5:22-23; 2 Thess. 2:13

Figure 7.4   The Spirit's ministry, according to Luke, John, and Paul

B. Luke emphasizes God's plan to fill all believers with the Holy Spirit.

The work of the Holy Spirit in Christ's ministry shows Him as the promised Prophet who was to be the new Moses (Deut. 18:15, 18; Acts 3:22, 7:37). Like Moses, Christ is empowered for service (Luke 4:14, 18). Just as Moses passed that anointing on to the seventy elders, so Christ, the new Moses, passes the Spirit anointing on to His disciples (Num. 11:10-30; Acts 1:5). This time, it is not limited to a few men. As Joel predicted, this gift would be available to all classes of believers (Joel 2:28-29; Acts 2:17-18).

Q 9 *Does Luke teach that all believers are filled with the Spirit at conversion? Defend your view.*

Luke also consistently uses the phrases *"baptized with the Spirit"* (three times) and *"filled with the Spirit"* (nine times). He uses the first phrase to refer to an initial experience of "commissioning for service." He uses the phrase *"filled with the Spirit"* to describe "continuous power for service." Luke **never** uses these phrases to refer to regeneration or salvation.

Q 10 *Why do you think Luke emphasizes being baptized with the Spirit and filled with the Spirit?*

#	Acts	Setting	Outward Evidence of the Inner Filling
1.	2:1-4	The Day of Pentecost	All 120 spoke in new languages as they were filled with the Holy Spirit.
2.	8:14-19	The believers at Samaria	Something happened that caused Simon to offer money.
3.	9:17-19	The conversion and filling of Saul	We know that Paul often spoke privately in languages he did not know (1 Cor. 14:18).
4.	10:44-46	The home of Cornelius	They spoke in new languages.
5.	19:1-7	The believers at Ephesus	They spoke in new languages and prophesied.

Figure 7.5   The five places in Acts where believers were first filled with the Holy Spirit

The pattern Luke gives in Acts is: After or when you believe in Jesus, be filled with the Spirit *so you will have power to witness for Jesus*. The apostles lived with, walked with, learned from, and ministered with Jesus for over 3 years. Then He appeared to them and others for 40 days after the Resurrection. They were followers of Jesus. **Yet to become powerful witnesses of Jesus, they needed to be filled with the Spirit.** After Pentecost, the apostles stopped hiding. They preached the Word with boldness, and did powerful signs and wonders through the Spirit.

Q 11 *According to Luke, how does the purpose of being filled with the Spirit differ from repenting and believing in Christ?*

Luke shows us a pattern of believers being saved and filled with the Spirit. He wants us to understand that God has a gift for all who choose to follow Jesus. God promises this gift of being filled with the Spirit to all who repent and are baptized in water. The promise of being filled with the Spirit is a gift for all believers—to us and our children, and all God calls—to be saved and to serve (Acts 2:38-39). On the Day of Pentecost, the crowd saw disciples of Jesus filled with new power, and they heard them glorifying God in languages they had never learned. Peter explained that a new era had dawned. The age of the Spirit that Joel prophesied had come. God had begun to pour out His Spirit on all flesh. And this gift of the Spirit is available to sons and daughters, young and old, of all nations. Throughout Luke's writings, he emphasizes this powerful gift of being filled with the Holy Spirit. Why? For what purpose do we need the Spirit? To witness that through Jesus Christ, God offers salvation to all nations.

C. Luke emphasizes Pentecostal power in six waves of church growth in Acts.

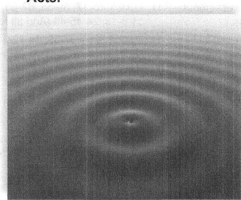

Figure 7.6   Throw a rock into a pond of water and watch the ripples go in all directions.

Throw a rock into a pond of water. The rock will cause a circle of waves to go out in all directions. These waves will continue, moving further away from where they started. So it is with the power of the Holy Spirit and witnessing. God "threw the rock into the pond" when He poured out the Holy Spirit on the Day of Pentecost. Acts 1:8 describes **three waves of witnessing** about salvation through Jesus Christ. The first wave expanded in Jerusalem (Acts 1–7). The second wave spread into Judea and Samaria (Acts 8–12). And the third wave expanded all the way to Rome itself (Acts 13–28).[8] This witnessing through the power of the Spirit in Jerusalem, Judea and Samaria, and to Rome is a simple way to remember Acts.

Q 12 ↗ *How does Luke connect salvation and the Church?*

For Luke, salvation means receiving Jesus as Savior and Lord—and becoming a member of God's Church. Luke shows the growth of the Church in **six waves** of expansion (Figure 7.6). Each wave ends with a comment that summarizes the spiritual and numerical growth of the church. We see Luke's focus on being filled with the Spirit with the evidence of tongues, prophecy, and powerful witness as a major theme in Acts.

In Acts 2:1-4, the Jewish disciples in Palestine receive the gift of the Spirit. Peter preaches and explains that this is the promised outpouring of the Spirit for all believers. The Spirit was no longer limited to leaders and prophets. Since the Day of Pentecost, **all believers—regardless of their gender, race, or social standing—can be filled with the Spirit** (Acts 2:17-18).

Q 13 ↗ *According to Luke, what made it possible to spread the gospel of salvation?*

Q 14 ↖ *What big truth about the Spirit does Acts 2:17-18 emphasize?*

We notice that the Spirit baptism of the Samaritans was delayed until the "witnesses" from Jerusalem could observe the event (Acts 8:14-17). How amazing that the early Jewish Christians could accept the Samaritans as brothers! Were they convinced because they witnessed a repeat of the speaking in tongues as on the Day of Pentecost?

Q 15 ↗ *What amazing event caused the Jews to welcome Samaritans into the Kingdom?*

Believers in Jerusalem criticized Peter for going into the home of Cornelius, a Gentile (Acts 10:44-48). Then Peter explained that God had filled these Gentiles with the Spirit—just as He had filled the 120 at Pentecost (Acts 11:16-18). Thus the experience of being filled with the Spirit united the Jewish and Gentile believers. Luke is emphasizing that being filled with the Spirit is *important for all believers.* God wants Jews and Gentile believers to receive this power to serve. Later, at the Council in Jerusalem, Peter emphasizes what happened at the household of Cornelius (Acts 15:6-9). The filling of all believers with the Holy Spirit is a big theme in Acts.

Q 16 ↖ *From all the events Luke could have chosen, why did he write about Cornelius?*

During Paul's third missionary trip, another "Pentecost" occurs at Ephesus after water baptism (Acts 19:1-7). Luke used this event to emphasize that God wants **all** believers be baptized in the Spirit. When Jews in Jerusalem heard about this, it helped unite them with believers far away in Ephesus.

Q 17 ↖ *Why does Luke emphasize believers being filled with the Spirit in Jerusalem, Samaria, Syria (Paul), Caesarea, and Ephesus? Why does he hammer this nail so much?*

Keep in mind that Luke wrote a selective history. No doubt the Church grew in many directions. But Luke emphasized that the church grew in the direction of Rome.

Q 18 ↖ *To what does Luke link the expansion of the Church? What theological and practical point is he making?*

Acts also includes a more complex report of how witnessing expanded. Unlike Acts 1:8, this report emphasizes six stages of expanded witnessing (See Figures 7.6 and 7.7).

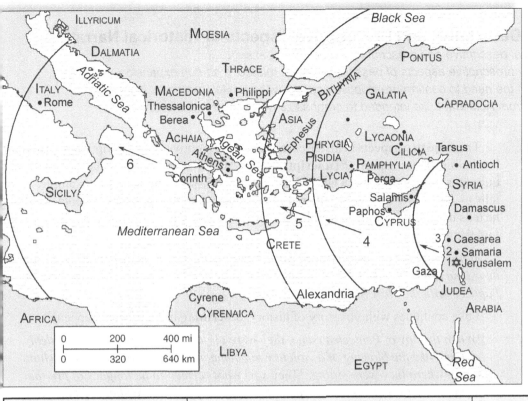

Figure 7.7
The Church spread from Jerusalem to Rome in six stages.[9]

Six Waves of Growth: in the Spirit, in Numbers, and in Unity	The Role of Being Baptized in the Holy Spirit (or Being Filled With the Spirit)	Summary in Acts About Growth in Numbers and Faith
1. **Jerusalem:** The church expands with great growth. It struggles to include Jews who speak Greek. (Acts 1–7)	**Event:** Jesus promises the baptism in the Spirit (Acts 1:5), and this gift is given at Pentecost (Acts 2:1-41). **Sermon:** Peter explains that Joel's prophecy is being fulfilled—God is pouring out His Spirit on all flesh (Acts 2:17, 18, 38, 39).	*"So the word of God spread. The number of disciples in Jerusalem increased rapidly, and a large number of priests became obedient to the faith"* (Acts 6:7).
2. **Samaria:** The church reaches out to the Samaritans, an African eunuch, and Saul. (Acts 8:1–9:31)	**Event:** Philip, a deacon, evangelizes the Samaritans. They believe and are baptized in water. Peter and John pray for the Samaritans, and they are baptized in the Holy Spirit. This helps the Jews accept the Samaritans as brothers (Acts 8:14-17).	*"Then the church throughout Judea, Galilee and Samaria enjoyed a time of peace. It was strengthened; and encouraged by the Holy Spirit, it grew in numbers, living in the fear of the Lord"* (Acts 9:31).
3. **Caesarea:** The church extends to the Gentile part of Palestine up to Antioch. (Acts 9:32–12:25)	**Event:** The household of Cornelius receives the Holy Spirit and speaks in tongues (Acts 10:44-48). **Sermon:** Peter explains that the miracle continues to fulfill Christ's promise of Spirit baptism—and shows that God accepts Gentiles (Acts 11:16-18).	*"But the word of God continued to increase and spread"* (Acts 12:24).
4. **Antioch, Syria, and Galatia:** Jerusalem leaders accept Gentiles as equal believers—without keeping Jewish customs. (Acts 13:1–16:5)	**Sermon:** The church council hears the report of Peter, Paul, and Barnabas concerning the Gentiles. Because Gentiles had a similar Pentecostal experience, Jews accepted them without circumcision (Acts 15:8-19). Note that this council also applied to the churches of Galatia, which Paul had just planted on his first missionary trip, A.D. 46-48.	*"So the churches were strengthened in the faith and grew daily in numbers"* (Acts 16:5).
5. **Ephesus:** Paul plants churches in Eastern Europe and Asia Minor. (Acts 16:6–19:41)	**Event:** Another Pentecost takes place in Ephesus (Acts 19:1-7).	*"In this way the word of the Lord spread widely and grew in power"* (Acts 19:20).
6. **Rome:** Paul meets with kings, and the Word of God reaches Rome. (Acts 20–28)	**Events:** No Pentecost is reported in these chapters. But we see the result of previous fillings, since Paul and others prophesied, and Paul healed many.	*"Boldly and without hindrance he preached the kingdom of God and taught about the Lord Jesus Christ"* (Acts 28:31).

Figure 7.8   Acts records that the Church expanded in six waves—through the baptism in the Holy Spirit.

> **Lesson 24**
>
> # Discerning Descriptive and Prescriptive Aspects of Historical Narrative
>
> **Goal A:** *Contrast descriptive and prescriptive aspects of a passage.*
> **Goal B:** *Identify prescriptive aspects of passages in Acts, related to church expansion.*
> **Goal C:** *Explain the need to confirm prescriptive aspects with parallel passages. Illustrate.*
> **Goal D:** *Show from Acts that Luke intended to emphasize being filled with the Spirit.*

Q 19 *What questions do the descriptive aspects of a story answer?*

There are **two aspects** in historical narrative: descriptive and prescriptive. Every story has both of these aspects. ***Descriptive** aspects of a story give us details—answering questions that begin with: when, where, who, what, why, and how. For example, Luke tells us *how many* believers gathered in an upper room in Jerusalem at Pentecost. And he tells us *why* these believers gathered. They were obeying the command of Jesus, who told them:

[4] *"Do not leave Jerusalem, but wait for the gift my Father promised, which you have heard me speak about.* [5]*For John baptized with water, but in a few days you will be baptized with the Holy Spirit"* (Acts 1:4-5).

Q 20 *What questions does Luke's description of Acts 2:1-4 answer?*

Luke continues with this story of history, **describing** more of what happened:

[1]*When the day of Pentecost came, they were all together in one place.* [2]*Suddenly a sound like the blowing of a violent wind came from heaven and filled the whole house where they were sitting.* [3]*They saw what seemed to be tongues of fire that separated and came to rest on each of them.* [4]*All of them were filled with the Holy Spirit and began to speak in other tongues as the Spirit enabled them* (Acts 2:1-4).

Q 21 *How do the details in a story's description help us?*

The details of a story draw us into the setting, help us identify with the characters, touch our emotions, and preserve the truth in a form that is easy to understand and remember. Some have called stories of history the perfect form of communication. Perhaps this is why stories are the most common way that God reveals truth to us in the Bible.

Q 22 *What are the prescriptive aspects of a story?*

Q 23 *How are the descriptive aspects of a story different from the prescriptive aspects of a story?*

*Prescriptive aspects of a story tell us what we should *believe, discern, be,* and *do.* As you interpret the historical narrative of Acts, follow the same rules that we studied for historical narratives of the Old Testament and the Gospels. As we studied in chapter 1, when we study historical narrative, we should answer three questions:

Q 24 *What 3 questions should we ask about any story in Acts?*

- What is God revealing to us about Himself? (What does He want us to know and believe about Him?)
- How does the story relate to God's plan of salvation that reaches completion in Christ—and expands to all nations and peoples? (If there is a healing or a miracle, *discern* that this is part of God's *broader plan of salvation*—for eternity.)[10]
- What does God want us to be and do? (What actions should we avoid? What should we imitate?)

Q 25 *In Acts 2, 8, 10, and 19, what is Luke indirectly* **prescribing** *as he describes believers being filled with the Spirit?*

In Acts 2, 8, 10, and 19 Luke *describes* what happened as believers were filled with the Spirit. His purpose in describing these fillings is to *prescribe* this powerful filling of the Spirit for all believers.

Q 26 *What behavior was Jesus prescribing by telling the story of the Good Samaritan?*

Q 27 *What behavior was Jesus prescribing by telling the story of the unmerciful servant?*

Q 28 *What behavior was Jesus prescribing by telling the story of the sheep and the goats?*

Q 29 *Do you think the apostles and other disciples of Jesus learned to teach by telling stories? Defend your view.*

Q 30 *What are some things that the stories of Acts prescribe for us to believe about God?*

The stories of Acts teach us to **believe** in God—in His power, love, holiness and faithfulness. They teach us to discern that His plan of salvation is for all nations.

Likewise the stories teach us to be holy, righteous, and filled with the Spirit—depending on the Spirit to empower us as God's servants.

Q 31 ↖ *What are some things that the stories of Acts teach us to be and do?*

Q 32 ↖ *Complete column 2 in Figure 7.9 on the emphasis of salvation in the Old and New Testaments.*

Emphasis of Salvation in the Old Testament	Emphasis of Salvation in the New Testament
God redeemed Israel from slavery to Egypt.	
Israel focused on conquering physical enemies.	
Israel focused on entering a physical land.	

Figure 7.9   Practice seeing salvation moving from physical aspects in the Old Testament to moral and spiritual aspects in the New Testament.

In Scripture, we see **salvation** moving from physical aspects in the Old Testament to moral and spiritual aspects in the New Testament.[11] In the Old Testament, God redeemed Israel from slavery to Egypt. In the New Testament, God redeems us from slavery to sin. In the Old Testament, salvation focused on conquering physical enemies and entering a physical land. In the New Testament, we wrestle not with flesh and blood, but with spiritual enemies, as well as the sinful tendencies within us.

Stories in Acts have prescriptive aspects—they tell us what to believe, discern, be, and do. Above we noted some of the descriptive aspects of Acts 2:1-4. But Luke is also prescribing by telling us this story. He told this story to guide believers. On the Day of Pentecost, the apostles and over 100 other disciples were obeying Jesus. These people were already believers and followers of Christ. But they needed to be filled with the Spirit to become the powerful witnesses Jesus wanted—in character, words, and deeds. So by telling us this story of Acts 2, Luke is emphasizing that all believers need this same power that comes as we are filled with the Spirit. He prescribes this *filling of the Spirit* throughout the book of Acts. As a doctor prescribes medicine, Luke the beloved physician prescribes being filled with the Spirit! He uses history for the theological purpose of emphasizing being filled with the Spirit.

Q 33 ↖ *What is Luke prescribing (telling believers to do) through the story of Acts 2:1-4?*

Q 34 ↖ *For what theological purpose does Luke use the historical stories of being filled with the Spirit (Acts 2, 8, 10, and 19?*

Guidelines: In *Hermeneutics 1* you studied the six circles of literary context. We must compare *prescriptive* aspects with any parallel passages: in the same book (Circle 3), in a different book by the same author (Circle 4), and a different author in the same testament (Circle 5). A passage is prescriptive, *if and only if* we find other passages that teach the same truth. Also, remember to state prescriptive aspects as *principles*, in the form of a command, a promise, a warning, or a timeless truth.

In this lesson you will practice identifying descriptive and prescriptive aspects of a story.

A. Confirm prescriptive aspects with parallel passages.

Q 35 ↖ *Fill in the empty parts of Figure 7.10.*

Acts	Some Descriptive Aspects (Who what, where, when, why, how)	Prescriptive Aspects (Principles on believing, discerning, being, and doing)	Parallel Passages
2:1-4	120 disciples gathered in an upper room in Jerusalem. As they were filled with the Spirit, He empowered them to praise and worship in languages they had not learned.	Be filled with the Spirit. Worship God in a new language as the Spirit enables you.	(Circle 3) Acts 10:44-46; 19:1-7 (Circle 5) 1 Cor. 14:18; Eph. 5:18
4:32-35			
6:1-6			
8:36-38			

Figure 7.10   Practice identifying descriptive and prescriptive aspects of a story.

Q 36 *Why do the stories Luke chose for Acts have great weight?*

Q 37 *Can a pattern in Acts serve as a basis for doctrine? Defend your answer.*

Q 38 *Outside of Acts, what evidence is there that Paul and others spoke in tongues?*

Q 39 *Is appointing deacons a pattern in Scripture? Is there more than one method of appointing deacons?*

Q 40 *Complete Figure 7.11 filling in the blanks in both columns.*

Q 41 *Shall we select deacons or leaders by casting lots? Defend your answer.*

The interpreter should first look for **direct statements** to determine if a practice is prescriptive. For example, when Paul says, *"Be filled with the Spirit,"* we recognize that he is prescribing—telling us behavior to imitate (Eph. 5:18). But a **pattern** can also serve as the basis for doctrine. For example, Acts gives **three** examples showing that believers spoke in tongues when they were baptized in the Holy Spirit. We see a **pattern** in three of the four times that a group receives the gift of the Spirit (Acts 2:4; 10:46; 19:6). The one possible exception is found in Acts 8:15-19. This passage does not directly mention that the Samaritans spoke in tongues upon receiving the Holy Spirit, but it suggests it. Luke records that a dramatic sign accompanied the receiving of the Holy Spirit in Samaria. Something visible or audible must have occurred when these believers were baptized in the Spirit. Why else would Simon the sorcerer offer money for the power to impart the Spirit (Acts 8:18-19)? **Luke wrote history with a purpose.** Acts covers 30 years of Church history, but Luke recorded only *a few things*. So the examples he chose have *great weight*. His examples of being filled with the Spirit guide us to *expect* believers to speak in tongues when they receive the gift of the Spirit. At the same time, the fire and wind of Acts 2:1-4 are *never repeated*, so we conclude that these details were descriptive, not prescriptive.

The New Testament relates two other situations (parallel passages) where the evidence of tongues is implied. Ananias told Paul to *"be filled the Holy Spirit"* (Acts 9:17). Later, Paul told the Corinthians, *"I thank God that I speak in tongues more than all of you"* (1 Cor. 14:18). This was not a gift restricted to the apostles, for Paul wrote to Corinthian believers, *"I would like every one of you to speak in tongues"* (1 Cor. 14:5).

On another topic, do Acts 2:44 and Acts 4:32-35 teach *Christian communism*? No, the sharing of possessions was *voluntary*. And both Scriptures refer to the same historical crisis. In another passage, Christians are encouraged to give *only a part* of their income as an offering for suffering believers in Jerusalem (1 Cor. 16:1-2). Paul even suggests that the Macedonians gave far more than what was expected of them (2 Cor. 8:1-4). So we see that Acts 2:44 and 4:32-35 describe but do not prescribe behavior.

What about appointing deacons for church ministry? We see this in Acts 6:1-6, but is it a prescriptive pattern? Scripture supports appointing deacons to assist in the ministry (Acts 14:23; 1 Tim. 3:8-12; Tit. 1:5; Phil. 1:1). But the method of selecting deacons may vary. In Acts 6, the leaders set the standard for candidates and the congregation voted. In other instances, leaders such as Paul and Barnabas selected deacons (Acts 14:23). Scripture mentions various ways to appoint deacons.

B. We cannot base a doctrine or prescriptive practice on only a single event.

Acts	Descriptive Events (Illustrations)	Broader Principles of Scripture
1:26	Casting _____ to find a leader	We must seek God when choosing leaders.
5:15	Peter's shadow and _____	It is the power of God, not a method, that brings healing. God heals in many ways.
19:19	Burning books that teach _____	Believers should not keep anything that tempts them to return to a life of sin.
21:24	Joining in purification rites in the _____	To lead people into the future, we must relate to their _____ and _____.
27	People were saved when a boat sunk.	_____

Figure 7.11   Practice linking descriptions of an event to a broader principle in Scripture.

A one-legged stool lacks balance. We must not base a doctrine on a single passage or a lone event. Casting lots to choose a church leader occurs only once in the New Testament. In contrast, praying before selecting a leader is repeated (Acts 1:24; 13:2). We do not recommend using rolling dice, choosing lots, or drawing straws to select a pastor. But the Scriptures guide us to pray and study each candidate's character and reputation when choosing church leaders (1 Tim. 3; Titus 1).

We have one example of a shadow bringing healing (Acts 5:15). But one event does not give us a biblical pattern. We should not use this passage to restrict healing services to daylight hours on sunny days—when a shadow is possible! Likewise, we should not expect people to be healed through a cloth from an apostle's body (Acts 19:12). This cloth was probably a band that Paul wore around his forehead to soak up sweat as he sewed tents. And he wore an apron around his waist to hold tools and protect his clothes from wear and dirt. Note that a "sweat rag" would be impossible to get from many who call themselves apostles today, since they do not work enough to sweat!

Q 42 ⟫ *Why do we not teach that healing comes through shadows and cloths?*

It would be foolish to teach that Christians should maintain the sacrificial system based on the example of Paul in Acts 21:26. A single event, such as the resurrection or ascension of Christ, can have great value. But to use an event to establish doctrine, there must be other Scriptures that confirm or explain its significance. If something just happened once without further commentary, it is not prescriptive—it is not a basis for doctrine.

Q 43 ⟫ *Does Acts teach that we should offer animal sacrifices today? Defend your view.*

C. A prescriptive action must reflect the intent of the author.

You may be wondering, "What value are descriptions if they do not teach doctrine?" Sometimes they illustrate broader principles. So we must look for the principle that a story illustrates (Figure 7.10).

To interpret, we must always ask, "Did the author intend to prescribe this teaching or practice? Note that this question relates to the author's purpose, which you identified in the historical/cultural practice. For example: Did Luke intend to prescribe being filled with the Spirit and speaking in tongues? There is strong evidence that Spirit anointing for ministry is a major theme of Luke in both his Gospel and in Acts. We also see a pattern in Acts that emphasizes the baptism in the Holy Spirit, and speaking in tongues, throughout Acts.

The parallels between Luke and Acts indicate a pattern of Spirit empowerment for prophetic ministry—speaking through the anointing. Roger Stronstad, in his book *The Charismatic Theology of St. Luke*, emphasizes themes of the Gospel of Luke and Acts. One of the main themes in both of Luke's volumes is the anointing of the Spirit—with power to speak and serve. In Luke and Acts, almost every time a person receives the Spirit or is filled with the Spirit, the result is some sort of *prophetic ministry—speaking through the anointing.*[12]

Q 44 ⟫ *Which well-known scholar emphasizes that anointed speaking is a theme in Luke and Acts?*

Questions	Answers and Explanations
Do you think Luke intended to teach that believers should be baptized in water?	:
Do you think Luke intended believers to be filled with the Spirit and speak in tongues?	
Do you think Luke intended to teach that the Church needs signs and wonders to expand?	
Do you think Luke intended to teach that believers are exempt from persecution?	
Do you think Luke intended to teach that apostles are wealthy, and respected by all?	

Figure 7.12 Practice analyzing Luke's intentions.

Test Yourself: Circle the letter by the *best* completion to each question or statement.

1. What is Luke's main concern?
a) History
b) Theology
c) Geography
d) Eschatology

2. How many ministries of the Spirit does Luke emphasize?
a) 1
b) 2
c) 3
d) 4

3. How many ministries of the Spirit does Paul emphasize?
a) 1
b) 2
c) 3
d) 4

4. Why does Luke want people to be filled with the Spirit?
a) To be saved
b) To live a holy life
c) To serve
d) To grow

5. Which of these is *only* descriptive?
a) Believe on the Lord Jesus Christ.
b) They all began to speak in tongues.
c) Repent and be baptized.
d) Then they cast lots.

6. Which of these is prescriptive?
a) The islanders showed us unusual kindness.
b) After prayer, Paul placed his hand on him and healed him.
c) "Paul, you must stand trial before Caesar."
d) After three months we put out to sea.

7. Which passage in Acts is prescriptive?
a) You will receive power when the Holy Spirit comes on you.
b) May his place be deserted.
c) Peter's shadow healed people.
d) Stephen's face glowed like an angel.

8. Which passage is parallel to Acts 2:4?
a) Acts 3:15-17
b) Acts 7:14-16
c) Acts 10:44-46
d) Acts 12:10-12

9. Which passage in Acts is parallel to the rushing wind at Pentecost?
a) The wind of the Spirit at conversion (John 3)
b) A gentle south wind (Acts 27:13)
c) A wind like a hurricane (Acts 27:14)
d) No passage

10. Which chapters show that Luke intended to emphasize being filled with the Spirit?
a) Acts 1, 2, 6, 13, and 19
b) Acts 2, 4, 8, 14, and 20
c) Acts 1, 2, 8, 10, and 19
d) Acts 1, 7, 11, 18, and 27

Essay Test Topics: Write 50-100 words on each of these goals that you studied in this chapter.

- Summarize the relationship of history and theology in Luke's writings.
- Compare and contrast what Luke, John, and Paul emphasize about the Spirit.
- Explain and illustrate the Lucan purpose of being filled with the Spirit.
- Contrast descriptive and prescriptive aspects of a passage.
- Identify prescriptive aspects of passages in Acts, related to church expansion.
- Explain the need to confirm prescriptive aspects with parallel passages. Illustrate.
- Show from Acts that Luke intended to emphasize being filled with the Spirit.

Chapter 8:
Interpreting the Epistles

Introduction

Some time ago I was sitting in an airport, and a stranger sat down beside me. He said, "Why did you want to talk to me?" I asked, "Excuse me?" He looked annoyed and turned away. Just then I saw a telephone wire hanging from his ear. He continued his conversation on his phone with his back to me.

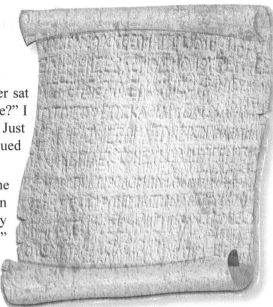

Reading the Epistles is like overhearing one end of a phone conversation. If you try hard, you can guess the conversation on the end you cannot hear. If a woman says, "I am so happy for you. I know you wanted a boy. How much does he weigh?" you can assume the person on the other end of the line has a *baby boy*. It is unlikely that the woman beside you would ask about the weight of a *boyfriend!* In the same way, if the writer of an epistle stresses a teaching or repeats an exhortation, this gives us a clue about the problems, issues, or spiritual conditions of the first readers.

Figure 8.1   In New Testament times, scrolls were a common way of sending letters.

The Epistles are *not* written to us directly. We are reading someone else's mail—from the first century. In the New Testament, out of 27 books, God gave us 22 letters. This method of communication is more powerful and interesting than sermons or a list of commands. Yet these letters weave history, culture, and teachings. So this genre can challenge the interpreter.

Lessons:

Epistles: Letters to Help With Specific Problems

Goal A: *Use the historical and cultural background to help interpret a passage.*
Goal B: *Use parallel passages to help interpret a text.*
Goal C: *Analyze word usage and relationships and literal and figurative language to interpret.*

Epistles: More Practice Interpreting

Goal A: *Use the historical and cultural background to help interpret a passage.*
Goal B: *Use parallel passages to help interpret a text.*
Goal C: *Analyze word usage and relationships and literal and figurative language to interpret.*

 Key Words and Phrases

historical cultural background—refers to the setting of the original writing; who wrote to whom? what was their relationship? when did he write? for what purpose? what was happening where they lived? what was their social status or setting?

literary context—the written verses that come before and after a verse; verses that come before it, surround it, and come after it provide the true meaning of a particular verse.

parallel passages—passages on the same subject or topic; used to compare the same author in a different book, a different author of the same Testament, or an author in the other Testament

literal language—understanding words in their usual or primary sense without symbolic meaning

figurative language—not literal; having symbolic meaning

Lesson 25 Epistles: Letters to Help With Specific Problems

Goal A: *Use the historical and cultural background to help interpret a passage.*
Goal B: *Use parallel passages to help interpret a text.*
Goal C: *Analyze word usage and relationships and literal and figurative language to interpret.*

Setting

Figure 8.2 lists some verses that have challenged interpreters.

Verse in the Epistles	Reference
What I want to do I do not do, but what I hate I do.	Rom. 7:15
Greet one another with a holy kiss.	Rom. 16:16
All things are yours.	1 Cor. 3:21
"Everything is permissible for me."	1 Cor. 6:12
It is good for a man not to marry.	1 Cor. 7:1
Eat whatever is put before you without raising questions of conscience.	1 Cor 10:27
A woman should pray with her head covered.	1 Cor. 11:5
A woman ought to have a veil on her head when she prays.	1 Cor. 11:10
If a man has long hair, it is a disgrace to him.	1 Cor. 11:14
Women should not ask their husbands questions during church.	1 Cor. 14:35
Slaves, obey your earthly masters.	Eph. 6:5
Have self-employed pastors.	2 Thess. 3:7-8
If a man will not work, he shall not eat.	2 Thess. 3: 10
Lift your hands when praying.	1 Tim. 2:8
Dress modestly, ...not with braided hair or gold or pearls or expensive clothes.	1 Tim. 2:9

Figure 8.2   Verses in the Epistles that have been difficult to interpret

In *Hermeneutics 1* you studied all you need to know to interpret the Epistles. But there was a lot to learn in that course. So let us review four keys (A–D) for interpreting letters of the New Testament. We will give you an example first, and then guide you to practice.

Let us begin with an example of interpreting 1 John 2:27.

As for you, the anointing you received from him remains in you, and you do not need anyone to teach you. But as his anointing teaches you about all things and as that anointing is real, not counterfeit—just as it has taught you, remain in him (1 John 2:27).

Note: As we work through sections A–D, we will summarize answers to questions that are the most helpful.

A. Search for clues in the *historical/cultural background (of 1 John 2:27).

5 questions about the author of the book or letter:	Answers:
Who was he?	The apostle John
When did he write the book?	About A.D. 85-95
What setting was he in?	Asia
What relationship did he have with those to whom he wrote?	John was an elder—like a father to his readers.
What was his purpose?	To refute and correct false teachings of the Gnostics

3 questions about the receivers of the book:	Answers:
Who were they?	The letter is addressed to unknown believers.
What was their city or town like?	They were probably in the province of Asia, over which John had apostolic responsibility.
What was their social status?	Low

141

3 questions about the passage in the book:	Answers:
How does the specific passage relate to the author's purpose?	As we examine 1 John, we find many references to the heresy of Gnosticism, which John wrote to correct.
Are there any specific historical details to explain?	Gnosticism plagued the second generation of the Church. Gnostics claimed that a person could not be saved without extra knowledge that was not in the Bible. Gnostic teachers required their followers to pay for knowledge (*gnosis*). The Gnostics believed that the body was bad and the spirit was good. For this reason, they did not accept that Jesus could have a human body and still be the Christ. They taught that the spirit of Christ descended on Jesus at His baptism in water—and departed before His death on the cross. Gnostics said that Jesus and the Christ were not the same. Jesus was flesh, and the Christ was spirit. They claimed that the Christ never came in the flesh—and did not shed blood on the cross. Now read the passages below. Does the historical context help you understand why John wrote these verses? *"Every spirit that acknowledges that Jesus Christ has come in the flesh is from God"* (1 John 4:2). [Notice how John puts Jesus Christ as the title of one person.] *"This is the one who came by water and blood—Jesus Christ. He did not come by water only, but by water and blood"* (1 John 5:6). [Notice that John joins Jesus and Christ, and mentions the water (of baptism) and the blood (of the cross).] The Gnostic teachers denied the true gospel. First John 2:27 emphasizes that believers do not need teachers *like* the Gnostics. We already have the truth about Christ, and the anointing of the Spirit to guide us into truth. It would be foolish to pay Gnostic teachers for their false doctrines.
Are there any specific cultural details to explain?	None

B. Consult *parallel passages (Figure 1.2).

These parallel passages can be by the author in the same book or in a different book; by a different author of the same Testament; or, if necessary, by an author in the other Testament. Recall that parallel passages are illustrated in the six circles of literary context (Figure 1.2).

To clarify 1 John 2:27, it is helpful to recall parallel passages by Paul, a different author of the same Testament.

Scripture	Summary:
Eph. 4:11	After Jesus rose, he gave *some* to be pastors and *teachers*.
2 Tim. 2:2	Paul told Timothy to *teach* others, so they could also *teach*.

Conclusion: Godly teachers are a gift from God, and are vital to the church. First John 2:27 does not mean we do not need *any* teachers; it means we do not need *false* teachers like the Gnostics.

C. Analyze word usage and relationships.

You will need to explain key words, phrases, conditions, and promises.

Explain:	Summary:
All things	Refers to matters of salvation
Teach	Believers do not need *teachers* who claim to have secret knowledge that is not part of the gospel of the apostles.

D. Discern *literal and *figurative language.

Does the literal meaning of your passage make sense? Does the context explain the meaning of your text? Are there figures of speech to explain?

Response: The historical context explains the meaning of 1 John 2:27. The literal language of the passage makes sense. There are no figures of speech to interpret in 1 John 2:27.

Student Practice: Interpreting 1 Corinthians 7:1

It is good for a man not to marry (1 Cor. 7:1).

Note: As you work through sections A and B, summarize answers to questions we supply for you.

A. Search for clues in the historical/cultural background (1 Cor. 7:1-40).

5 questions about the author of the book or letter:	Answers:
Who was he?	
When did he write the book?	
What setting was he in?	
What relationship did he have to believers in Corinth?	
What was his purpose?	

3 questions about the receivers of the book:	Answers:
Who were they?	
What was their city or town like?	
What was their social status?	

3 questions about the passage in the book:	Answers:
How does the specific passage relate to the author's purpose?	
Are there any specific historical details to explain? Yes: • Why did Paul write about the topic of marriage (1 Cor. 7:1)?	
Any cultural issues to explain? Yes: • How did life in Corinth affect the question of marriage?	

B. Consult parallel passages (By the author in the same book or in a different book; by a different author of same Testament, or, if necessary, by an author in the other Testament).

Scripture	Your Summary:
1 Cor. 7:8-9	What counsel does Paul give about marriage?
1 Cor. 7:29-31	How does this passage summarize Paul's concerns about marriage?
1 Cor. 9:5	Did Paul think it was wrong for other apostles to marry? Explain.
Matt. 19:10-12	What counsel did Jesus give about marriage?

Lesson 26 — Epistles: More Practice Interpreting

Goal A: *Use the historical and cultural background to help interpret a passage.*
Goal B: *Use parallel passages to help interpret a text.*
Goal C: *Analyze word usage and relationships and literal and figurative language to interpret.*

Student Practice 1: Interpreting 1 Corinthians 3:21

All things are yours (1 Cor. 3:21).

Note: As you work through sections A–C, summarize answers to questions we supply for you.

A. Search for clues in the historical/cultural background (of 1 Cor. 3:21).

You may skip the five questions about the author and the three questions about the receivers of Paul's letter to the Corinthians since you covered these questions in lesson 26.

3 questions about the passage in the book:	Answers:
How does the specific passage relate to the author's purpose? • In the outline of 1 Corinthians, which section contains 1 Corinthians 3:21? (Give chapters and verses.) • What is the topic of the section that contains your text?	
Are there any specific historical details to explain? Yes: • Why were the Corinthians divided? • What were they arguing about?	
Any cultural issues to explain? Yes: • How did the culture of Corinth influence some (1 Cor. 1:10-31)?	

B. Consult parallel passages
(By the author in the same book or in a different book; by a different author of same Testament, or, if necessary, by an author in the other Testament).

Scripture	Your Comments:
1 Cor. 4:8-13	Did the apostles walk at the front or the end of the parade? Explain. _____ Did Paul believe that spiritual believers must be wealthy on earth?_____
Phil. 4:11-13	Was Paul wealthy by earthly standards? Explain. _____
Eph. 4 11-12	Relate Ephesians. 4:11-12 to the meaning of 1 Corinthians 3:21._____

C. Analyze word usage and relationships. (Explain key words, phrases, conditions, and promises.)

Scripture	Your Analysis and Answers:
1 Cor. 3:21-23	How does **belonging to Christ** affect what belongs to the Corinthians?_____
1 Cor. 3:21	To what does **all things** refer? _____

Student Practice 2: Interpreting Romans 7:15

What I want to do I do not do, but what I hate I do (Rom. 7:15).

Note: As you work through sections A–C, summarize answers to questions we supply for you.

A. Search for clues in the historical/cultural background (of Rom. 7:15).

5 questions about the author of the book or letter:	Answers:
Who was he?	
When did he write the book?	
What setting was he in?	
What relationship did he have to believers in Rome? • Had Paul been to Rome when he wrote Romans?	
What were Paul's purposes for writing to the Romans? • What do you think Jews and Gentiles in Rome had heard about Paul? • How would his letter help Romans know Paul better?	

3 questions about the receivers of the book:	Answers:
Who were they? Where was Rome?	
What was their city like?	
What was their social status?	

3 questions about the passage in the book:	Answers:
How does the specific passage relate to the author's purpose? • In the outline of the book of Romans, which unit and chapters contain Romans 7:15? • What is the theme of the unit that contains Romans 7:15? • How does the unit that contains Romans 7:15 relate to the other units?	
Are there any specific historical details to explain? Yes: • How did corruption in Rome affect living a holy life?	
Any cultural issues to explain? Yes: • What types of temptations did believers face in Rome?	

B. Consult parallel passages (By the author in the same book or in a different book; by a different author of same Testament, or, if necessary, by an author in the other Testament).

Scripture	Your Summaries:
Rom. 6:1-2	Shall we go on sinning? _____
Rom. 8:4	What happens when believers are led by the Spirit, and not the flesh? _____
1 Cor. 6:9-11	How can we recognize those who will not inherit the kingdom of God? _____
Gal. 5:16	What is the key to living a life of victory over sinful desires of the flesh? _____
Romans	What examples of sin does Paul give in Romans? _____
Gal. 5:19-21	What examples of sin does Paul give in Galatians? _____
Gal. 5:16-26	How do Paul's examples of flesh versus Spirit in Galatians 5:16-26 help you interpret Romans 6–8?

C. Analyze word usage and relationships. (Explain key words, phrases, conditions, and promises.)

Questions	Your Analysis and Answers:
How does Paul define sin?	_____
Give examples of sin from Romans.	_____
Do you think Romans 7:15 describes Paul as an apostle, led by the Spirit? Or does Romans 7:15 describe Paul as a sinner, led by the flesh, who needed to meet Christ and be filled with the Spirit? Defend your answer.	_____

Test Yourself: Circle the letter by the **best** completion to each question or statement.

1. What helps us understand 1 John 2:27: *"You do not need anyone to teach you"*?
a) Historical knowledge of Jewish teachers
b) Historical knowledge about Judaism
c) Historical knowledge about the Gnostics
d) Historical knowledge about the Libertarians

2. Who denied that Jesus Christ came in the flesh?
a) Celtics
b) Gnostics
c) Heretics
d) Agnostics

3. In *"This is the one who came by water and blood,"*
a) water refers to physical birth.
b) water refers to spiritual life.
c) water refers to what poured from His side.
d) water refers to baptism.

4. What cultural insight helps us interpret Romans?
a) Understanding Jewish thoughts about Moses
b) Understanding the Roman government
c) Understanding Roman policies on freedom
d) Understanding what Jews thought of Rome

5. What passages helps us interpret 1 John 2:27?
a) Matthew 5:13 – *"You are the salt of the earth."*
b) Ephesians 4:11-12 – God gave pastors and teachers.
c) Philippians 2:8-10 – God will supply all our needs.
d) 1 Corinthians 8:1 – *Knowledge puffs up.*

6. What helps us interpret Paul on marriage in 1 Corinthians 7:1?
a) God's comment on marriage in Genesis 2:18
b) Peter's words on marriage in 1 Peter 3
c) Christ's words about marriage in Matthew 19:10-12
d) John's illustration of a miracle at a marriage in John 2

7. Which passage helps us interpret Romans 8:4?
a) John 3:16
b) Romans 3:23
c) Galatians 5:16-26
d) Romans 9:16

8. In Romans 7:23, what *law* was at work in Paul's body?
a) The law of Moses
b) The law of sin
c) The law of liberty
d) The law of slavery

9. What does 1 Corinthians 10:4 mean: *"They drank from the rock that accompanied them, and that rock was Christ."*
a) The rock was Christ, the solid rock.
b) All living water comes from Christ.
c) Jesus is the water of life.
d) The rock was a symbol of Christ.

10. How are we like *living* stones (1 Pet. 2:5)?
a) As God dwelt in the temple, He now dwells in us.
b) Believers are, like Peter, solid as a rock.
c) We are like the white stones of Revelation 2:17.
d) Some believers are stepping stones to Christ.

 Essay Test Topics: Write 50-100 words on each of these goals that you studied in this chapter.

- Use the historical and cultural background to help interpret a passage.
- Use parallel passages to help interpret a text.
- Analyze word usage and relationships and literal and figurative language to interpret.

Chapter 9:

Interpreting Apocalyptic Passages

Ezekiel saw a vision of God on a throne that had wheels. Unlike all other thrones, God was on a throne that moved from place to place. Around Him were four living beings (Ezek. 1:10). Each had four faces—a man, an ox, a lion, and an eagle. Each had four wings and could move at fast speeds. In motion, the four creatures sounded like the roar of rushing waters. The throne sat on wheels that shone like crystal dotted with eyes. Within each wheel was another intersecting wheel. The person on the throne looked like a man, but glowed brightly. Above his head was a great sky, sparkling like ice, with a rainbow.

Ezekiel's message to the slaves in Babylon was that God's presence was not restricted to Jerusalem. His throne was on wheels! Ancient kings used to travel in chariots. Likewise, high above all kings of earth, God moved with His people. He was with them, even while He disciplined them for their sins in Babylon—a journey of 900 miles from home.

Figure 9.1
In captivity in Babylon, Ezekiel saw the Lord on a throne that moved from place to place. The Jews were far from their homeland and temple. During this period of 70 years, God encouraged them with a vision and great truth: God is not confined to one building or one place. He is with His people, wherever we are.

Q 1 *How many principles will we study in this chapter? How will you locate them?*

This vision is in Ezekiel 1 and again in chapter 10. The passage is a type of literature that reaches its highest point in the book of Revelation. The name of this genre or form is apocalyptic. It is based on the Greek word *apocalypsis*—which means "to unveil." Apocalyptic passages are found in: Isaiah 24–27; Daniel 2, 7–12; Ezekiel 1, 10, 40–48; Zechariah 9–14; Matthew 24; Mark 13; Luke 21; Revelation.

 In this final chapter we will explore seven principles (A–G) for interpreting apocalyptic passages.

Lessons:

Principles for Interpreting Apocalyptic Passages—Part 1

Goal A: *Explain 2 ways that Revelation focuses on and reveals Jesus.*

Goal B: *Illustrate that the authors of apocalyptic passages often interpret their symbols for us.*

Goal C: *Illustrate how the historical/cultural background can help us interpret.*

Goal D: *Identify at least 10 characters in Revelation. Summarize their roles.*

Principles for Interpreting Apocalyptic Passages—Part 2

Goal A: *Demonstrate the skill of using parallel passages to discern the big story of an apocalyptic passage.*

Goal B: *Identify contrasts in Revelation to help you interpret apocalyptic passages.*

Goal C: *Admit what you do not see clearly in Revelation. Give examples.*

 Key Words

apocalyptic—types of books like Daniel and Revelation that unveil or reveal the future

symbols—images that represent a person, concept, or kingdom

Day of the Lord—occasions when God reveals Himself to punish the wicked and reward the righteous, in times of great distress in the world; the *final* Day of the Lord comes after the millennial reign of Christ, after Satan is loosed for a season and then judged forever.

Principles for Interpreting Apocalyptic Passages—Part 1

Goal A: *Explain 2 ways that Revelation focuses on and reveals Jesus.*
Goal B: *Illustrate that the authors of apocalyptic passages often interpret their symbols for us.*
Goal C: *Illustrate how the historical/cultural background can help us interpret.*
Goal D: *Identify at least 10 characters in Revelation. Summarize their roles.*

A. Keep the focus on the King and His kingdom (Rev. 1:1).

The revelation of Jesus Christ, *which God gave him to show his servants what must soon take place* (Rev. 1:1).

The book of Revelation is a blend of three genres: *apocalyptic, prophecy, and epistle. But most of Revelation is apocalyptic. The word *revelation* comes from the Greek word *apocalypsis*—"to reveal, unveil, or to pull away the cover that is hiding something." Revelation removes a veil **from Jesus** in two ways. *First*, it lets us see Jesus in His glory. *Second*, Revelation unveils future events—climaxing in the return of Jesus to conquer evil and to reign in His kingdom. Do not divorce the **person** from the **prophecy** of the future. In Revelation, John weaves two themes together—the glorious King, and His future victory and reign in His kingdom.

Q 2 *What does the Greek word "apocalypsis" mean?*

Q 3 *Which 2 themes does Revelation weave together in revealing Jesus?*

Revelation is both *from* Jesus and *about* Jesus. It is a *prophecy* from Jesus about *"what must soon take place"* (Rev. 1:1-3; 19:10). But Revelation is also a book about Jesus. Remember that Jesus is the Person who will conquer evil in the future. "Do not divorce the person from the prophecy."[1]

The greatest value of Revelation is not what it teaches about the dragon, the beast from the sea, or the beast from the earth. Nor is the highest value of Revelation in what it teaches about the new heaven, the new earth, and the New Jerusalem. The supreme value of Revelation is what the book teaches about **Jesus**. All of the treasures of wisdom and knowledge are hidden in Christ (Col. 2:3).

Q 4 *What is the highest value of Revelation? Explain.*

Revelation gives us insights about Jesus that no other book gives. The list that follows shows some of the things Revelation reveals about Jesus. Enjoy these. Do not be in a hurry. This is a good time to worship.

Q 5 *Complete Figure 9.2 by filling in the blanks.*

Revelation	Revelation Reveals Jesus As:
1:1	The One who _____ the future.
1:5	The faithful witness, *_____ from the dead, and ruler of the kings of earth.
1:5	The One who loves us (now) and _____ us from our sins by His blood.
1:6; (5:10)	The One who made us to be a _____ and priests to serve God.
1:7	The One coming with _____ whom all the peoples of earth will see and mourn over.
1:8	The _____ and _____, who was, and is, and is to come, the Almighty.
1:13; (2:1)	The One walking among the *_____.
1:14-15; (2:18)	The One with white _____, eyes like _____, feet like _____, a voice like _____.
1:16; (2:1; 3:1)	The One holding His _____ in His right hand.
1:16; (2:12, 16; 19:15)	The One with a _____ flashing from His mouth and a face shining like the sun.
1:17-18; (2:8)	The First and the Last, the _____ One who died and is alive forever.
1:18	The One who holds the _____ of death and *Hades*.
2:2	The One who knows when believers _____, do good deeds, persevere, cannot tolerate _____ men, and expose false _____.
2:4	The _____ of every believer.

Figure 9.2   Continued on next page

Continued from previous page

2:5, 16, 22; 3:3, 19	The One who calls the churches to _____.
2:6	The One who hates the deeds of the _____.
2:7, 11, 17, 29; 3:3, 6, 13, 22	The One who emphasizes we should hear what the _____ says to the churches.
2:7, 11, 17, 28	The One who gives each _____ the right to eat from the tree of life, safety from the second death, hidden manna, a white stone, and the morning star.
2:9	The One who knows the afflictions, _____, and spiritual condition of believers.
2:9	The One who knows _____ and those who slander true believers.
2:10	The One who tells us not to be afraid of _____.
2:10	The One who promises to give those who are faithful to death a _____.
2:13	The One who knows where we _____.
2:13	The One who knows the name of every faithful _____ and witness, such as Antipas.
2:14-15, 20	The One who knows when people in the church follow _____.
2:19	The One who knows our _____, faith, service, perseverance, and _____.
2:23	The One who searches hearts and minds and will _____ each person for his deeds.
2:26	The One who will give each overcomer authority to _____.
3:1-2	The One who knows the false _____ and true _____ of each church.
3:3; (16:15)	The One who will come like a thief to those who are _____.
3:5	The One who will not _____ of overcomers from the book of life (See 2 Tim. 2:12).
3:7-8	The One who is _____ and _____, with the key of David, who _____ a door that no man can _____ and _____ a door that no man can _____.
3:8	The One who knows when a believer has only a little _____.
3:9	The One who will make those who _____ fall at the feet of believers and confess that God loves them.
3:10	The One who will keep patient believers from the _____ that will come on the whole world.
3:11	The One who is coming _____ and warns believers not to lose their crowns.
3:12	The One who makes overcomers a _____ in the temple of God, and writes a new name on them.
3:14	The Amen, the faithful and true _____, the _____ of God's creation.
3:15-16	The One who will _____ out of His mouth.
3:18	The One who offers believers spiritual _____, _____, and insight.
3:19	The One who _____ and _____ those He loves.
3:20	The One who knocks on the door of each believer's _____, desiring to fellowship.
3:21	The One who _____ and is our example of _____.
3:21	The One who sits with His Father on His throne and gives _____ the right to sit with Him.
5:9-10	The One who gave His life's blood _____ men for God and made them a kingdom and priests who will serve God as they reign on earth.
5:11-14	The One whom the angels and every creature declare _____ to receive power, wisdom, strength, honor, glory, and praise.
6:16-17	The One who with the Father will pour out _____ on the wicked of the earth.
7:9-17	The One who is worshiped by the _____ who come out of the Great Tribulation, and who will protect them forever.
7:17	The _____ at the center of the throne.
7:17	The _____ of those who come out of the Great Tribulation.
11:15	The One who will reign forever over the _____ of the world.
12:5; (19:15)	Israel's _____ who will rule the nations with an iron *scepter (rod).
13:8	The One who owns the _____.
14:14-16	The Son of Man, seated on a cloud, wearing a gold crown, holding a _____.
17:14	The One who overcomes the _____.
19:7	The _____ who will come for His _____.
19:10	The theme of _____.
19:11	The rider who is called _____ and _____.
19:13	The One whose name is the _____.
19:14	The One who leads the _____ of heaven.

Figure 9.2   Continued on next page

Continued from previous page

19:15, 19-21	The One who strikes down the nations with the _____ of His mouth.
19:15	The One who _____ of the wrath of God Almighty.
19:16	The KING OF KINGS AND _____.
20:4	The One who reigns _____.
21:9	The _____ who is married to the bride.
21:22-23	The temple and the lamp of the Holy City, _____.
22:4	The One who will show us His _____ and put His name on our _____.
22:7, 12, 20	The One who is _____.
22:7; (1:3)	The One who _____ those who keep the words of the _____ of Revelation.
22:12	The One who _____ each one according to what He has done.
22:13	The Alpha and the _____, the First and the _____, the Beginning and the _____.
22:16	The Root and _____ of David and the bright _____.

Figure 9.2   Practice enjoying what Revelation reveals about Jesus, and keeping the focus on Him as you interpret.

All else is poverty compared to the wealth of knowing Jesus Christ. Study each of the seven seals on the scroll. This is interesting. But it is nothing compared to rejoicing over the One in heaven who is worthy to open the scroll! Let us bow with the thousands of angels, the elders, the four living creatures, and all of creation to worship the Lamb (Rev. 5:6-14). Study the seven trumpets one by one. They teach about terrible judgments that are coming. But the trumpet that means the most to us is the one that will announce the return of our beloved Savior (1 Thess. 4:15-18). Tremble as you read about the seven bowls of God's wrath (Rev. 15–16). God pours out these bowls as the Antichrist reigns on seven hills. But what is all of this compared to the fact that God poured out His love for us on the hill of Calvary? May it never be the false christ on a white horse who captures the attention of the saints (Rev. 6:1-2). The true Christ returning on a white horse with His saints is what lifts our spirits (Rev. 19:11-16). All that thrills our souls is Jesus! Pastor, lift Him up as you preach and teach the apocalyptic book of Revelation! Lead your people to praise and worship Him. He is worthy! It is too soon to know all we desire to know about the future. But we can enjoy our Savior's presence, even now!

Q 6 *What are at least 5 things that Revelations exalts Jesus above?*

B. When possible, let the author explain the symbols he uses.

Apocalyptic writings reveal the future through *symbols in dreams or visions. The prophet sees many images. Some readers today would like to have words of explanation. But apocalyptic writing uses **symbols**—images that represent a person, concept, or kingdom.

Images last longer than words. And the symbols of apocalyptic writing capture our attention. All over the world, people are fascinated with apocalyptic literature. The images of Ezekiel's dry bones, Daniel's beasts, and the plagues, characters, and symbols of Revelation appear in art, books, video, television, and on the Internet. Most people do not understand what the images mean. Still, they are fascinated with them. We can almost imagine ourselves in a dream as we read these descriptions. Many of the visuals are far from normal. They are like a painting of the future—a film of things to come.

Q 7 *What are 2 reasons why God chose to reveal truth through symbols?*

Look for the meaning of symbols in the passage or book you are interpreting. In Daniel's visions, an angel often explains the symbols. The reader soon learns that the statues and beasts symbolize the great empires that are or will control Judah: Israel, Babylon, Assyria, Greece, and Rome. The final empire is Christ's kingdom—a stone that strikes the statue, and fills the earth.

Q 8 *Where is the best place to find the meaning of a symbol? Explain.*

In Revelation, the author tells us that the seven candlesticks are seven churches (Rev. 1:20), and the smoke coming from the altar of incense is the prayers of the saints (Rev. 5:8; 8:3-4). The author tells us that the dragon in Revelation is Satan (Rev. 12:9; 20:2).

Q 9 *Fill in the meanings John gives for some of his symbols in Revelation (Figure 9.3).*

Revelation	Symbol	Meaning	Revelation
1:12-13	7 lampstands		1:20
1:16	7 stars		1:20
2:28	The morning star		22:16
3:7	Key of David	Power to open and close doors	3:7-8
4:5	7 lamps		4:5
5:6	The Lamb		17:14
5:6	7 eyes		5:6
5:8	Golden bowls full of incense		5:8
6:1-8	4 horses and riders		6:1-8
9:1	Fallen star		9:1
12:3; 20:2	Red dragon, old serpent		12:9; 20:2
12:4	1/3 of the stars of heaven		12:7-9
12:14	A time, times and ½ a time		12:6
13:1-10; 17:8-12	The beast out of the sea, with 7 heads and 10 horns		17:11
13:1; 17:3, 7	7 heads of the beast		17:9-10
13:1; 17:3, 7	10 horns of the beast		17:12-13, 16-17
13:11-17	The beast out of the earth		19:20
17:1-7	The great harlot, Babylon the Great who sits on a beast with 7 heads and 10 horns		17:9, 18
17:1	The waters on which the woman sits		17:15
19:8	Fine linen		19:8
19:11-16	The rider of the white horse		19:16
22:16	The Root of David		22:16

Figure 9.3   Practice identifying John's explanations of symbols in Revelation.[19]

Q 10 ↖ *Studying the details of Revelation 12, who do you think the woman is? Defend your interpretation.*

Sometimes the writer does not give a direct explanation of his symbols, but the *details of the text* help explain the symbol. Consider how Revelation 12 describes *the woman in travail*. Taken literally, this woman would appear to be Mary because she gave birth to Christ. Some have leaped on this literal interpretation and presented Mary in paintings and illustrations *"clothed with the sun, with the moon under her feet and a crown of twelve stars on her head"* (Rev. 12:1). But other aspects of this mystery woman in Revelation 12 cannot relate to Mary. When would Mary have spent 1,260 days in the desert (Rev. 12:6)? When did she have two wings to flee from Satan (Rev. 12:14)? When did Satan try to destroy her (Rev. 12:15)? Who are *"the rest of her offspring"* with whom Satan will make war (Rev. 12:17)?

A more reasonable explanation of the woman in Revelation 12 is that she is *a symbol of Israel*. The sun represents the glory of Israel's Messiah. The twelve stars are symbols of Israel's 12 tribes whom Joseph saw in dreams (Gen. 37:9). The moon under the woman's feet may represent that she is over lesser glorious things, such as the Law, the temple, and the promises (Rom. 9:4).[2] The attack and protection in the desert (Rev. 12:6) are during the Great Tribulation (Exod. 19:4; Dan. 12:7; Rev. 12:14). The offspring of the woman are the spiritual heirs of Israel's promises (Rev. 12:17).

C. Look for meaning in the history and culture of the writer.

Note that we are emphasizing the historical and cultural contexts. We covered this in *Hermeneutics 1*, and reviewed it in chapter 1 of this course. In every genre, the historical and cultural contexts are important to study. Sometimes the writers of apocalyptic literature used symbols that their readers understood *because of history or culture*. The letters to the seven churches in Revelation 2–3 contain several examples of symbols that are clear through the lenses of history and customs.

Q 11 ↗ *What does the white stone in Revelation 2:17 represent? (See Figure 9.5.)*

Figure 9.4   Remains of pillars at the temple of Diana in Sardis

Q 12 ↖ *What practices today are similar to the dedicated pillar of Revelation 3:12?*

Revelation	Symbols	Historical/Cultural Meaning
2:17	The white stone	There are a dozen interpretations of the white stone. Jurors used white and black stones to give a verdict. Roman emperors gave white stones to citizens as tokens, to exchange for food; victors at public contests received white stones; gladiators who received a white stone could retire from fighting. *Here*, the white stone seems to have the believer's name on it, and represents a personal guarantee to enter the joys of heaven.[3]
2:20	Food sacrificed to idols	All members of trade guilds, such as carpenters or masons, were expected to attend feasts, where food was sacrificed to their gods. After offering the sacrifice, the members ate the meat at a wild party that included drunkenness and prostitution. Those refusing to attend the celebrations were excluded from having jobs or social connections.
3:3	The thief in the night	Sardis was the capital of the kingdom of Lydia in 550 B.C. Cyrus, king of the Medes and Persians, conquered it. His soldiers discovered a secret entrance to the fortress on top of a mountain. They entered Sardis in darkness, like a thief in the night. (For the full story see *Faith & Action* course *Revelation & Daniel,* chapter 4, Introduction.)
3:12	The engraved pillar	One way to honor a person in a city like Philadelphia, was to engrave a pillar in the temple, and dedicate the pillar to him. To this day, some pillars of the original city are still standing. (See Figure 9.4, showing pillars at Sardis.)
3:15	The lukewarm water	The water supply for Laodicea warmed as it traveled through the stone aqueduct. It had a nauseating taste, since people prefer hot or cold water. Jesus used the lukewarm water of Laodicea as a symbol of believers who were neutral, or had a weak commitment to spiritual things. The Lord wanted them to be loyal and have passion for His kingdom.

**Figure 9.5   The meaning of some symbols becomes clear and powerful
when we understand the historical and cultural context.**

D. Remember that apocalyptic literature, such as the book of Revelation, is a story with characters.

Relate the characters and their roles to the plot—and to the big message of the story.

Q 13 ↖ *How did the lukewarm condition of believers at Laodicea relate to their historical context?*

Q 14 ↖ *Fill in column one of Figure 9.6, the characters of Revelation.*

Character	Explanation in Revelation
1.	The book reveals Him in such ways as: One like a *Son of Man* (1:13; 14:14), the *Lamb* (6:5), the *Lion* (5:5), a *Male Child* (12:5), the *Rider* on the white horse (19:11), and the One on the great white throne (20:11).
2.	He is seated on the throne (4:1-11), and referred to throughout the story.
3.	He is referred to as the 7-fold Spirit of God (1:4; 4:5; 5:6). John was in the Spirit on the Lord's Day (1:10). The Spirit speaks to the seven churches (2:1–3:22), and is active throughout the story.
4.	He sees the visions and narrates or tells the story to us (1:9-19). Also, he often shares his feelings and responses to the visions.

Figure 9.6   Continued on next page

Continued from previous page

5.	Jesus speaks to these in chapters 2–3. They remain in the background the rest of the book. All of Revelation was written for these churches and the churches that they represent.
6.	He is the main enemy in Revelation, and is referred to as the devil, Satan, and the Dragon (12:3–13:1; 20:1-10).
7.	These may represent all of creation. They appear often (4:6, 8; 5:6, 8, 14; 6:1, 6; 7:11; 14:3; 15:7; 19:4).
8.	These may represent all whom God has redeemed (4:4, 10; 5:8; 11:16; 19:4).
9.	These are active throughout the book. An _____ brought the revelation to John (1:1). They worship God and the Lamb (4–5), declare judgment (10:1-11), and fight in heavenly warfare (12). They blow the seven trumpets (8:2), and pour out the seven bowls and seven plagues (15–16). An _____, perhaps the one of Revelation 1:1, showed John many things (22:8).
10.	These dress in black clothes and call sinners to repent. Likewise, they prophesy and declare God's judgment (11).
11.	The _____ is the ruler of the beast, which is his kingdom. Sometimes John refers to the _____ as the beast. This is because a king and his kingdom are one. The beast has seven heads and ten horns (13). Five of these heads were in the past (17:10). We believe that these represent the world kingdoms of Egypt, Assyria, Babylon, Medo-Persia, and Greece. The sixth head of the beast was present in John's day. That head was Rome. We believe that the seventh head is a revised form of the Roman Empire. The Antichrist is the horn that arises to rule over it. The ten horns on the head of the seventh beast are ten kings. They reign a short time with the Antichrist.
12.	This person represents the Antichrist as the Holy Spirit represents Christ. Satan, the Antichrist, and the _____ form an unholy trinity (Rev. 1:4-5; 20:10). *beast & false prophet*
13.	John tells us that the _____ is the capital city of the Antichrist (17:18). This great city represents the world and its values. In John's day this capital city was Rome. John referred to it as Babylon to protect believers. Caesar was considered to be the Antichrist in John's day. But we believe there will be a final Antichrist who will rule the world from a great city.
14.	The _____ is the Church, the body of Christ (19:7-8). The bride includes those who go up in the Rapture (1 Thess. 4:13-18), and all those saved during the Great Tribulation (7:9-17). The bride is united with Christ when He comes to conquer evil.
15. Others	There are many more characters in Revelation. These include Jezebel (2:20-23), the riders on horses (6:5-8), the woman (12), the martyrs, kings, merchants, sailors, followers of the beast, faithful witnesses of the Lord, slaves, rich and poor people, the 144,000, a great multitude in white robes, all the dead who came to life, and people on thrones.
	Likewise, we meet things and creatures who act like humans. An eagle cries with a loud voice (8:13). The earth opens its mouth (12:16). An altar responds to God (16:7). The New Jerusalem comes as a bride (21:9-10). Finally, death and *Hades* are judged like God's other enemies. Thus Revelation has a great and varied list of characters. All of these play a part in the story of God's final victory over evil.

Figure 9.6   Characters in the story or drama of Revelation

Principles for Interpreting Apocalyptic Passages—Part 2

Lesson 28

Goal A: *Demonstrate the skill of using parallel passages to discern the big story of an apocalyptic passage.*

Goal B: *Identify contrasts in Revelation to help you interpret apocalyptic passages.*

Goal C: *Admit what you do not see clearly in Revelation. Give examples.*

Q 15 *Fill in the blanks in column 3 of Figure 9.7.*

Symbols	Old Testament Apocalyptic	New Testament Parallels in Revelation
Living creatures	Ezek. 1:5-14	
Rainbow	Ezek. 1:28	
Seal or mark on the forehead	Ezek. 9:4	Rev. 7:3-4
Son of Man	Dan. 3:25; 7:13	Rev. 1:13
Beasts	Dan. 7:1-7	
Morning star	Dan. 12:3	
Four horsemen	Zech. 1:8-11	
The great angel	Zech. 1:11	Rev. 10:1-11

Figure 9.7   Apocalyptic passages of the Old Testament can help us understand New Testament apocalyptic passages.

In this final chapter we are exploring the remainder of the seven principles (A–G) for interpreting apocalyptic passages. Review principles A–D in Lesson 28.

E. Compare symbols and events in parallel passages, to see the big picture of salvation.

A **symbol** in an apocalyptic passage of the Old Testament tends to have the same meaning in a parallel passage of the New Testament. Figure 9.7 gives a few examples of apocalyptic parallels.

Events. *In the Old Testament, apocalyptic writings reflected times of crisis for the Jews.* Daniel and Ezekiel reflect the violence that Judah suffered from Babylon and Persia. Ezekiel and Daniel saw a brighter day in the future. They prophesied that God would destroy Israel's enemies. The Son of David would reign. Jerusalem would be restored. The Jews would return to their land and would worship God.

Revelation shows a fulfillment of the prophecies of Ezekiel and Daniel. Like Old Testament days, Revelation describes a war raging between Babylon and Jerusalem. In Revelation, the new Babylon (Rome) is destroyed—and the New Jerusalem comes down from heaven. Christ rules from His temple, and His people return to worship Him. *Apocalyptic writings encourage those under the new covenant by using images of the past in prophecies about the future* (Figure 9.8). As God's people sang after crossing the Red Sea (Exod. 15), believers will sing by a sea of glass after overcoming the beast, his image, and his mark (Rev. 15:2-3). So *relate the past and the future.* As you learned in chapter 1, answer the question: *How does the story you are interpreting relate to God's whole plan of salvation that reaches completion in Christ?*

Apocalyptic writing stresses the ***final chapter*** of salvation. Apocalyptic passages refer often to *events* of biblical history. One scholar estimated that the book of Revelation refers 350 times to the Old Testament.[4] It is ironic, but we can best understand some prophecies by reviewing the past. When we know what God *has been doing*, it is easier to see what He *is going to do* in the future. Figure 9.8 lists some events in God's big plan of salvation.

Q 16 What type of circumstances surrounded apocalyptic writings? Illustrate.

Q 17 How do the circumstances of Revelation mirror the days of Daniel?

Q 18 See the big picture of salvation by completing column 3 of Figure 9.8.

Early Events in the History of Salvation	Old Testament	Final Events in the History of Salvation	Revelation
God created the heavens and earth.	Gen. 1:1		21:1
God created the sun.	Gen. 1:16		21:23-24
God created the night.	Gen. 1:5		22:5
God created the seas.	Gen. 1:10		21:1
A river flowed through Eden.	Gen. 2:10		22:1
Sin entered the human race.	Gen. 3:6-8		22:14-15
God judges the serpent temporarily.	Gen. 3:14-15		12:9; 20:10
The curse began.	Gen. 3:14-18		22:3
Death began.	Gen. 3:19		21:4
Humans were driven from the tree of life.	Gen. 3:22-24	*tree in Eden*	22:2
Sorrow and pain began.	Gen. 3:16-17		21:4
Humans were separated from God physically and spiritually.	Gen. 3:3, 23-24		21:3
Paradise was lost.	Gen. 3:23		22:3-5
God judges Sodom and Gomorrah with fire and brimstone.	Gen. 19		11:18; 19:20
God judges the Egyptians with plagues for persecuting His people.	Exod. 7–12		8, 9, 16
Those redeemed by God from Egypt sing the Song of Moses after they cross the Red Sea.	Exod. 15		15:2-4
God judges Babylon	Dan. 5		18

Figure 9.8 Apocalyptic passages about the future refer to events of salvation in the Old Testament. Together, passages of the Old Testament and the New Testament show us the big picture—the big story of salvation.

Apocalyptic passages reveal the big picture: conflict between heaven and earth—over thousands of years. The prophets who recorded apocalyptic prophecy lived during times of crisis. Isaiah's generation faced the threat of Assyria. Ezekiel and Daniel were slaves in Babylon. Zechariah faced danger from Persia. And the apostle John wrote to Christians enduring persecution from Rome. No doubt these believers wondered why God did not help them. Why did evil triumph, while God remained silent?

Q 19 How long do you think the conflict between good and bad angels has been going on? Defend your view.

Vision in Daniel 2	Vision in Daniel 7	Daniel 8:1-7, 20-21	Daniel 8:8, 22	Daniel 8:9-12, 23-25
1. Head of Gold (**BABYLON**) 626–539 B.C.	Winged Lion (**BABYLON**) Nebuchadnezzar			
2. Chest and Arms of Silver (**MEDO-PERSIA**) 539–330 B.C.	Bear (**MEDO-PERSIA**) Darius and Cyrus	Ram (**MEDO-PERSIA**)		
3. Belly and Thighs of Bronze (**GREECE**) 330–63 B.C.	4-Headed Leopard (**GREECE**) Alexander the Great and his 4 generals	Goat (**GREECE**) Alexander the Great (336–323 B.C.)	Goat (**GREECE**) Alexander's 4 generals	Goat (**GREECE**) Antiochus Epiphanes (175–164 B.C.)
4A. Legs of Iron (**ROME**) 63 B.C.–A.D. 486	Terrifying Beast (**ROME**)			
4B. Feet of Iron and Clay (**REVISED ROME**) Future date	Terrifying Beast (**REVISED ROME**)			

Figure 9.9   Visions in Daniel span thousands of years.

In these times of crisis, God pulls back the curtain of time and **puts the entire crisis in context**. The prophet and his generation are *part of the war taking place over thousands of years—involving heaven and earth*. God's people seem to be traveling through a dark tunnel, and for a time the enemy is winning. But there is a purpose and a limit to their suffering. *At the end of the darkness, the prophet sees a bright light of victory. He sees Christ coming to rule the earth and restore a kingdom of peace*. This conflict is obvious in John's Revelation. Note John's references to: the dragon (Rev. 12; see Dan. 7:7, 20); the beast (Rev. 13:1-10); kings of the earth (Rev. 19:19); Satan's earthly army (Rev. 20:7-9).

Apocalyptic passages reveal the Day of the Lord—the final chapter of human history. The New Testament writers saw the period from Christ to the end of the age as the *last days*. In the apocalyptic writings, the prophets focus on the *Day of the Lord and the reign of Christ. The Day of the Lord occurs in times of great distress in the world— occasions when God reveals Himself, to punish the wicked and reward the righteous. The *final* Day of the Lord comes after the millennial reign of Christ, after Satan is loosed for a season and then judged forever.

The messages of apocalyptic passages are often gloomy, but they always end with hope and victory. The purpose of apocalyptic writings is to show the reader that God is in charge and He and His people will win. The prophet does not deny the suffering—but looks beyond it to the mountaintop of glory. Negative images dominate the parts of Revelation. There is chaos on earth as evil reigns. John sees the powerful Antichrist, and the Great Tribulation. But throughout John's story of the end, there are scenes of victory. John moves freely in Revelation, from earth up to heaven, and from suffering to glimpses of victory. And at the end of the book, Christ is the victor. Evil is judged. We see the blessings of the millennial reign, a new heaven, a new earth, and a new Jerusalem. There is feasting, and Christ dwells among His people. Salvation history stretches from tree to tree, and river to river—from Eden to heaven on earth. Revelation reveals Jesus as the Ultimate Victor. And those who overcome the world, sin and Satan will reign and rejoice with Him forever.

Q 20 ⟋ *What is the one big message of apocalyptic writings? Describe it.*

F. Identify contrasts in the book of Revelation, to help you interpret apocalyptic passages.

The big picture of Revelation is clearer when we recognize the contrasts John gives in this apocalyptic book.

Q 21 ⟍ *Read the contrasts in Figure 9.10 and fill in the blanks.*

A	Revelation	B	Revelation
The *dependable* one: who was, is, and is to come	1:4, 8; 4:8	The *undependable* one: who was, now is not, and will come	17:8, 11
The *holy* Trinity: the Father, the Son, and the sevenfold Spirit	1:4-5	The *evil* trinity: _____ , _____ , and _____	20:10
The description of *Christ*	1:12-16	The description of the *Antichrist*	13:1-3
The Ephesians' *lack of tolerance* for wicked men or false apostles	2:2	Thyatira's *tolerance* of Jezebel, the false prophetess	2:20
The past love of the Ephesians	2:4-5	The love of the Ephesians at the time John wrote to them	2:4
The Ephesians' hate for the deeds of the Nicolaitans	2:6	Those at Pergamum and Thyatira who followed Nicolas, Balaam, and Jezebel	2:14-15, 20-24
The *crown of buildings* at Smyrna		The *crown of life* Jesus promised believers at Smyrna	2:10
Faithfulness unto *death*	2:10	The crown of _____	2:10
The *reputation* of believers at Sardis	3:1	The *condition* of believers at Sardis	3:1
The *deeds* of Ephesus, Thyatira, and Philadelphia	2:2, 19; 3:8	The *incomplete deeds* of Sardis	3:2

Figure 9.10 Continued on next page

Continued from previous page

The *rebukes* Christ gave 5 of the 7 churches	2:1-7, 12-28; 3:1-6, 14-22	The *lack of rebuke* to _____ and _____	2:8-11; 3:7-13
The *good things* he said to 6 of the 7 churches	2:1–3:13	The *absence of any praise* to Laodicean believers	3:14-22
The *confession* of Laodicean believers	3:17	The *condition* of Laodicean believers	3:17
The *fame* of Laodicea for business, cloth, and eye salve		The *spiritual poverty*, nakedness, and blindness of Laodicean believers	3:17-18
Those *who have ears* to hear what the Spirit says	2:7, 11, 17, 29; 3:6, 13, 22	Those *who do not have ears* to hear what the Spirit says	
_____ to overcomers in all 7 churches	2:7, 11, 17, 26-28; 3:5, 12, 21	*Warnings* to those who are overcome	2:5, 16, 22-23; 3:3, 5, 11, 16; 21:8; 22:15
The *Lord God Almighty* on his throne in heaven	4:2-3	*Earthly rulers* on earthly thrones	
Our God who is *holy* and *eternal*	4:8	The beast who is *evil* and *temporary*	13:5
The _____	4:11	All *created things*	4:11
He who *was*, and *is*, and *is to come*	4:8	The beast who _____, _____, and *is going to destruction*	17:11
The Lamb who alone is *worthy* to open the scroll	5:7-10	All in heaven, on earth, and under the earth who are *not worthy* to open the scroll	5:3
The _____ who *shed his blood* so men could worship God	5:9	The _____ who *sheds men's blood* because they refused to worship him	13:15
The white horse rider with one temporary *stephanos* crown	6:2	The white horse rider with many permanent *diadem* crowns	19:11-12
The *fifth* seal: martyrs resting in heaven, praying, "*Avenge us!*"	6:9-11	The *sixth* seal: sinners trembling on earth, saying, "*Hide us!*"	6:12-17
The *silence* before the scroll is opened	8:1	The *roar* of great multitudes in heaven shouting, "*Hallelujah!*"	19:1-6
_____ years of *hell* on earth with the Antichrist	11:2-3; 12:6, 14	_____ years of *peace* on earth with Christ	20:2-6
The *anger of the nations*	11:18	The _____ of God	11:18
Rewarding the prophets, saints, and those who respect God	11:18	*Judging* the dead and destroying those who destroy the earth	11:18; 20:12
The woman *out of* the serpent's reach	12:14	The woman's children *within* the dragon's reach	12:17
Those with the name or *mark of the beast* on their foreheads	13:16-17	Those with the *name of God* on their foreheads	9:4; 14:1; 22:4
The *lost who never find rest*, tormented in the lake of fire	14:10-11	The *saved who find eternal rest* in the presence of God	14:13
The *vile* dress of the _____ of the Antichrist	17:3-4	The *pure* dress of the _____ of Christ	19:7-8
The city of *Babylon* in ruins	18:2	The city of the *New Jerusalem* in glory	21:2
The *sinful* citizens of Babylon	18:4-5	The *holy* citizens of the New Jerusalem	22:14-15
Mourning of kings, merchants, and seamen over Babylon's fall	18:9-19	*Rejoicing* of saints, apostles, and prophets over Babylon's fall	18:20
The *Wedding Supper* of the _____	19:9	The *great supper* of _____	19:17-18
The *first* _____	20:5-6	The *second* _____	20:12-13
_____, children of God who *inherit the New Jerusalem*	21:7	Cowards, unbelievers, the vile, murderers, the sexually immoral, those who practice magic, idolaters, and liars who *inherit the lake of fire*	21:8
Those whose names are written in the *Lamb's book of life	21:27	Those who do shameful or deceitful deeds	21:27
Those who are _____ and _____ *right*	22:11	Those who are *vile* and _____ *wrong*	22:11
Come	22:17	_____	20:15

Figure 9.10   Contrasts in Revelation make some passages clearer.

Q 22 ⟋ *How can Deuteronomy 29:29 help us on some passages in Revelation?*

Q 23 ⟍ *What are some things you do not understand well in Revelation?*

Q 24 ⟍ *What happens when leaders speak with authority about things they do not understand well? Illustrate.*

G. Admit what you do not yet see clearly.

There is a great contrast between Daniel and Revelation. Daniel was a closed book. God told Daniel, *"Close up and seal the words of the scroll until the time of the end"* (Dan. 12:4). But God told John the opposite of what He told Daniel. The Lord said to John, *"Do not seal up the words of the prophecy of this book, because the time is near"* (Rev. 22:10). We are living in the last days. Therefore, God wants us to understand what is near. Unlike Daniel, Revelation is an open book.[5]

Even so, most of the prophecies of Revelation are still for the future. We may understand the general message, but find it hard to know specifics. For example, we may understand a lot about the Antichrist. But Revelation does not tell us his name. Great leaders like Martin Luther and John Calvin were wrong in their interpretation of Revelation. These men thought the 1,260 days stood for 1,260 years and that the Antichrist was the pope. John Wesley also erred by believing the 1,260-year theory. He expected the pope to be conquered by Christ in 1836.[6] If such spiritual giants as these erred in interpreting Revelation, surely we should not jump to conclusions.

10

A voice from heaven told John to seal up what the seven thunders said (Rev. 10:3-4). This shows us that there are some things about the future that remain the secrets of God. We should be humble and admit what we do not yet know. Paul's advice to the Corinthians is good for us. *"Do not go beyond what is written"* (1 Cor. 4:6). Likewise, the words of Moses may help us. *"The secret things belong to the LORD our God, but the things revealed belong to us and to our children forever"* (Deut. 29:29).

Q 25 ⟋ *How can Deuteronomy 29:29 help us on some passages in Revelation?*

Bible teachers today have different views on the beast. Recall the lesson of the seven thunders (Rev. 10:4). God keeps some secrets until the end of the age (Deut. 29:29). It is not good to thunder about things we do not see clearly. Therefore, we only whisper about the seven heads of the beast! If we were more certain, we would state who the seven heads are with more authority. However, we have given the view we think is best.

Q 26 ⟍ *What are some things you do not understand well in Revelation?*

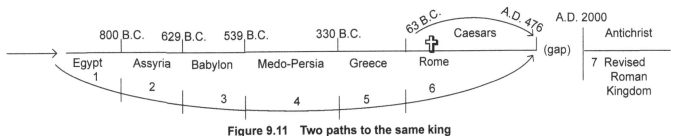

Figure 9.11 Two paths to the same king

Note that there are two paths to the same king! Some think the seven heads are Roman Caesars. Others think the seven heads are seven world rulers—from Egypt to Rome. But most agree that the Antichrist rules over the Revised Roman Kingdom. Therefore these two views—Caesars or world rulers—are two paths to the same Antichrist, who rules a revised Roman kingdom. So why argue about who the first six rulers were?

Q 27 ⟍ *What happens when leaders speak with authority about things they do not understand well? Illustrate.*

Test Yourself: Circle the letter by the *best* completion to each question or statement.

1. What does Revelation emphasize most?
a) The conflict between good and evil
b) The ultimate victory of Jesus
c) The final defeat of evil
d) The triumph of the saints

2. What does *apocalyptic* mean?
a) Mysterious
b) Visionary
c) Unveiling
d) Eschatological

3. The best way to interpret symbols is:
a) Compare parallel passages.
b) Pray and research.
c) Search the historical context.
d) Ask the author.

4. Contrasting characters in Revelation are:
a) the harlot and the bride.
b) the Antichrist and false prophet.
c) the first and the last.
d) the dragon and the beast.

5. What helps us understand *lukewarm?*
a) Laodicea's spiritual condition
b) Laodicea's response to Christ
c) Laodicea's source of water
d) Laodicea's climate

6. What helps us interpret the tree in Revelation 22?
a) The fruit on the tree
b) The tree in Eden
c) The first Psalm
d) The wooden cross

7. The parallel to Revelation 15—singing by the sea—is in
a) Genesis 6.
b) Exodus 15.
c) John 3.
d) Revelation 22.

8. Apocalyptic literature was written in
a) the worst of times.
b) the best of times.
c) good and bad times.
d) in-between times.

9. Which 2 cities does Revelation contrast?
a) Sodom and Jerusalem
b) Cairo and Jerusalem
c) The earthly Jerusalem and New Jerusalem
d) Babylon and the New Jerusalem

10. Who was wrong about identifying the Antichrist?
a) Luther
b) Augustine
c) Stott
d) Barclay

Essay Test Topics: Write 50-100 words on each of these goals that you studied in this chapter.

- Explain 2 ways that Revelation focuses on and reveals Jesus.
- Illustrate that the authors of apocalyptic passages often interpret their symbols for us.
- Illustrate how the historical/cultural background can help us interpret.
- Identify at least 10 characters in Revelation. Summarize their roles.
- Demonstrate the skill of using parallel passages to discern the big story of an apocalyptic passage.
- Identify contrasts in Revelation to help you interpret apocalyptic passages.
- Admit what you do not see clearly in Revelation. Give examples.

Definitions

The right-hand column lists the chapter in the textbook in which the word is used.   **Chapter**

abolish—to put an end to the existence or practice of a custom or institution; [It is good to abolish slavery, but Jesus did not come to abolish the ethical principles of the Law.]

2

already but not yet—the new age of the Kingdom has *already* begun at the coming of Jesus, but it is *not yet* complete until He returns.

6

antinomianism—against the Law; a belief that Christians are released from the obligations of observing the moral law—that they are freed from the moral law by virtue of grace as set forth in the gospel

2

antithesis—the direct opposite; contrast or opposition between two things

3

antithetic—against or opposite; in poetry having antithetic parallelism, the second line is the opposite of the first line in order to give a clear contrast.

3

antithetic parallelism—in poetry, having the second line opposite of the first line in order to give a clear contrast

3

apocalyptic—types of books like Daniel and Revelation that unveil or reveal the future

9

Assyria—a strong and cruel nation northeast of Israel, whose capital was Nineveh; Assyria took the ten northern tribes (Israel) into exile in 722 B.C. Babylon conquered Assyria in 612 B.C.

5

bridle—related to the headgear used to control a horse; to bring under control; to hold back or restrain [as one's tongue from speaking in anger]

4

ceremonial laws—laws that pertain to religious rituals such as circumcision, laws for priests, concerning the tabernacle, sacrifices, and cleansing

2

chiasm—parallel poetry in which lines 1 and 2 say the same thing, but the second line inverts the order of thought: the last thought of line 1 is the first thought of line 2. [named after the Greek letter "X" (chi) because of the "X" pattern]

3

civil laws—laws that guide relationships; laws forbidding the religious practices of the Canaanites and guiding the Jews in relating to each other

2

climactic parallelism—parallelism that builds up to a climax

3

covenant—an agreement between two parties—with duties and promises that each side agrees to perform; in the Old Testament, the agreement between God and the Israelites; in the New Testament, the agreement between God and believers; [When God creates a covenant, He alone decides the conditions and blessings. Humans cannot change God's covenant, but they may choose to accept or reject it.]

2, 5

Day of the Lord—occasions when God reveals Himself to punish the wicked and reward the righteous, in times of great distress in the world; the *final* Day of the Lord comes after the millennial reign of Christ, after Satan is loosed for a season and then judged forever.

9

descriptive aspects of a story—those parts that give us details of the narrative—answering questions that begin with *when, where, who, what, why,* and *how;* [providing the setting, characters, and action of the story]

7

duration—the length of time something endures, such as the time that Old Testament ceremonial and civil laws continue (temporary) compared to moral laws (eternal)

2

eschatological—about the future and the end times; refers to the *not yet*

5

eschatology—about the end, when God brings this age to a close | 6

ethics of the kingdom—God's standards of behavior for us to live by now, in this present age; the commands of Jesus in the Gospels guide the ethics or behavior of believers in the Kingdom. Many of the commands of Jesus are in the context of teaching on the [moral] Law of the Old Testament, which Jesus came to fulfill and not to abolish. | 6

fable—a supernatural story, not based on fact, that a person creates or invents to teach a principle or moral truth; often a tale with animals or inanimate objects as characters to teach a moral lesson | 1

figurative language—not literal; having symbolic meaning | 8

firstborn—in Revelation 1:5, refers to Jesus as the first person to conquer death, permanently | 9

foil—a person or thing that makes another seem better by contrast | 1

foretellers—prophets who spoke about the future, warning of God's judgment to come while calling people to repent, and promising God's help to those who obeyed. [Foretelling strengthens the message of responsibility to the covenant.] | 5

forthtellers—prophets who spoke forth the Word of God to the people among whom they lived; those who spoke what God said to them, functioning as a mouth and a voice for God | 5

genre—type of writing; a distinctive literary type | 1

goad—a spiked stick used for urging cattle forward; a prod; anything that pricks or wounds like a stick; anything that irritates or stimulates | 4

historical context—the setting of a story. The three aspects are *physical* [the place, objects, and people], *cultural* [customs, values, beliefs, attitudes, and actions], and *temporal* [politics, government, and events]. | 1

historical/cultural background—refers to the setting of the original writing of a passage of Scripture: the unique history of the author, those involved in the narrative, and the receivers of the book; also refers to people's values, customs, beliefs, and practices that relate to the passage of Scripture | 1, 8

historical narrative—true stories of history; scholars tend to refer to biblical stories as historical narrative; most often the stories about Jesus as recorded in the Gospels | 1, 6

Imprecatory Psalms—psalms in which the author prays for God to curse or judge the wicked; those that invoke judgment, calamity, or curses upon one's enemies or those perceived as the enemies of God | 3

kingdom of God—the realm over which God rules; although this is everywhere, His kingdom is more vibrant in the lives of those who are in relationship with Jesus Christ and where God's will is being obeyed. [At Creation, God's kingdom was present; at the coming of Jesus, the kingdom of God came into history; when Jesus returns, the Kingdom will be fully realized.] | 6

Lamb's book of life—a book Christ has of all who love God and make peace with Him through Jesus | 9

lampstands—in Revelation 1:12-19, seven different stands, where each held up or supported an oil lamp, represent the seven churches of Asia Minor | 9

literal language—understanding words in their usual or primary sense without symbolic meaning | 8

literary context—the written verses that come before and after a verse; the paragraph surrounding a verse that provides the true meaning of that verse. [Ultimately, the context of a verse begins with the paragraph, but also concerns the subdivision of a chapter, the same author in a different book, a different author in the same Testament, and authors in the other Testament.] | 1, 8

mandrake—a poisonous, narcotic plant with white or purple flowers and large yellow fruit; since the root resembles the human form, it was thought to enhance conception (See Genesis 30). | 1

Messiah—a word from Hebrew that means "anointed one;" in Greek, this word is translated "Christ." God announced the coming of this King and Deliverer through the prophets.   5

messianic—inspired by hope or belief in the Messiah, the promised and expected deliverer of the Jewish people; writings foretelling events concerning Jesus Christ   3

moral laws—laws that teach what is always right or wrong, such as the Ten Commandments   2

parallel passages—passages on the same subject or topic; used to compare the same author in a different book, a different author of the same Testament, or an author in the other Testament   1, 8

parallelism—referring to two things that are side-by-side, going in the same direction; a main characteristic of Hebrew poetry—two lines of poetry side by side, with the first and second lines expressing the same or opposite thought [thus one line helps give understanding of the other]   3

parties—individuals or organizations who participate in forming an agreement, usually legally   2

plot—the storyline; the plan, scheme, or main story; includes the introduction, conflict, crisis, resolution, and conclusion of a story   1

prescriptive aspects of a story—those parts that tell us what we should *believe, discern, be,* and *do;* refers to the interpretation of the narrative; must be able to be stated as principles that can be found in parallel passages of Scripture   7

progressive revelation—the advancement of light or revelation from God in stages; God's provision to mankind of more understanding concerning Himself through time. The old covenant often revealed an infant form of truth, but the new covenant reveals mature, full-grown truth.   2

scepter—a short rod used as a symbol of authority; usually held by a king or ruler   9

stanza—in poetry, the block of thought formed by several parallel lines; similar to several sentences making one paragraph of thought; several parallelisms of similar length, meter, or rhyme grouped into one sub-theme; [strophe: a group of lines forming a section of a lyrical—meant to be sung—poem]   3

superscription—the writing [heading] above 116 psalms that gives information to better understand the psalm [its author, historical setting, how it was used, and such]   3

symbols—images that represent a person, concept, or kingdom   9

synonym—a word that means the same as another word   3, 6

synthetic—that which is blended together as a whole; in poetry having synthetic parallelism, all of the lines together give the whole thought or big picture.   3

synthetic parallelism—in poetry, having all of the lines together to give the whole thought or big picture   3

the Prophets—usually refers to the 16 biblical prophets who wrote from 760–460 B.C.; 4 major prophets and 12 minor prophets, based on the length of their writings, who each warned of God's coming judgment to Israel and Judah because of the people's sins   5

theocracy—a form of government in which God is recognized as the supreme civil ruler, with the laws being interpreted by the priestly authorities; the system of Jewish government from Moses, through the Judges, until the monarchy   2

vertical—spiritually, referring to the relationship of God to man   2

Zion—originally the hill of Jerusalem on which the city of David and the temple were built; now, the kingdom of God in heaven; the final gathering place of true believers   3

God's Plan of Salvation

1. Introduction: God is holy, good, and pure—completely righteous. *"God is light; in him there is no darkness at all"* (1 John 1:5).

2. The Problem: Our sins have separated us from God. Because we have sinned— done things we know are wrong—we cannot fellowship with God. Our sins make us too dirty to come into God's holy presence. As we cannot enter a clean room with muddy shoes, we cannot come into God's presence with our sins. *"All have sinned"* (Rom. 3:23). The wages for our sin is death—spiritual death—which is separation from God, now and forever. Those who reject Jesus will die in their sins. They will spend eternity tormented in the flames of hell, away from the presence of God.

3. God's Solution: God loves us so much that he sent Jesus to rescue us. Jesus said, *"I am the way and the truth and the life. No one comes to the Father except through me"* (John 14:6). His name is Jesus, which means Savior, because He saves us from our sins (Matt. 1:21). Jesus saves us from both the penalty and the power of sin–now and forever. Jesus, the Son of God, became a man and lived a perfect, sinless life (Jn. 1:14; Heb. 4:15). He died on the cross as our substitute—He took the penalty for our sins (Rom. 6:23; 2 Cor. 5:21; 1 Pet. 2:24-25. Those who submit their lives to Jesus—God declares to be forgiven, clean and righteous (Rom. 5:1-2).

4. God's Invitation: Jesus says, *"Here I am! I stand at the door (of your heart) and knock. If anyone hears my voice and opens the door, I will come in"* (Rev. 3:20). God's favorite word is "Come". He wants to come to all people, and He wants them to come to him. *"The Spirit and the bride say, "Come!" And let him who hears say, "Come!" Whoever is thirsty, let him come; and whoever wishes, let him take the free gift of the water of life"* (Rev. 22:17). Accept God's invitation. Come to Jesus. Repent of your sins, that is, turn away from what you know is wrong. Put your trust in Jesus as your Savior and Lord. Believe that He died to save you from your sins. Ask Him to forgive your past sins and free you from being a slave to sin. *"If we confess our sins, He is faithful and just and will forgive us our sins, and cleanse us from all unrighteousness"* (1 John 1:9). Welcome Jesus into your life and He will enter. To all who receive Him, He gives the right to become God's children (1 John 1:12).

5. Your Commitment: Welcome to the family of God! God's plan of salvation has a beginning, a middle, and a completion–when we reach heaven. By walking through steps 1-4 above, you have begun to follow God's plan of salvation. Your name is now written in God's book of life (Ph. 4:3; Rev. 3:5; 20:12). The middle part of God's plan is following Jesus as we live on earth. As a child of God, seek to obey the teachings of Jesus in the Bible (Mt. 28:19-20). As you follow Him, He will lead and strengthen you in your relationship with God. As a baby grows into an adult, you will grow from a new child of God into to a mature family member. Be baptized in water (Mt 28:19; Acts 8:36-38; Rom. 6:4; Mk. 16:16). Become part of a local church that preaches and teaches the Bible (Acts 2:41; 9:31). Seek to be filled with the Holy Spirit (Acts 1:8; 2:4; 4:31; 8:17; 10:44-46; 19:1-7; Eph. 5:18-20). Learn to walk in the Spirit, so you can overcome sinful desires that come through the flesh (Rom. 8:5; Gal. 5:16). Grow in grace, and in the knowledge of our Lord and Savior Jesus Christ, and in maturity (2 Pet. 3:18; 2 Pet. 1:5-18). Fellowship with other believers who will encourage you. Share your testimony with others, and lead them to Jesus (Jn. 1:40-42; 4:39). The completion of salvation occurs when Jesus Christ returns. At that time, He will give you a new body, and complete His glorious plan of salvation in your life (Rom. 8:18-25;1 Cor. 15:20-58;1 Th. 4:13-17). We do not know the exact time Jesus will return. For now, enjoy the presence of God, and His Spirit in you, as you grow in grace. You have been saved from your past sins. You are being saved daily, as you abide and grow in Christ. And your salvation has a glorious completion ahead.

Scripture List

Bibliography

Arnold, Bill T. and Bryan E. Beyer. *Encountering the Old Testament: A Christian Survey.* Grand Rapids, Michigan: Baker Book House, 1999.

Barker, Kenneth, gen. ed. *The NIV Study Bible.* Grand Rapids, Michigan: Zondervan Publishing House, 1985.

Barrett, David. *International Bulletin of Missionary Research.* January 2000, p. 25.

Douglas, J. D., ed. *The New Bible Dictionary.* Grand Rapids, Michigan: Wm. B. Eerdmans Publishing Co., 1978.

Fee, Gordon D. and Douglas Stuart. *How to Read the Bible for all its Worth: A Guide to Understanding the Bible,* first edition. Grand Rapids, Michigan: Zondervan Publishing House, 1982.

_____. *How to Read the Bible For all It's Worth,* fourth edition. Grand Rapids, Michigan: Zondervan, 2014.

France, R. T. *Tyndale New Testament Commentaries: The Gospel of Matthew,* Vol.1. Grand Rapids, Michigan: Wm. B. Eerdmans Publishing Co., 2007.

Geisler, Norman. *A Popular Survey of the Old Testament.* Grand Rapids, Michigan: Baker Book House, 1981.

Gilbrandt, Thoralf. *Complete Biblical Library: Leviticus–Numbers.* Springfield, Missouri: World Library Press, Inc., 1995.

_____. *Complete Biblical Library: Proverbs.* Springfield, Missouri: World Library Press, Inc., 1998.

Graham, Ron. Chart in http://www.simplybible.com/f01p-psalms-about-christ.htm

Harrison, Everett F. *Baker's Dictionary of Theology.* Grand Rapids, Michigan: Baker Book House, 1975.

Horton, Stanley M. *The Ultimate Victory: An Exposition of the Book of Revelation.* Springfield, Missouri: Gospel Publishing House, 1991.

Kaiser, Walter C. Jr. *Back Toward the Future: Hints for Interpreting Biblical Prophecy.* Grand Rapids, Michigan: Baker Book House, 1989.

_____. *Toward an Exegetical Theology: Biblical Exegesis for Preaching and Teaching.* Grand Rapids, Michigan: Baker Book House, 1998.

_____. *Toward Old Testament Ethics.* Grand Rapids, Michigan: Academie Books, Zondervan Publishing House, 1991.

Klein, William W., Craig L. Blomberg, and Robert L. Hubbard, Jr. *Introduction to Biblical Interpretation.* Dallas, Texas: Word Publishing, 1993.

Ladd, George Eldon. *The Blessed Hope, A Biblical Study of the Second Advent and the Rapture.* Grand Rapids, Michigan: Wm. B. Eerdmans Publishing Co., 1975.

Marshall, I. Howard. *Luke: Historian and Theologian.* Downers Grove, Illinois: IVP Academic, 1978.

Mathewson, Steve. http://thegospelcoalition.org/blogs/tgc/2011/02/27/preaching-the-gospel-in-judges/#_edn1

Menzies, William W. and Robert Menzies. *Spirit and Power.* Grand Rapids, Michigan: Zondervan Publishing House, 2000.

Mounce, Robert H. *The New International Commentary on the New Testament: The Book of Revelation,* Rev. ed. Grand Rapids, Michigan: Wm. B. Eerdmans Publishing Co., 1998.

Osborne, Grant R. *The Hermeneutical Spiral: A Comprehensive Introduction to Biblical Interpretation.* Downers Grove, Illinois: InterVarsity Press, 1991.

Radmacher, Earl D., Ronald B. Allen, and H. Wayne House, eds. *Nelson's New Illustrated Bible Commentary: Spreading the Light of God's Word Into Your Life.* Nashville, Tennessee: Thomas Nelson Publishers, 1999.

Ryken, Leland. *How to Read the Bible as Literature.* Grand Rapids, Michigan: Zondervan Publishing House, 1984.

_____. *Words of Delight: A Literary Intro to the Bible,* 2nd Rev. ed. Grand Rapids, Michigan: Baker Book House, 1992.

Ryken, Leland and Tremper Longman III. *A Complete Literary Guide to the Bible.* Copyrighted by Ryken and Longman; contact Grand Rapids, Michigan: Zondervan Publishing House, 1993.

Stamps, Donald C., gen. ed. *The Full Life Study Bible,* New International Version. Grand Rapids, Michigan: Zondervan Publishing House, 1992. Introduction to Psalms and Ezra written by J. Wesley Adams.

Stein, Robert H. *The Method and Message of Jesus' Teachings,* Rev. ed. Louisville, Kentucky: Westminster, John Knox Press, 1994.

Stronstad, Roger. *Spirit, Scripture & Theology.* Baguio City, Philippines: Asia Pacific Theological Seminary Press, 1995.

_____. *The Charismatic Theology of St. Luke.* Peabody, Massachusetts: Hendrickson Publishers, 1984.

_____. *The Prophethood of All Believers: A Study in Luke's Charismatic Theology.* Springfield, Missouri: ICI University Press, 1998.

Traina, Robert A. *A Methodological Bible Study.* Grand Rapids, Michigan: Zondervan Publishing House, 2002.

Turnbull, Ralph G. *Proclaiming the New Testament.* Grand Rapids, Michigan: Baker Book House, 1972.

Virkler, Henry A. *Hermeneutics: Principles and Process of Biblical Interpretation.* Grand Rapids, Michigan: Baker Book House, 1981.

Wesley, John. *Explanatory Notes on the New Testament,* Vol. 1. Grand Rapids, Michigan: Baker Book House, 1983.

Wiersbe, Warren. *The Bible Exposition Commentary: Ephesians–Revelation,* Vol. 2. Wheaton, Illinois: Victor Books, 1989.

http://literarydevices.net/foil/

http://prepareinternational.org/wp-content/uploads/2009/12/e-understandingthegenreofthebook.pdf
in conjunction with Fee and Stuart, *How to Read the Bible for all its Worth;* Leland Ryken, *How to Read the Bible as Literature;* Phyllis A. Bird, *The Bible as the Church's Book;* Walter Bruggemann, *The Bible Makes Sense.*

Endnotes

Chapter 1

[1] Adapted from http://prepareinternational.org/wp-content/uploads/2009/12/e-understandingthegenreofthebook.pdf in conjunction with Fee and Stuart, *How to Read the Bible for all its Worth;* Leland Ryken, *How to Read the Bible as Literature;* Phyllis A. Bird, *The Bible as the Church's Book;* Walter Bruggemann, *The Bible Makes Sense.*

[2] http://literarydevices.net/foil/

[3] Gordon D. Fee and Douglas Stuart, *How to Read the Bible for all its Worth: A Guide to Understanding the Bible* (Grand Rapids, Michigan: Zondervan Publishing House, 1982), p. 74.

[4] Walter C. Kaiser, Jr., *Toward an Exegetical Theology: Biblical Exegesis for Preaching and Teaching* (Grand Rapids, Michigan: Baker Book House, 1998), p. 11.

[5] Fee and Stuart, first edition, p. 79.

[6] Steve Mathewson, http://thegospelcoalition.org/blogs/tgc/2011/02/27/preaching-the-gospel-in-judges/#_edn1

[7] Steve Mathewson, http://thegospelcoalition.org/blogs/tgc/2011/02/27/preaching-the-gospel-in-judges/#_edn1

[8] Adapted by permission from Steve Matthewson, http://thegospelcoalition.org/blogs/tgc/2011/02/27/preaching-the-gospel-in-judges/#_edn1

Chapter 2

[1] Everett F. Harrison, *Baker's Dictionary of Theology,* Article by G. L. Archer, Jr. (Grand Rapids, Michigan: Baker Book House, 1975), pp. 142-144.

[2] Walter C. Kaiser, Jr., *Toward Old Testament Ethics* (Grand Rapids, Michigan: Academie Books, Zondervan Publishing House, 1991), pp. 75-78.

[3] Henry A. Virkler, *Hermeneutics: Principles and Process of Biblical Interpretation* (Grand Rapids, Michigan: Baker Book House, 1981), p. 145.

[4] For example, see R. T. France, *Tyndale New Testament Commentaries: The Gospel of Matthew,* vol. 1 (Grand Rapids, Michigan: Wm. B. Eerdmans Publishing Co., 2007), pp.64-67.

[5] Kaiser, *Toward Old Testament Ethics,* p. 45.

[6] Kaiser, *Toward Old Testament Ethics,* p. 116.

[7] Thoralf Gilbrandt, *Complete Biblical Library: Leviticus–Numbers* (Springfield, Missouri: World Library Press, Inc., 1995), p. 677.

Chapter 3

[1] Donald C. Stamps, gen. ed. *The Full Life Study Bible,* New International Version (Grand Rapids, Michigan: Zondervan Publishing House, 1992). Introduction to Psalms written by J. Wesley Adams, p. 759.

[2] Robert A. Traina, *A Methodological Bible Study* (Grand Rapids, Michigan: Zondervan Publishing House, 2002), p. 69.

[3] Norman Geisler, *A Popular Survey of the Old Testament* (Grand Rapids, Michigan: Baker Book House, 1981), p. 179.

[4] Earl D. Radmacher, Ronald B. Allen, and H. Wayne House, eds., *Nelson's New Illustrated Bible Commentary: Spreading the Light of God's Word Into Your Life* (Nashville, Tennessee: Thomas Nelson Publishers, 1999), p. 685.

[5] Fee and Stuart, first edition, p. 220.

[6] Adapted from Fee and Stuart, first edition, pp. 223-225.

[7] Adapted from Fee and Stuart, first edition, pp. 223-225.

[8] Grant R. Osborne, *The Hermeneutical Spiral: A Comprehensive Introduction to Biblical Interpretation* (Downers Grove, Illinois: InterVarsity Press, 1991), p. 183.

[9] Adapted from Fee and Stuart, first edition, pp. 226-228.

[10] Leland Ryken, *How to Read the Bible as Literature* (Grand Rapids, Michigan: Zondervan Publishing House, 1984), p. 118.

[11] Adapted from chart by Ron Graham, http://www.simplybible.com/f01p-psalms-about-christ.htm

[12] Adapted from Fee and Stuart, first edition, pp. 230-231.

Chapter 4

[1] Bill T. Arnold and Bryan E. Beyer, *Encountering the Old Testament: A Christian Survey* (Grand Rapids, Michigan: Baker Book House, 1999), p. 317.

[2] Thoralf Gilbrandt, *Complete Biblical Library: Proverbs* (Springfield, Missouri: World Library Press, Inc., 1998), pp. 87-88.

[3] William W. Klein, Craig L. Blomberg, and Robert L. Hubbard, Jr., *Introduction to Biblical Interpretation* (Dallas, Texas: Word Publishing, 1993), p. 159.

[4] Leland Ryken, *Words of Delight: A Literary Intro to the Bible,* 2nd rev. ed. (Grand Rapids, Michigan: Baker Book House, 1992), p. 334.

[5] Arnold and Beyer, p. 327.

[6] Geisler, p. 218.

Chapter 5

[1] Stamps, *The Full Life Study Bible,* NIV, Introduction to Ezra written by J. Wesley Adams, p. 648.

[2] Arnold and Beyer, p. 341.

[3] Roger Stronstad, *The Prophethood of All Believers: A Study in Luke's Charismatic Theology* (Springfield, Missouri: ICI University Press, 1998), pp. 71-95.

[4] Arnold and Beyer, pp. 342-344.

[5] J. D. Douglas, ed., *The New Bible Dictionary* (Grand Rapids, Michigan: Wm. B. Eerdmans Publishing Co., 1978), p. 1037.

[6] Fee and Stuart, *How to Read the Bible For all It's Worth,* fourth edition (Grand Rapids, Michigan: Zondervan, 2014), pp. 190-191.

[7] Fee and Stuart, fourth edition, p. 211.

[8] Adapted from Arnold and Beyer, pp. 347-348.

[9] David Barrett, *International Bulletin of Missionary Research* (January 2000), p. 25.

[10] Fee and Stuart, fourth edition, pp. 208-210.

Chapter 6

[1] Harrison, Article by George Eldon Ladd, pp. 308-314.

[2] John Wesley, *Explanatory Notes on the New Testament,* vol. 1 (Grand Rapids, Michigan: Baker Book House, 1983), comments on Matthew 11:11.

[3] Fee and Stuart, first edition, pp. 119, 138.

[4] Walter C. Kaiser, Jr., *Back Toward the Future: Hints for Interpreting Biblical Prophecy* (Grand Rapids, Michigan: Baker Book House, 1989), p. 118.

[5] Based on Fee and Stuart, first edition, p. 132.

[6] Fee and Stuart, first edition, p. 132.

[7] Adapted from Fee and Stuart, first edition, pp. 131-134.

[8] Fee and Stuart, first edition, p. 105.

[9] Fee and Stuart, first edition, p. 117.

[10] Robert H. Stein, *The Method and Message of Jesus Teachings,* rev. ed. (Louisville, Kentucky: Westminster John Knox Press, 1994), pp. 90 -114.

[11] Fee and Stuart, first edition, p. 118.

Chapter 7

[1] William W. Menzies and Robert Menzies, *Spirit and Power* (Grand Rapids, Michigan: Zondervan Publishing House, 2000), p. 41.

[2] Bill Lasley, Missionary and editor at Global University, Interview on the relationship between history and doctrine, July, 2000.

[3] Roger Stronstad, *Spirit, Scripture & Theology* (Baguio City, Philippines: Asia Pacific Theological Seminary Press, 1995), p. 42.

[4] Kenneth Barker, gen. ed., *The NIV Study Bible* (Grand Rapids, Michigan: Zondervan Publishing House, 1985), p. 1642.

[5] I. Howard Marshall, *Luke: Historian and Theologian* (Downers Grove, Illinois: IVP Academic, 1978), p. 18.

[6] Marshall, p. 18.

[7] Stronstad, *Spirit, Scripture, & Theology,* pp. 189-192.

[8] Ralph G. Turnbull, *Proclaiming the New Testament* (Grand Rapids, Michigan: Baker Book House, 1972), p. 8.

[9] Based on *The NIV Study Bible,* pp. 1643, 1668.

[10] Marshall, p. 96.

[11] Marshall, p. 94.

[12] Roger Stronstad, *The Charismatic Theology of St. Luke* (Peabody, Massachusetts: Hendrickson Publishers, 1984), p. 11.

Chapter 9

[1] Warren Wiersbe, *The Bible Exposition Commentary: Ephesians–Revelation,* vol. 2 (Wheaton, Illinois: Victor Books, 1989), p. 566.

[2] Stanley M. Horton, *The Ultimate Victory: An Exposition of the Book of Revelation* (Springfield, Missouri: Gospel Publishing House, 1991), p. 172.

[3] Robert H. Mounce, *The New International Commentary on the New Testament: The Book of Revelation,* rev. ed. (Grand Rapids, Michigan: Wm. B. Eerdmans Publishing Co., 1998), pp. 82-83.

[4] Leland Ryken and Tremper Longman III, *A Complete Literary Guide to the Bible* (copyrighted by Ryken and Longman; contact Grand Rapids, Michigan: Zondervan Publishing House, 1993), p. 465.

[5] Wiersbe, p. 566.

[6] George Eldon Ladd, *The Blessed Hope, A Biblical Study of the Second Advent and the Rapture* (Grand Rapids, Michigan: Wm. B. Eerdmans Publishing Co., 1975), p. 33.